Woodturning & Design
RAY KEY.

KT-438-371

# WOODTURNING
## A Foundation Course

# WOODTURNING

## A Foundation Course

### KEITH ROWLEY
With a foreword by
Bert Marsh

GUILD OF MASTER CRAFTSMAN PUBLICATIONS

First Published in 1990 by
Guild of Master Craftsman Publications Ltd,
Castle Place, 166 High Street,
Lewes, East Sussex BN7 1XU

Reprinted 1991, 1992, 1993

© KEITH ROWLEY 1990

ISBN 0 946 819 203

**All rights reserved**

No part of this publication may be reproduced, stored
in a retrieval system, or transmitted in any form or by
any means without the prior permission of the
publisher and copyright holder

**Illustrations and photography by G Ford**

**Designed by Teresa Dearlove**

Printed and bound in Great Britain by
Hillman Printers (Frome) Ltd. Frome, Somerset

# Contents

# Dedication

This book is dedicated to the memory of my late father who taught me to appreciate the beauty of trees and wood and persuaded me to follow a trade working with them. Also to my wife, Jean, who has always provided unfailing support and encouragement in both the professions I have followed.

# Acknowledgements

I should like to thank Geoff Ford who has spent many hours in my workshop preparing the photographs and the line drawings, which are as good as any I have seen. I consider you to be a very talented man in your field Geoff. Thank you very much.

I would also like to express my thanks to a neighbour, friend and 'workshop assistant', Robert Ollerhenshaw, a retired engineer, who has given me considerable assistance with certain aspects of the book.

I would finally like to thank Mr Malcolm Haddon of the South East Derbyshire College of Further Education, who on numerous occasions has had to 'rescue' me when I have got into trouble with the word processor I used to write this book. (You will be pleased to know Malcolm that I am now quite proficient in using it.)

**Important Note**
Readers are strongly recommended to read the section on safety, pages 145 to 146, before attempting any of the *practical* work in this book.

# Foreword

People may argue the reasons why, but no one can disagree that recently there has been a great upsurge in interest in woodturning. Numerous enthusiasts with a thirst for knowledge have been watching demonstrations, attending seminars and courses and initially being inspired, but becoming frustrated when finding themselves alone in their workshop. This is often because the proper groundwork has not been laid down, and this book will, I am sure, help to encourage the development of the necessary basic skills, which will lead to both greater satisfaction and enjoyment in woodturning.

It is especially good to see someone writing a book from the depth of their experience, rather than regurgitating recently read or discovered facts. Keith, a professional woodturner who, to use his own words, 'Had a life-long love affair with woodturning', has succeeded especially in writing a book which provides a safe basis for beginners. The title, Woodturning: A Foundation Course, describes the book exactly. A foundation is a firm base to build on, and I am sure that this is what the book will provide for many readers, who by following its advice will go on to become accomplished turners.

I remember talking to Keith soon after he had set out to write this book. He was very pleased to tell me he had moved into the twentieth century, the era of technology. 'I bought myself one of those computer, word processor things,' he said. Then he proceeded to tell me how, after reading the instruction manual, he quickly set about enthusiastically on the first chapter. After a time, very pleased with his efforts – a screen full of text – he pressed the button to print. Oh dear – wrong button! The script disappeared for ever. With a gleam in his eye, he said, 'That was the best thing I have ever written.' This may be the case, but somehow I doubt it, and thank goodness the urge to push that particular button was overcome.

With the text finished, and the addition of a considerable number of excellent photographs and very well produced drawings, this is a book to be valued and referred to by amateur and professional woodturners alike for many years to come.

Certainly I am sure that many turners and would-be turners will be most grateful that Keith got the buttons right on his computer.

**Bert Marsh,** Brighton, 1990

# INTRODUCTION

**B**eing born into a mining community in south Derbyshire, where on leaving school most of the lads went to work in the mines, I was destined to work for 'the company' in some capacity.

My father, a miner too, was equally determined I was not going to follow in his footsteps and insisted that I learn a trade.

His advice went something like, 'Get a trade behind thee, lad, it will always stand thee in good stead, in any case it's worth five quid a week to see the sunshine and the crows fly over. You don't want to be stuck down the pit.' (£5 was an awful lot of money in those days.)

Thus I went into the joiners' shop to serve my time, working on projects such as ventilation doors for the mines, pit-pony shafts and carts, wheels, general joinery, and furniture making and restoration for the company offices and estate houses.

Most of all I liked to use the huge woodturning lathe in the corner of the workshop. Perhaps this was understandable when you consider we had very few woodworking machines and the majority of dimensioning, mortising, moulding, etc. had to be done by hand.

While such labours developed my wrists and forearms to blacksmith proportions, the hard physical labour was in marked contrast to the ease (after instruction and much practice of course) with which I was able to fashion newels, balusters, chair and table legs, and so on, using gouges and chisels on the lathe.

My 'love affair' with woodturning therefore started very early, and my father, being very proud of the fact that I had followed his advice, bought a new 8' x 6' shed and an early model Coronet lathe for me to practise on at home.

Almost 40 years on the shed is still standing and the lathe is still in use, which speaks volumes for both the shed manufacturer and the Coronet engineers, and I can sincerely say that I still derive as much pleasure and satisfaction from 'making the shavings fly' as I did in those early days.

The demise of the coal industry in the Erewash Valley of south Derbyshire came in the late fifties and meant I was faced with the choice of moving to another NCB area, or seeking alternative employment. By this time I was a married man with a family, and a millstone called a mortgage hanging round my neck. I therefore plumped for a secure job and joined the Nottingham City Police.

Almost 20 years of my service was spent in the CID, and the ability to commit often extremely complicated cases to paper in a chronological, easy-to-understand manner was a vital part of the business. I took advantage of the early retirement facility about eight years ago and I have been woodturning professionally ever since, combining commercial turnery with the private courses of instruction I offer. For much of the same period, I have also been qualified to teach woodturning at the South East Derbyshire College of Further Education.

Travelling up and down the country and demonstrating at the various woodworking shows has brought me into contact with hundreds of aspiring woodturners. I enjoy talking to them immensely, and the dialogue invariably gets round to the difficulties and problems encountered with turning, and the same queries are raised over and over again. I hope that now I can suggest causes of and remedies for these problems and incorporate them into my teaching methods and general approach.

I have described my background and experience in order to inspire confidence in my methods, and hopefully to persuade you that I am a practical man who understands the difficulties beginners face. Additionally my 20 years experience of 'putting it on paper' leaves me with no excuses for making other than a fair job of the script!

This book is written for the relative newcomer to the craft, the purpose being to impart a thorough understanding of its basic, safe and correct techniques. If the beginner can lay solid foundations, he will be able to build on them with confidence and develop into a proficient woodturner.

While there is no better way of learning a trade or craft than actually being shown by a competent craftsman/teacher, a good deal can be learned from a well-written textbook if the student is sufficiently enthusiastic, determined and diligent.

If after reading the book I have convinced you that you too can become a competent woodturner', and gone some way to firing your enthusiasm for what is a very satisfying and relaxing hobby, then I shall have achieved what I set out to do.

# Chapter 1
## TREES AND WOOD

**M**y love of nature was probably inherited from my father. For most miners, the countryside and fresh air were a means of escape from the dark, dusty and dangerous environment in which they spent almost a quarter of their lives.

Some of my earliest and fondest recollections are of exploring with my father the extensive countryside and woods near my childhood home. It was on such excursions that I was made to appreciate 'the best thing any mortal hath are those which every mortal shares'.

My nature education therefore started very early. My father taught me how to identify wild flowers, wild animals and birds by their call, colour, flight and song.

And then there were the *trees*.

One has only to reflect for a short time to realize what an important part they play in our lives, and to appreciate why they are regarded as amongst the best chosen gifts of nature to man. In their natural state they adorn the landscape and perform an important ecological function. They vary considerably in shape and outline, and when fully clad in leaf, spike or needle, they vary even more in shades of colour.

Trees are things of beauty, and have inspired writers, poets and artists over the centuries. One of the saddest sights the countryside holds for me is the demise of the magnificent English Elm. Once very common, its numbers have been devastated by Dutch Elm disease, and in many districts all that remains is their skeletal, ghostly forms silhouetted against the skyline.

While for many the fascination of trees lies in their sheer beauty, it is in their converted state that they serve man more than any other living organism. When felled and sawn, timber varies tremendously in colour, grain and texture. It also varies in the uses it can be best put to, some humbler varieties being used for rough carpentry and firewood. Others, with richer grain and texture, are used for the highest grades of cabinetmaking.

It is incumbent upon all of us to play our part not only in conserving this most precious gift of nature, but also applying our best endeavours in every project we undertake with wood.

It is also incumbent on every woodworker to be able to identify as many different varieties of timber as possible, and to know their properties so as to be able to put them to their best uses.

# TIMBERS SUITABLE FOR WOODTURNING

While almost every species of wood can be turned, some are eminently more suitable than others. More and more turners are realizing that although some varieties of the foreign exotic hardwoods are beyond compare for certain types of turning, some home-grown species are not far behind in their general appeal.

The following list is by no means exhaustive, but it should provide the beginner with sufficient information to be able to identify and be aware of the properties of the most useful species.

### Native Timbers (UK)

**Ash** A large elegant tree, and after the oak probably the most useful native timber in the UK. Recognition is easy. The pale grey bark is smooth when young but in maturity develops a network of ridges and furrows. The winged seeds, green at first, turn to brown and often stay on the tree all winter. It is easily worked, yet very tough and elastic, qualities which make it the ideal timber for such things as handles for tools, garden and farm implements, and for sporting equipment. In the past, it was also a timber frequently used by the wheelwright and carriage builder, and in toughness and resistance to shock, ash can only be equalled by hickory.

It is now used extensively in furniture making, high-class joinery and shop-fitting. The timber is pale in colour but often tinged with pink, and the heartwood is generally light brown. Ash turns very well despite its coarse texture, and I consider it underestimated as a turnery timber.

**Olive Ash/Ripple Ash** These are two unusual characteristics normally found in more mature parkland trees which have had a chance to develop fully in girth rather than height. The 'ripple' effect runs at right angles to the grain and is combined with the grey/brown streaks running along the length of the grain. These very attractive features make this variety of ash much prized by all woodturners, which is reflected in the price you have to pay for it.

**Beech** A tall, stately tree which with good reason has been referred to as the 'queen of the forest'. Its silver-grey bole and branches make it one of the easiest trees to identify, and its huge domed crown forms a great circle of shade when in full leaf.

The timber is hard and close grained and has a fine, even texture. There is no marked difference between the spring and summer wood and the colour is generally pinkish/buff. Beech turns particularly well and was the timber predominantly used by the Chiltern pole-lathe turners. While not possessing the elastic qualities of ash, it does lend itself to steam-bending and for this reason was used extensively in the furniture trade.

**Spalted Beech** Again, much prized by woodturners. The 'spalted' effect is obtained from logs which have lain on the ground for some time after felling and are affected by a fungus which causes the attractive black lines and spots.

**Chestnut (Sweet)** A large, handsome tree which develops a deeply fissured, spiralling bark. There is no mistaking this tree when it bears the prickly green husks which protect the golden-brown nuts. The timber bears a strong resemblance to oak, although it does not show the medullary rays that give oak its 'silver grain' when quarter sawn. This timber is increasingly being used for high-quality work and is very suitable for turnery.

**Elm (English)** A magnificent, tall and stately tree which has been the victim of the most disastrous setback to native hardwoods in recent times – Dutch Elm disease. While by no means as valuable as ash or oak, elm was indispensable for many reasons. Village carpenters and wheelwrights appreciated its qualities of strength, durability and resistance to splitting, features which make it an ideal timber for chair seats, wooden pumps, wheel hubs and felloes, etc. In colour it varies from the yellowish/white of its sapwood to the light brown of its heartwood. Its wild, irregular grain makes it, for me, one of the most attractive of timbers.

Although the coarse and irregular grain means it is not the easiest of timbers on which to achieve a good finish, patience, sharp tools and a good turning technique will reward the user with beautiful results. It is particularly suited to bowl-turning in both 'green' and seasoned states.

**Elm (Wych)** In outline a much smaller and more rounded tree than the English elm, but with very similar properties. Many examples have distinctive green streaks running through them which enhance their appeal and look well on bowlwork.

**Elm (Burr)** Burrs occur on several species of tree and are formed by a curious wart-like growth which, in the case of the elm, is usually towards the base of the trunk. They are caused by the stunted growth of a number of buds and when cut through, the burr reveals the characteristically large number of closely grouped miniature knots. Such burrs are indeed beautiful and make extremely attractive bowls and platters.

**Hornbeam** A smallish tree with silver-grey bark. The boles of the more mature trees tend to become deeply fluted and twisted. It is not in great supply, but one of my favourite timbers for turning and is particularly suited to long-stemmed and translucent goblets. The timber, yellowish-white in colour, is strong, tough and difficult to split, qualities which make it ideal for such things as cogs, plane stocks, skittles and mallets.

**Oak** Very few Englishmen are unable to identify the most revered of our native trees. It is one of the latest trees to leaf and the unique shape of the leaves, together with the acorns, makes it impossible to confuse with other species. Its properties are well known. For durability and strength, it is beyond compare. The possibilities with oak are seemingly endless, and it has been used for centuries for such things as ecclesiastical woodwork, furniture, roof supports and trusses, wheelwrighting, agricultural implements, timber-framed buildings, etc. But of course it is best known for the construction of sea-going vessels, the 'hearts of oak' which formed the British fleet.

Oak is by no means easy to turn to a good finish and demands a combination of very sharp tools and sound technique to achieve good results.

**Sycamore** A splendid and hardy tree. Its distinctive leaf form and yellow-green tassel-like flowers, followed by winged seeds, make identification easy. In its converted form, the timber is whitish, with a close fleck grain. Some logs have wonderful rippled markings across the grain and are in great demand, not only by woodturners but also for veneers and the bodywork of stringed instruments. (It is often referred to as 'fiddle-back sycamore'.)

'Sweet is sycamore as a nut' – a fact appreciated by the old rural woodturners, and it was extensively used for making dairy and kitchen implements such as churns, butter scoops, mashers, rolling pins and bowls. It is certainly a joy to turn!

**Walnut** A tree that might well be referred to as the 'aristocrat' of the woodlands because of its delicious nuts and the regal quality of the timber it yields. The leaves of the tree, late to show, are reddish-brown before changing to green. This characteristic, together with the unmistakable deeply fissured grey bark, again make identification easy.

The timber varies from a pale buff colour to dark brown and has a fine, even grain and texture. Besides being fairly hard and durable, walnut is capable of being worked to a smooth, lustrous finish. It possesses a beautifully attractive figure and occasionally throws up a 'ripple' effect such as occurs in sycamore. These qualities, together with its renowned stability, made it the favourite timber of the cabinetmakers of the Queen Anne period.

Supplies of this valuable timber are limited and if the woodturning beginner is fortunate enough to acquire some, I suggest that it should be saved until sufficient skill is attained to do justice to it.

**Yew** One of our three native conifers, and although it is a softwood, its timber is very dense and harder than many hardwoods. The myths and legends surrounding the yew tree are endless, but it is without doubt best known for its use as a longbow, as captured in the lines of Sir Arthur Conan Doyle: 'What of the bow? The bow was made in England, of true wood, of yew wood, the wood of English bows...'

Yew is the longest-living tree in Europe and some specimens are reputed to be as old as the churches in whose yards they stand. The leaves, bark and fruit are poisonous and children should be educated to identify the tree and to be aware of its dangers.

It is without doubt my favourite wood for turning. The colours vary tremendously from the whitish sapwood to the rich brown heartwood, which is often tinted with purple streaks and spots.

All the above are timbers of commerce, and are available, albeit some more easily than others, from sources which advertise regularly in the monthly woodworking magazines.

There are other smaller native timbers equally suitable for woodturning, which are not really 'timbers of commerce'. These smaller trees and shrubs, from gardens, orchards and hedgerows, are not generally on sale from timber merchants, although many turners feel they are most suitable for woodturning and prefer to work with them.

Furthermore, not only are such timbers suitable to turn, but many have beautiful grain and colour which can match even the most exotic of imported species, although the sizes and sections are understandably small. Accordingly, contact with tree surgeons, park officials and local authorities may well prove a valuable source of varieties such as those listed below:

**Apple** Although a very difficult timber to season satisfactorily, it is well worth experimenting with. Despite being very hard and tough, it turns easily and provides a very pleasing reddish-brown coloured timber with attractive grain.

**Blackthorn** A common hedgerow bush that heralds the first signs of spring when its bare black twigs are covered in the familiar masses of pure white flowers. It yields tough strong timber which has a very attractive reddish-brown heartwood and yellowish sapwood.

**Cherry (Wild and Cultivars)** Most desirable and beautiful timbers to turn. The wild cherry provides a slightly scented golden-brown timber which is much valued for high-class furniture, veneers and turnery. It is a tough, strong wood but easy to turn and polishes extremely well.

**Holly** A tree that is familiar and recognizable to everyone with its glossy, dark green prickly leaves. It yields a white timber which is very close-grained and turns easily. This makes it ideal for the 'green' turning of thin-walled bowls and platters, etc. for which many turners are now using it.

**Laburnum** There are few more welcome and striking springtime sights than the laburnum when it 'puts forth its gay blossom'. The timber it yields is equally beautiful and comes a close second to yew as my favourite timber to turn. It is hard and heavy, with a rich brown heartwood marked with golden flecks, contrasting strongly with the pale yellow sapwood.

**Pear** This is another of my favourites to turn. It is remarkably free from knots, hard and even-grained. Its pinkish, pale appearance is sometimes enhanced by the same 'ripple' effect found in sycamore.

**Plum** Very difficult to obtain in large sizes, but if you are fortunate enough to do so, make something special with it because the even-textured timber, which varies from a pale yellow to dark brown and purple, is absolutely beautiful.

In addition to the above non-commercial timbers, I suggest you experiment with others such as lilac, box, rowan, hawthorn and sumac (stagshorn). You will be pleasantly surprised not only by the ease with which they turn, but also by the beauty they reveal in their grain and colour.

**Scots Pine** A valuable commercial softwood, it is used extensively in the building and construction trade. You may have read that it is not suitable for turning, but I disagree. With the recent increased demand for pine bedroom and kitchen furniture, and the use of turned components, woodturners are realizing the full potential of this attractive timber. It matures to a rich honey colour when finished with clear lacquer.

Pine is an ideal timber to practise on. When you can get a good finish on pine straight off the tools, then you can consider yourself accomplished. I use it a great deal when demonstrating to convince people it is a suitable timber to turn, and that a good finish is possible without recourse to heavy sanding.

An important advantage of using this timber, particularly for practice, is that you can often acquire suitable off-cuts fairly cheaply, and additionally the workshop is filled with the pleasant aroma of pine shavings.

## Imported and Exotic Timbers

I will not discuss the imported and exotic timbers in any great detail here, as I consider them unsuitable for novice woodturners until a fair degree of proficiency has been attained. Mistakes on projects made in these exotics can be very costly indeed. Moreover, the sight of an expensive piece of timber whirling round on the lathe can make the operator too cautious and inhibited when he should be aiming for a relaxed attitude and fluency in tool use.

However, here is a simple list of a number of exotics which have proved to be ideal for turnery:

**Amarello** Origin – South America. A dense yellow/cream timber.

**Blackwood** Origin – Africa. A hard, dense and extremely heavy timber. The heartwood is black in colour, as you would expect.

**Bubinga** Origin – West Africa. It is purplish-brown in colour, sometimes having a mottled effect in deeper tints.

**Cocobolo** Origin – South America, and one of my favourites. A rosewood species, it provides an extremely attractive colour variation ranging from purple to yellow and black markings.

**Ebony** Origin – India and the Far East. It is not always black, as many believe, but may be medium to dark brown. A fine even texture and extremely dense.

**Olivewood** Origin – Europe, and another of my personal favourites. It is yellowish-brown in colour, with variegated darker streaks, and affords a fine lustrous finish.

**Rosewoods** Origin – Central and South America, and from India. There are many varieties of rosewood and all are suitable for turnery. All are very expensive but the timber is absolutely beautiful.

**Zirocote** Origin – Central America and West Indies. An exceptionally beautiful, hard and heavy timber with a fine close grain. It is a dark grey colour with irregular black lines and comes up to a smooth lustrous finish.

There are now dozens of varieties of exotic timbers coming on to the market and those interested in buying such woods should study the woodworking magazines to find reliable suppliers.

Finally, as regards timber species, even a brief account of tropical trees cannot omit:

**Mahogany** The excellence of this timber was recognized as long ago as the Spanish colonization of the New World – in fact some of the vessels of the Spanish Armada were made of mahogany.

For over a century it was the favourite wood of the cabinetmaker. This was because of its dimensional stability, the ease with which it could be worked by hand tools, and its beautiful rich appearance.

**Brazilian Mahogany** Widely used by woodturners and cabinetmakers and still available in very wide boards up to about 30" wide. It is ideal for reproduction wine tables, dumb waiters, Victorian-style tea tables, etc., where dimensional stability is absolutely vital.

# WITH A LITTLE UNDERSTANDING

Understanding all the peculiarities and the unpredictability of timber demands a lifetime's study. The only real way to begin to understand is to work with it. However, it is desirable for any woodworker to have a basic understanding of the growth, structure, seasoning, shrinkage and defects of the timber tree. Such knowledge will enable him to choose the best species for a particular job and anticipate its problems.

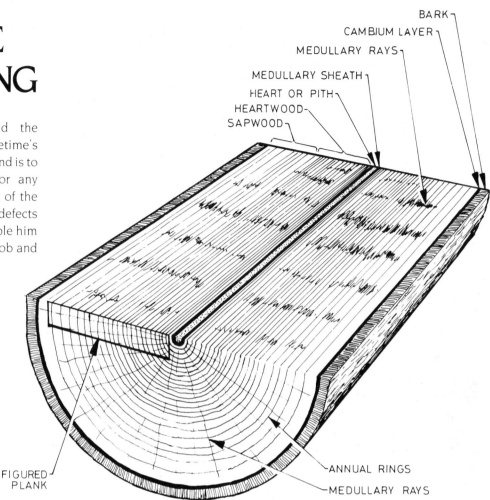

Fig 1.1 Section of an oak tree.

# STRUCTURE OF A TREE

Fig 1.1 shows a section of an oak tree, illustrating the structure common to most trees.

**The pith** is the original seedling, sometimes hardly visible. It remains soft and is commercially useless. It should be cut out.

**The heart** represents the first few years of growth in the young tree. This part dries up and is cut away during conversion, since it is unsuitable for constructional work.

**Heartwood** is the most durable timber and is the part of the tree between the heart and the sapwood.

**Sapwood** is the later growth of the tree and is quite porous. It is not suitable for constructional woodwork, but a mixture of heartwood and sapwood in 'green' bowl-turning is very popular and produces spectacular variations of colour.

**Annual rings,** each indicating one year's growth, give an accurate indication of the tree's age and are formed by differing rates of growth in spring and summer.

**The cambium layer** consists of living cells which form new wood on one side and bark on the other side.

**Bark** acts as a protective covering.

**Medullary rays** radiate from the centre of the tree and are found in all woods, though they are discernible in few. They are very distinct in woods such as oak (silver-fleck grain), beech and plane.

# SEASONING

The object of seasoning is to remove the sap and moisture which are present when the tree is felled. If this were not done, timber used for constructional work would shrink considerably, causing warping and open joints and a consequent loss of strength.

The two most common methods of seasoning are:

**Natural seasoning** This is without doubt the best method but can take many years. The planks, boards, logs, etc. are stacked in the open air but protected from direct sunlight and water by a roof. Laths or skids placed between the layers ensure a free circulation of air. The rule of thumb calculation for seasoning time is one year for each inch of timber. Thus a plank three inches thick would take approximately three years to season.

**Unseasoned or 'green'** This kind of turning is much in fashion these days, particularly for bowl work. Many examples can be seen where the blanks have been turned extremely thin and allowed to find their own shape.

**Kiln drying** Timber is placed in a closed chamber through which hot air is circulated, which speeds up the seasoning process. Inevitably it makes the timber more costly. It is also very much an exact science, and timber which is incorrectly kilned loses its elasticity and tends to become brittle.

## Shrinkage

Shrinkage is caused by evaporation of the moisture in the wood. The unequal distribution of this moisture (the majority being located in the sapwood) means that shrinkage is not uniform. Thus in logs, shrinkage is obviously greater on the outside, and this causes cracks to occur on the outside first and run towards the centre (Fig 1.2).

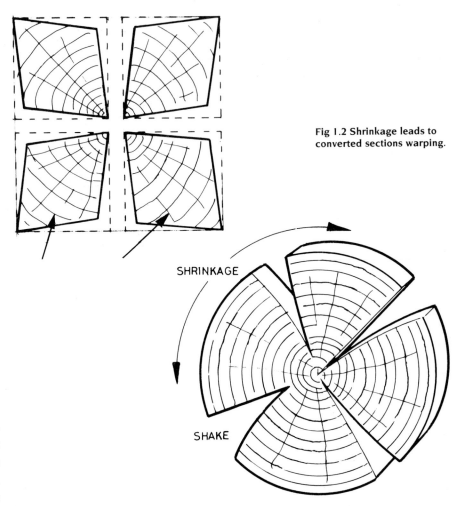

Fig 1.2 Shrinkage leads to converted sections warping.

SHRINKAGE

SHAKE

## Warpage

This unequal shrinkage causes planks and boards to become warped or 'dished'. It follows that the rounded side always appears on the heart side of the timber. Accordingly, allowances must be made for such warpage in all branches of woodwork, including turning (Fig 1.3).

# DEFECTS IN TIMBER

Using timber which is unsound or defective for woodturning can be dangerous. Every piece of wood to be mounted in the lathe should first be examined. Some of the most common defects are as follows:

**Heart shake** This develops if the heart of the tree decays, or the wood inside the growing tree shrinks.

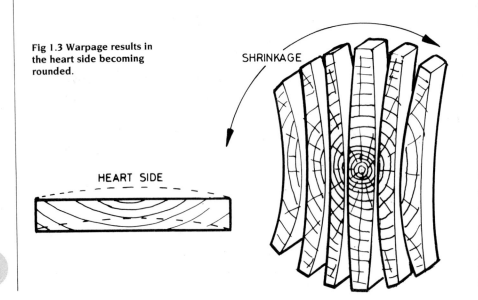

Fig 1.3 Warpage results in the heart side becoming rounded.

SHRINKAGE

HEART SIDE

Heart shakes radiate outwards from the pith and badly affected pieces should be discarded (Fig 1.4).

**Star shake** This begins on the outside of the stock and follows the medullary rays inwards. Star shakes are usually caused by unequal shrinkage, as outlined above. This type of shake can be extremely dangerous to the woodturner (Fig 1.5).

**Cup or ring shake** Cracks appear on the annual rings and are caused by a growth defect, probably as a result of high winds or of fungal or insect ravages. Again, they can be dangerous to the turner (Fig 1.6).

**Knots** There are many kinds. 'Sound' knots which are solid and hard, although not easy to cut, present no danger to the turner. 'Dead' or loose knots are a different matter and can cause injury to the turner if they 'fly'.

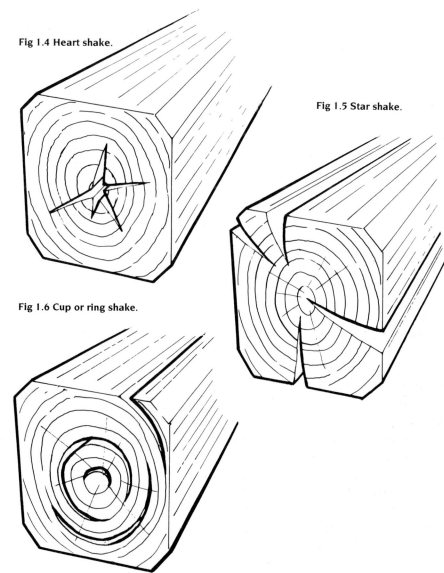

Fig 1.4 Heart shake.

Fig 1.5 Star shake.

Fig 1.6 Cup or ring shake.

# HAZARDOUS TIMBERS

There are a number of timbers, generally imported species, which can be harmful when being machined, turned or sanded. The fine dust from the mahoganies, rosewoods and many other exotic woods can cause irritation to the eyes, nose, throat and lungs. I adamantly refuse to work iroko, which badly affects me, even though I wear a protective mask and use an extractor. Makore, mansonia, padauk, guarea and partridge wood all affect me and prolonged exposure to dust from such timbers is obviously highly inadvisable.

# SOURCES OF TIMBER

Timber is expensive, so the aspiring turner would be well advised to apply his thoughts to obtaining wood from cheap sources. As mentioned earlier, pine off-cuts can be obtained from most joinery manufacturers and are ideal for practice. Autumn is a good time to ask gardeners, park and local authority officials, tree surgeons, etc., for prunings and felled fruit trees.

# SUMMARY OF CHAPTER

**1** Teach yourself to be able to identify as many trees as possible, in both their natural and converted states.

**2** While learning, make do with off-cuts, soft or hardwood, together with hedgerow, orchard and garden trees and shrubs.

**3** Remember that green wood turns much more easily than seasoned timber and is comparatively cheap.

**4** Beware of defects such as shakes in timber – they can be dangerous. Beware also of the dust from imported hardwoods and wear a dust mask when sanding.

# Chapter 2

# THE WOODTURNING LATHE AND ACCESSORIES

# BRIEF HISTORY OF THE LATHE

Indulgence in a little nostalgia may indeed be good for the soul, and certainly no book on woodturning would be complete without mentioning the history of the lathe.

Some early lathes consisted of sturdy wooden base frames with a lath or springy piece of wood conveniently positioned and secured to generate energy by reflex action. A piece of cord was fastened to the lath, wrapped twice around the wood and then tied with a loop hanging about 12" from the ground.

The turner would insert his foot into the loop and depress the cord. This pulled the lath downwards and caused the wood to revolve. On releasing the downwards thrust, the lath would recoil or spring back to its original position, causing the wood to revolve in the opposite direction. Thus the wood was made to spin forwards and backwards, and the turner had to time the application of the tools to the work *only* on the revolutions towards him.

The 'loop' principle was eventually replaced by the more sophisticated treadle, and in the UK – particularly in the beech forests of the Chiltern Hills – pole-lathes, which were very similar in concept to the more primitive types, were in everyday use until forty years ago.

The turners, known as chair bodgers, produced chair components such as legs, stretchers and rails for assembly in the furniture centre of High Wycombe, established there because of the proximity of the beech forests.

The term 'bodge' is associated with inferior or shoddy workmanship today, but the chair bodgers certainly did not fit this description – they were highly skilled and industrious craftsmen. They hold a unique place in the history of woodturning in the UK. They set up their lathes in the woods and turned the timber almost *in situ*, rather than establish workshops in the towns or villages and have the timber carted to them. Simple and very often crude shelters were erected in the forest to house the turner and his pole-lathe. The trees were selected, felled and then cross-cut to a suitable length for the various chair components.

With the aid of heavy mallets, axes and draw knives, the logs were cleft and rough shaped before being mounted in the lathe and turned 'green'. The industry and speed with which the components were turned, bearing in mind the equipment being used, never fails to amaze. Many of the bodgers were capable of completing a chair leg in about two minutes, relying on a trained eye to a great extent to copy turn. Fig 2.1 gives some idea of what the shelter and pole-lathe would have looked like.

Demonstrations on such lathes are regularly featured at the various woodworking shows, and witnessing them in action makes one realize how skilled the operators were, and how much physical effort was required.

In rural England virtually every village had its own craftsmen, including wheelwrights and carpenters. These craftsman made use of lathes powered by an apprentice turning a handwheel or the more sophisticated treadle and flywheel. Such lathes were predominantly constructed of wood, metal fittings made by the village blacksmith being restricted to the 'drive' and 'dead' centres.

The Industrial Revolution heralded the introduction of heavy cast commercial lathes, several lathes often being powered by one electric motor through a system of pulleys, belts and shafts. Few people other than those earning a living from woodturning had access to a lathe. Techniques and methods were jealously guarded, which was understandable when you consider that the very livelihood of the turner was at stake.

Nowadays, with the increase in leisure time, there has been a tremendous resurgence of interest in the craft, on both a professional and a hobby basis. One has only to look through the various woodworking magazines to realize how great this interest is. Many companies are now producing lathes with electric motors which can be run off the domestic electricity supply.

Additionally, there is an increasing number of turning tools, lathe accessories and chucking devices available on the market. This can be extremely confusing to the newcomer to the craft, trying to determine what he requires in the way of basic tools and equipment to get started. The following goes some way towards clarifying the situation.

Fig 2.1 A chair bodger at work.

# TYPES OF MODERN LATHE

Although woodturning lathes vary from manufacturer to manufacturer, the basic requirements of the lathe dictate that all must be quite similar. Broadly speaking there are two types of lathe:

### Free Standing Lathes

These are generally the heavy duty variety used in the trade, and when rag-bolted into a concrete plinth are well able to cope with the sometimes extreme forces associated with large section turnings. These lathes, with their heavy castings, are very expensive and it is not suggested that the novice rushes out to buy one. However, if in the course of searching for a lathe, a reasonably priced second-hand model becomes available, then buy it *if* you have room.

Perhaps the best known lathe of this type is the Harrison Graduate, the design of which was influenced by the late Frank Pain, a renowned woodturner. These lathes are much sought after in the second-hand market. I acquired a second-hand Graduate Short Bed (Fig 2.2) which is ideal for turning table tops and large heavy bowls. Fig 2.3 shows the Long Bed.

### Bench Mounted Lathes

These are the type most beginners will buy for their first lathe. Bench mounted lathes vary considerably in size, weight and price, many professional turners and cabinetmakers using exclusively the heavier models of this type.

Bench mounted lathes can be further divided:

### Swivelling Headstock

The Coronet Number 3 model heavy duty lathe (Fig 2.4) is eminently suitable for the professional, being capable of large-diameter 'faceplate' *and* 'between centres' turnings. I have one of these lathes which will turn 48" between centres and up to a maximum of 30" diameter with the swivelling headstock facility (Fig 2.5). It is in regular use for the production of bar, shop and staircase fittings for which I find it completely satisfactory. It is also used

**Fig 2.2 The Harrison Graduate 'Short Bed'.**

**Fig. 2.3 The Harrison Graduate 'Long Bed'.**

**Fig 2.4 The Coronet No. 3.**

**Fig 2.5 The Coronet No. 3 showing the swivelling headstock.**

Fig 2.6 The Tyme Cub.

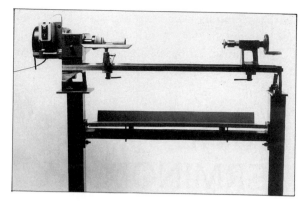

Fig 2.7 The Tyme Cub showing the swivelling headstock.

Fig 2.8 The Myford Mystro.

as a second teaching lathe and is extremely popular with the students.

A lighter duty example of this same type is the Tyme Cub (Fig 2.6). The swivelling headstock can be used to good advantage to turn a bowl (Fig 2.7). The Cub is a popular and proven smaller lathe, available in three different bed lengths and competitively priced.

The most recent addition to this type of lathe is the Myford 'Mystro' (Fig 2.8), which I have had the opportunity of testing for two weeks in my own workshop. This is a superb lathe and in my opinion the most positive and 'user friendly' lathe I have ever used. I subjected it to stringent tests on all aspects of turning and it came through them with flying colours.

All models are fitted with a totally enclosed fan-cooled motor, and supplied with a reversing/stop/start switch as standard. The reversing capability makes it much easier to obtain a superior finish on bowls and suchlike, even when notoriously difficult and coarse-grained timbers are being turned.

The headstock can be swivelled and locked on its vertical axis at any position between 0° and 180°. Three indent positions at 0°, 45° and 90° are also provided for convenience. A plunger locking mechanism facilitates not only the easy removal of faceplates and chucks but also the indexing of the spindle through 24 positions for such things as routing and boring operations.

The standard lathe is equipped with five step pulleys which provide a good range of speeds. The model I tested was fitted with an infinitely variable speed unit, which is a tremendous asset to the production turner.

Myford are to be congratulated on this new lathe. They have obviously listened to, and heeded, the advice of professional and production woodturners and have succeeded in producing a lathe which is a joy to use. Despite it being at the top end of the price bracket, I think the discerning woodturner will recognize it as being value for money. I shall definitely be investing in the 'variable speed' model.

With all lathes of this type, less space is required than with the other types and when undertaking large diameter turnings. This is an important consideration when space in the workshop is limited.

**Sliding Headstock**

Typical of this type of lathe is the Arundel K450 (Fig 2.9), a superbly engineered medium duty bench model lathe. Although by no means at the bottom end of the price range, it is suitable for both the beginner and the experienced turner.

By sliding the headstock along the twin bed bars, diameters up to 18″ can be turned by making use of the end turning assembly. I have had one of these lathes for some considerable time and use it for

**Fig 2.9 The Arundel K450.**

both teaching and demonstrating. I consider it ideal for both purposes.

Sufficient workshop space to enable the operator to work at the end of the lathe must of course be available.

# LATHE TERMINOLOGY

At the beginning of your venture into the craft of woodturning, it is important, as it is when you buy a new car, to get to know your machine thoroughly and as quickly as possible. Knowledge breeds self-confidence and makes for a more assured approach. The purchasing of spares and accessories can be quite a painful and embarrassing experience if you are not familiar with the characteristics and specifications of your own lathe.

I have said that lathes vary from one manufacturer to another, but the names of the main components do not alter. Fig 2.10 shows an example of a bench

**Fig 2.10 The components of the lathe.**

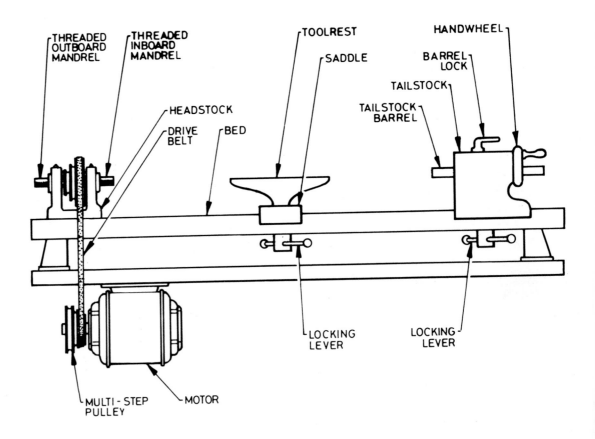

mounted lathe with the motor fixed underneath the lathe. (This is purely in the interests of clarity as the majority of this category of lathe have the motor mounted behind or to one side of the headstock.)

The 'business' end of the lathe is called the headstock, which on the better lathes is a casting of iron fixed to the bed at the left-hand side. The mandrel on to which drive pulleys are fixed is mounted in bearings, the quality of the bearings and distance between them being of paramount importance in smooth, vibration-free running.

Some mandrels are hollow to facilitate fittings being removed by tapping out with a round bar and hammer. The mandrel may be threaded on the inboard side only (as in the case of the swivelling headstock and sliding headstock types on pages 12 and 13), or on both the inboard and outboard, as shown in the drawing and in the case of the combined outboard and between centres models such as the Harrison Graduate Long and Short Beds, page 12.

To prevent attachments working loose on the outboard side, the mandrel is provided with a left-hand thread, which means both right- and left-hand accessories need to be obtained.

The inboard side of the mandrel is nearly always bored out with a decreasing tapered hole called a 'Morse taper' into which fit corresponding tapered fittings such as pronged drives, Jacobs chucks, etc.

The Morse tapers should be kept clean or they will not 'home in' correctly and this could result in 'chatter'. Check with your handbook and find out what size of Morse taper is fitted to your lathe. The files range from 1 to 3, although the majority of bench model lathes come with the number 1 size.

Power to the mandrel is supplied by the electric motor and activated by the drive belt fixed to the stepped pulleys mounted on both the motor and mandrel. These stepped pulleys also determine the speed at which the lathe will run.

When turning between centres, the wood is fixed between the headstock and the tailstock, the latter also normally being bored out to take Morse taper fittings. It can be slid along the bed of the lathe to the desired position and secured in place by the locking lever.

Additional adjustment can be made on the tailstock by means of the handwheel and threaded barrel. It is important, particularly when boring holes using a Morse taper chuck in the tailstock,

that there is at least 2″ of travel on the barrel or it will be painfully slow to bore.

The term 'swing over bed' means the largest possible diameter capable of being turned between centres. For example, if the height between the bed and the centre of the mandrel is 4½″, the 'swing' will be 9″. (Note, however, that the toolrest assembly will obviously reduce this maximum capability.)

Lathe beds are manufactured in a variety of sections such as single round bars, double round bars, square bars, angle iron and pressed steel. The most important demands on them are for stability and strength to prevent flexing and distortion in use. Unfortunately some of the cheaper lathes fail this requirement. Additionally, the lathe bed should be accurately machined to ensure that the tailstock and toolrest assembly slide easily along it.

# BASIC FITTINGS

### Toolrests

These come in all shapes and lengths. I consider about 15″ is the maximum length that can be adequately supported by a single stem. Rests longer than this will require two stems and the corresponding extra saddle.

The sections of some toolrests are totally unsuitable and make tool manipulation and control extremely difficult. Figs 2.11 and 2.12 show the two profiles I prefer. Fig 2.11 illustrates the type fitted to Harrison Graduate lathes and reduces leverage on

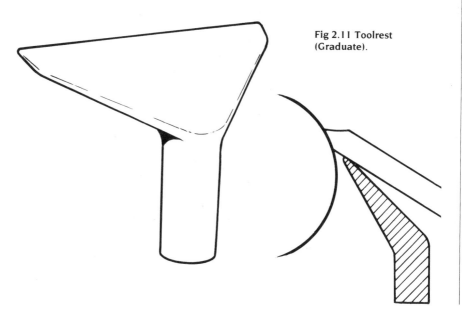

Fig 2.11 Toolrest (Graduate).

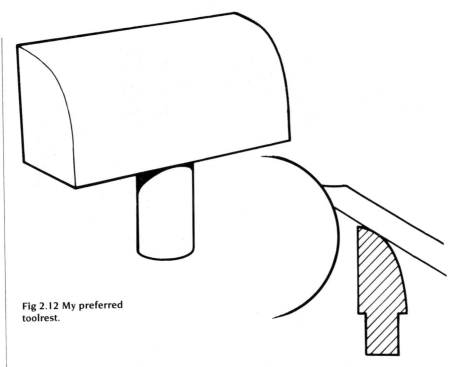

**Fig 2.12 My preferred toolrest.**

## Faceplates

These come in a range of sizes and I think for general purposes a 4" plate is the most useful. Traditionally, faceplates were the favourite method of many turners for bowl and platter work. Many now prefer the modern, sophisticated (and very expensive) specialist and multi-purpose chucks.

Faceplates are drilled to take a thick shanked screw to allow them to be fastened to the workpiece. I use the larger sizes for turning table tops, and they provide maximum support and prevent deflecting which can cause a heavy dig-in.

The faceplate is also employed in the making of a sanding-disc attachment and the mounting of scrap pieces of timber to serve as friction or 'jam fit' chucks.

# MINIMUM ACCESSORY REQUIREMENT

Generally speaking, a lathe comes with the basics such as a drive and a dead centre, one small toolrest and possibly a faceplate.

What then is the *minimum* requirement so far as accessories are concerned? First, if a faceplate is not included in the package, I would suggest you buy one.

Additionally, I suggest you buy a good woodscrew chuck. Unfortunately there are some very poor ones on the market, but I recommend you buy the 2½" screw chuck manufactured by the Coronet Lathe and Tool Co. which I consider to be by far the best individual screw chuck available.

Finally under this heading I recommend you purchase a Jacobs chuck which is a must for the many boring and drilling jobs on the lathe. It can be used in either the headstock or the tailstock by means of the Morse taper. However, in my opinion, the best type is the one where the Morse taper unscrews from the main body to enable it to be screwed on to the mandrel, so providing a much better hold when boring large holes. A few drills and bits can also be purchased to get you going.

The basic accessories shown in Fig 2.13 will enable you to carry out a wide variety of

the tool to a minimum, thereby providing easier control. Fig 2.12 shows the profile I prefer above all others, but I do not know of a manufacturer who produces such a design (the rests supplied with the Arundel lathes are the nearest thing to it) so I have them made by an engineer friend. The near vertical face of this rest affords easy traversing cuts and the radiused profile provides for the fulcrum being where it needs to be – that is, as close as possible to the wood.

### Drive and Tailstock Centres

You will probably get a four-prong drive centre and a dead centre supplied with your lathe, the pronged variety being fitted to the headstock and the dead centre to the tailstock.

Drive centres are made with either two or four prongs and vary in width across the prongs from about ½" to 1½". Dead centres (which means they are static, the wood revolving round them) are normally conical in shape and can create problems such as burning. loosening of the wood and the consequent 'chatter'.

The desirable alternative to the dead centre is the 'live' or 'revolving' centre fitted with a bearing allowing the centre to revolve with the wood. This eliminates friction, burning, loosening and 'chatter'. Beware, though, for there are some very poor examples on the market, fitted with extremely inadequate bearings with too much movement in them.

woodturning functions, and many turners derive a great deal of pleasure and satisfaction from making additional wooden chucking devices themselves.

# SPOIL YOURSELF ACCESSORIES

While in no way essential for mastering the various techniques in woodturning, the following instruments and devices can be extremely useful and will serve to speed up and simplify many operations:

**Measuring instruments and bits** such as calipers, dividers, rulers, twist bits etc. (Fig 2.14).

**Long hole boring kit** designed for the drilling of long holes for such projects as table and standard lamps (Figs 2.15 and 2.16).

**Combination or multi-purpose chucks.** There seems to be an ever-increasing supply of these sophisticated chucks from several well-known manufacturers. I possess both the Coronet (Fig 2.17) and the Precision Combination Chuck marketed by Craft Supplies Ltd (Fig. 2.18) for use on my courses.

**Fig 2.13 Basic accessories.**

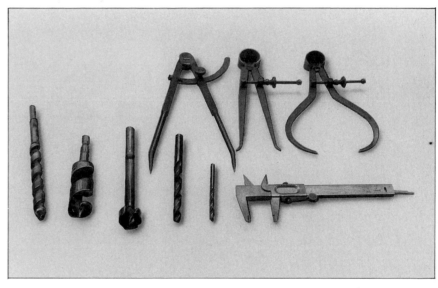

**Fig 2.14 Top, left to right: dividers, internal calipers, external calipers. Bottom, left to right: two machine wood augers, sawtooth machine bit, two engineer's twist bits, Vernier calipers.**

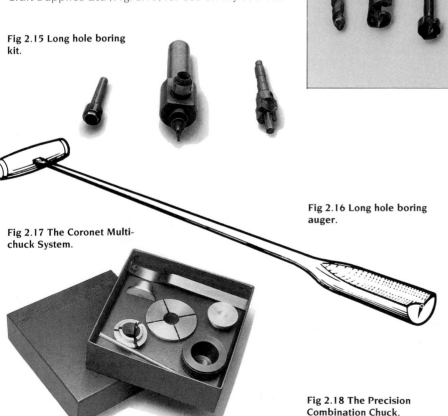

**Fig 2.15 Long hole boring kit.**

**Fig 2.17 The Coronet Multi-chuck System.**

**Fig 2.16 Long hole boring auger.**

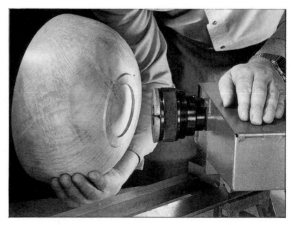

**Fig 2.18 The Precision Combination Chuck.**

# CONSIDERATIONS WHEN BUYING A LATHE

Ask yourself the following questions:

*What kind of turning do I propose to do or aspire to?*

*How much space have I got to site the lathe?* (If space is limited, remember the swivelling headstock type of lathe facilitates larger diameter turning without having to stand and work at the end of the lathe.)

*How much money have I got to spend?*

When you have the answers clear in your mind, you will need to compare the specifications of the lathes you are attracted to for such matters as:

The required distance between centres and the swing over bed.

The range of speeds available, (I consider you need no fewer than four different speeds ranging from approximately 500 rpm to 2000 rpm.)

Ease of adjustment to tailstock, speed changing and toolrests.

Consider whether the manufacturers are reputable and well established, whether they offer a good range of accessories and spares, and how long a guarantee they give.

If you decide on a combined outboard and between centres lathe, you must be prepared to spend extra on left- and right-hand attachments.

# GETTING THE BEST OUT OF YOUR LATHE

As with any other machine, thought has to be given to several factors to ensure you can use it to its full capability. Additionally, any machine needs to be well maintained and securely mounted.

If you take into account the factors listed below, you should ensure you derive maximum performance, comfort and satisfaction from your lathe.

## Siting

Make sure you site the lathe so that you are left with enough room at the tailstock end to use such accessories as the long hole boring kit. Similarly, if your lathe is of the outboard or sliding headstock type, you need at least 30" of extra space beyond the end of the lathe to work in.

Every turner needs the best possible light to work in, so it makes sense to position the lathe under a window. Daylight will of course need to be supplemented with perhaps strip lighting and/or a movable spotlight, which is particularly helpful when turning hollow ware.

## Maintenance

Bearings of the adjustable type need to be correctly set and lubricated in accordance with the manufacturer's instructions.

Drive belts need to be kept at the correct tension to provide adequate drive and to prevent 'belt slip'. (This can also occur if the drive pulleys work loose, so check these too and tighten the securing grub screws with an Allen key.)

Keep the toolrests in good order by occasionally running a file over the tool-bearing surface to remove any slight nicks. White spirit applied on a rag will remove oil and the resinous deposits which some timbers exude. It is a regular practice of mine to wipe a waxed cloth along the surface of the toolrest and this certainly makes for ease of tool traversing, particularly on long straight cylinders.

Keep the lathe bed clean by occasionally spraying it with something like WD-40 and rubbing with a fine wire wool. The threads on all the fixtures also need regular lubrication, and don't forget to use a small file to keep the prongs of the drive centres sharp.

Morse taper fittings (male and female) need to be cleaned. I use paraffin and wire wool. Oil obviously cannot be used or they will not 'bite'.

Time spent on cleaning and maintaining your lathe is time well spent. Not only does it make for ease of use, but it also ensures the lathe keeps or even enhances its value.

## Mounting

No matter how good a lathe is, if it is incorrectly mounted you will not get the best results. You should have stable, smooth running, otherwise you will encounter all kinds of problems.

Floor standing lathes are generally rag-bolted into a concrete plinth and this, combined with the very heavy weight of the lathe, provides for optimum performance and smoothness.

To get similar results from a bench mounted lathe, the bench needs to be as heavy and robust as possible. Below is a description of how to make a wooden bench like the one I made for my Coronet Number 3 lathe.

The construction of the bench is well within the capabilities of most people and the cost is small. The length will obviously have to be arrived at according to your particular lathe, but the method of construction will remain the same.

In the interests of a comfortable working posture, the *height* of the lathe is very important. As a rough guide the centre of the lathe mandrel needs to be approximately in line with the turner's elbow.

### Method of Construction

1  Set out the angles of splay on the bench ends by drawing out a section full size on a piece of plywood.

Now set your adjustable bevel to the angle so determined. Note that the height of the bench is arrived at by *adding* together the measurements of **(a)** distance between bottom of lathe foot and centre of mandrel and **(b)** any packing piece/cushion you choose to place under the lathe feet both to give more space for the hands and to damp out any slight vibration. (I used pieces of 1½" thick plywood and also pieces of ¼" thick rubber.)

Now *subtract* this measurement from the other relevant measurement (i.e. from ground level to elbow height) which will give you optimum bench height.

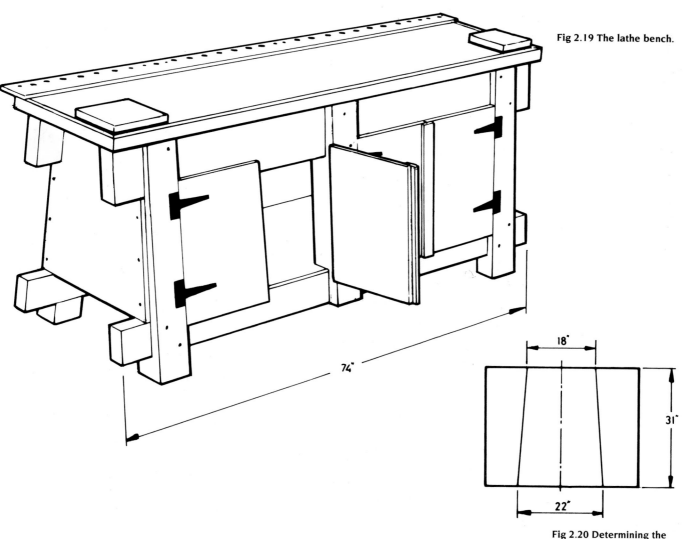

Fig 2.19 The lathe bench.

Fig 2.20 Determining the angle of splay.

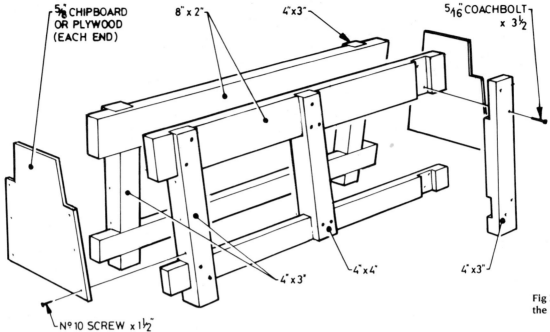

5/8" CHIPBOARD OR PLYWOOD (EACH END)

8" x 2"

4" x 3"

5/16" COACHBOLT x 3½"

4" x 3"

4" x 4"

4" x 3"

Nº 10 SCREW x 1½"

**Fig 2.21 The construction of the bench frame.**

**2** Set out the halving joints on the legs, top and bottom rails. These can be cut using a panel saw and chopped out with mallet and chisel. Now cross-cut the rails and the legs to length. Note that the legs at top and bottom will require cutting at the previously determined angle. The uppermost edges of all four rails will also need to be bevelled at the same angle along their full length with a hand plane.

**3** Glue and bolt the two main frames together.

**4** Cut the end panels as determined by the full-size drawing, drill and countersink for the screws and then assemble. You may well need some assistance to keep the side frames steady while you screw up the end panels.

**5** The bottom shelf now needs to be marked out, cut to fit around the protruding legs and inserted from the top of the bench. Failure to do this *before* fitting the top will mean that you cannot get the shelf fitted in one piece. Nail or screw the shelf in position.

**6** The top, which ideally should not be less than 1½" thick, is then screwed to the frame and lipped if desired with some ½" thick material, either soft or hardwood.

**7** The plywood back should now be fixed, preferably with woodscrews.

**Fig 2.22 Adding the base, back and top to the frame.**

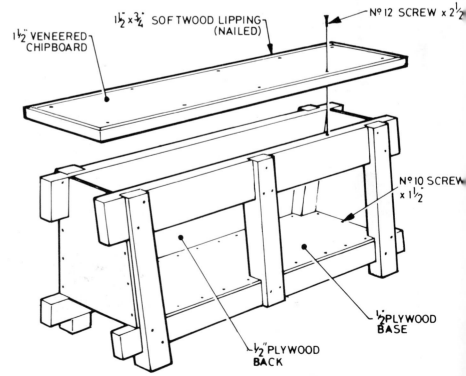

1½" x ¾" SOFTWOOD LIPPING (NAILED)

Nº 12 SCREW x 2½"

1½" VENEERED CHIPBOARD

Nº 10 SCREW x 1½"

½" PLYWOOD BASE

½" PLYWOOD BACK

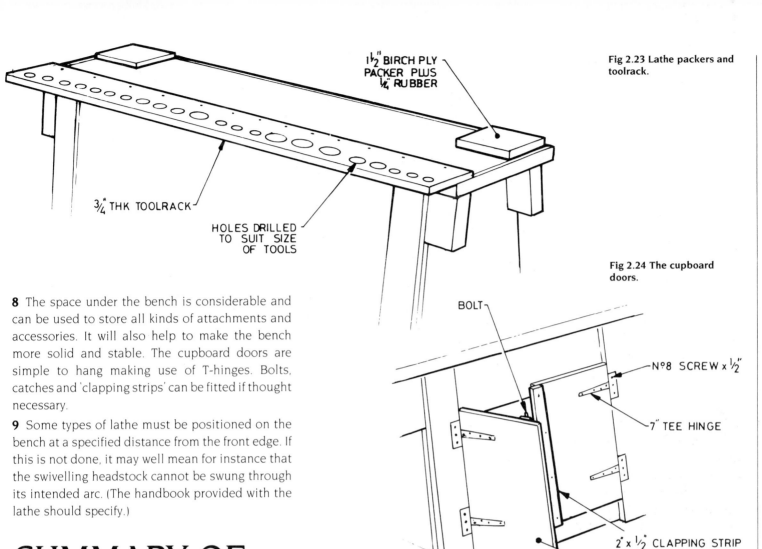

1½" BIRCH PLY
PACKER PLUS
¼" RUBBER

**Fig 2.23 Lathe packers and toolrack.**

¾" THK TOOLRACK

HOLES DRILLED
TO SUIT SIZE
OF TOOLS

**Fig 2.24 The cupboard doors.**

BOLT

N°8 SCREW x ½"

7" TEE HINGE

2" x ½" CLAPPING STRIP

¾" THK CHIPBOARD

**8** The space under the bench is considerable and can be used to store all kinds of attachments and accessories. It will also help to make the bench more solid and stable. The cupboard doors are simple to hang making use of T-hinges. Bolts, catches and 'clapping strips' can be fitted if thought necessary.

**9** Some types of lathe must be positioned on the bench at a specified distance from the front edge. If this is not done, it may well mean for instance that the swivelling headstock cannot be swung through its intended arc. (The handbook provided with the lathe should specify.)

# SUMMARY OF CHAPTER

**1** Choose the best lathe suited to your purposes after taking into account the advice given in this chapter.

**2** Read the manufacturer's handbook thoroughly and comply strictly with the advice on wiring, mounting and maintenance.

**3** Get to know your lathe as quickly as possible and familiarize yourself with lathe terminology.

**4** In the learning stages, buy as few accessories as possible, but buy the best you can afford.

**5** Add to your basic accessories as your skill increases – you will never be short of ideas for birthday and Christmas presents!

**6** A well-constructed, sturdy bench is essential for bench mounted lathes to ensure smooth, vibration-free running.

**Fig 2.25 The bench with the lathe mounted in position.**

# Chapter 3

## TOOLS
## OF THE
## TRADE

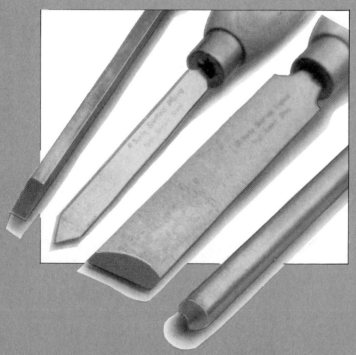

The greater part of my time-serving in the woodworking field was extremely enjoyable, despite the hard physical labour involved in the considerable amount of hand dimensioning.

It is difficult to explain the feeling of satisfaction derived from the slow but sure acquisition of skill: the skills of planing straight and square; of being able to saw straight and true; of being able to fashion all kinds of profiles with hand-moulding planes and of developing the 'feel' of the craft of woodturning.

One of the most important parts of the learning process is to acquire a comprehensive knowledge of all the tools available and to be able to use them to their full potential. The benefit of such knowledge is that unnecessary tool duplication is avoided, also any unnecessary expense.

My mentor always impressed upon me the importance of buying the best available tools for any branch of woodworking, stressing that quality work was easier and more pleasurable to achieve by using good-quality tools.

Quite clearly, making use of good-quality tools not only avoids the constant irritation and frustration you will inevitably experience when using inferior tools. It also instils a degree of confidence in the user. My advice, therefore, is the same as I had from my 'guvnor' 40 years ago – that is, buy the best available but buy only what you really need.

Broadly speaking, there are just two categories of woodturning. These are:

## Turning Between Centres

This is often referred to as *spindle turning*. The stock is driven by an attachment fitted into, or screwed on to, the headstock mandrel, and is usually (but not always) supported by the tailstock.

In this category of turning, the grain of the wood is usually longitudinal to the axis of the lathe bed, as shown in Fig 3.1.

The stock may be turned between centres without the support of the tailstock when accessories such as the screw chuck or the combination chuck are used in the making of hollow ware, e.g. goblets, vases or ornamental boxes. In such work, the grain of the timber is normally parallel to the axis of the lathe bed.

## Faceplate Turning

In this category, the wood is fixed to accessories such as a faceplate, screw chuck or spigot chuck and almost always the wood is not supported by the tailstock.

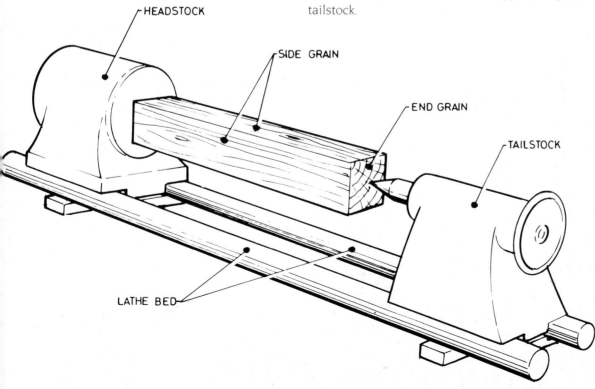

HEADSTOCK

SIDE GRAIN

END GRAIN

TAILSTOCK

LATHE BED

Fig 3.1 Turning between centres – the grain is parallel to the lathe bed.

Such turnings usually involve the turning of discs or bowl blanks where the grain runs along the *surface* of the wood and at right angles to the lathe bed. Thus, twice on every revolution of the stock, end grain will be encountered. Fig 3.2.

**Fig 3.2 Faceplate turning – the grain at right angles to the lathe bed.**

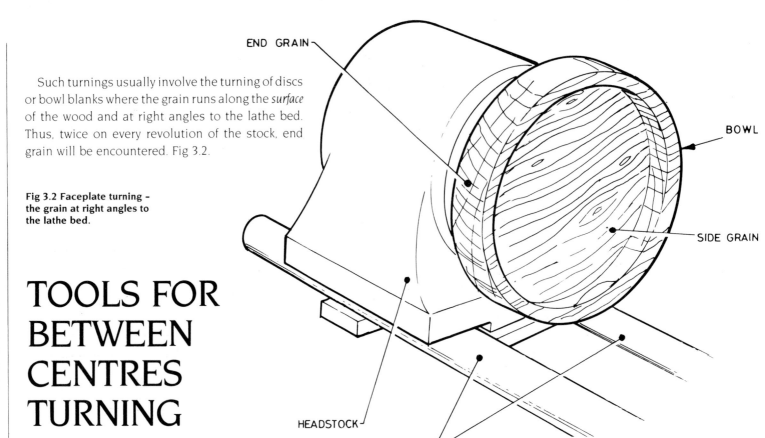

END GRAIN

BOWL

SIDE GRAIN

HEADSTOCK

LATHE BED

# TOOLS FOR BETWEEN CENTRES TURNING

**Gouges** These include roughing out and spindle gouges. Roughing out gouges are available in sizes between ¾" and 1½". Sizes ranging from ⅛" to ¾" are normally available in spindle gouges. Examples of both are shown in Figs 3.3 and 3.4.

**Fig 3.3 Profile of the roughing out gouge.**

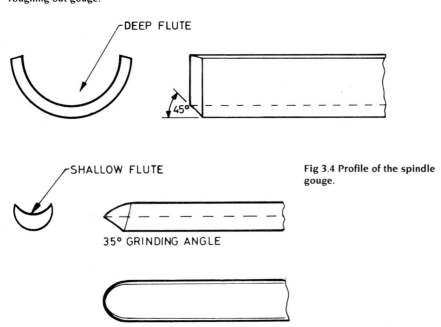

DEEP FLUTE

45°

SHALLOW FLUTE

35° GRINDING ANGLE

**Fig 3.4 Profile of the spindle gouge.**

**Chisels** These include beading tools as well as skew and square across chisels. They are available in widths from ½" to 1½". The profile of the skew chisel is shown in Fig 3.5.

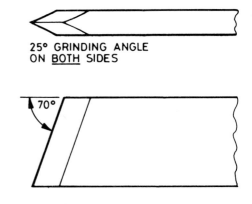

25° GRINDING ANGLE ON <u>BOTH</u> SIDES

70°

**Fig 3.5 Profile of the skew chisel.**

**Parting Tools** Strictly speaking these are chisels. They are available in a variety of widths and sections. I prefer and recommend the ¼" parallel parting tool, as shown in Fig 3.6.

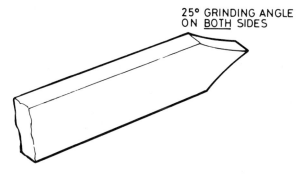

25° GRINDING ANGLE
ON <u>BOTH</u> SIDES

**Fig 3.6 Profile of ¼″ parting tool.**

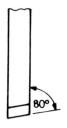

**Fig 3.9   Profile of 1″ domed end scraper.**

It is important to remember that gouges and chisels (including parting tools) are cutting tools and are generally used in the bevel rubbing mode. See Chapter 5 on the Laws of Woodturning.

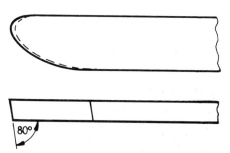

**Fig 3.10 Profile of ³⁄₈″ round nose scraper.**

# TOOLS FOR FACEPLATE TURNING

**Bowl Gouges** These are available in sizes from ¼″ to ¾″. The recommended ³⁄₈″ size is shown in Fig 3.7.

**Fig 3.7 Profile of ³⁄₈″ bowl gouge.**

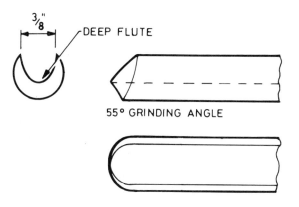

³⁄₈″

DEEP FLUTE

55° GRINDING ANGLE

**Scrapers** These are available in sizes ranging from miniature to massive heavy duty sections. All kinds of profiles are also available. The three recommended sizes and profiles are shown in Figs 3.8, 3.9 and 3.10.

**Fig 3.8   Profile of 1″ square end scraper.**

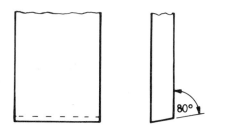

Again, it is important to remember that bowl gouges, like any other gouge, are generally used in the bevel rubbing mode, and that scrapers must be used in the trailing mode. See Chapter 5 on the Laws of Woodturning.

As a general rule, scrapers are not used on between centres turning. Spindle gouges may be used on faceplate turning and bowl gouges may be used on between centres turning, but my advice to the novice is to wait until considerable skill and control has been attained before using such tools in these ways.

The catalogue description of certain tools is sometimes prefixed 'L & S', which is an abbreviation for 'long and strong'. This simply means that the tool is normally heftier and longer than the standard tool (all bowl gouges are L & S) and consequently more expensive. The beginner will manage quite well with the standard strength variety.

The above information is summarized in chart form in Fig 3.11, providing a quick and easy reference guide.

Fig 3.11 Categories of
woodturning and types of
woodturning tools.

## THERE ARE TWO CATEGORIES OF WOODTURNING

### TURNING BETWEEN CENTRES

### FACEPLATE TURNING

(a) Grain runs parallel to lathe bed.

(b) Work driven by 'pronged' centres and usually supported by tailstock.

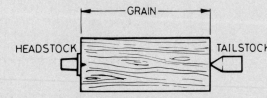

(c) Sometimes, the tailstock is not used, e.g. in holloware where 'open end' is necessary to shape the inside of goblets, egg cups, boxes, etc.

(d) In (c) the grain is usually in the same direction, but the work is driven and supported by accessories such as the screwchuck or combination chuck.

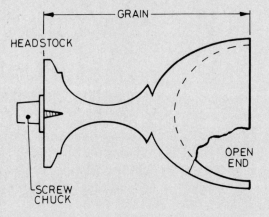

(a) Usually entails the turning of discs and bowl blanks, where grain runs on the 'surface'. Therefore end grain is encountered twice on every revolution on the edge of the blank.

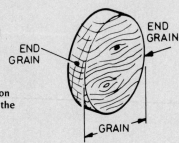

(b) Initial fixing is by means of either a screw chuck, faceplate or spigot chuck.

(c) Usually there is no support from the tailstock.

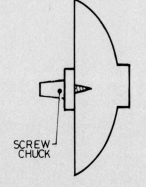

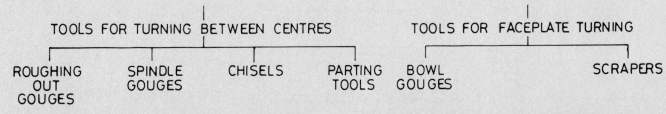

### TOOLS FOR TURNING BETWEEN CENTRES

### TOOLS FOR FACEPLATE TURNING

**ROUGHING OUT GOUGES**

**SPINDLE GOUGES**

**CHISELS**

**PARTING TOOLS**

**BOWL GOUGES**

**SCRAPERS**

(a) Available in sizes from ³/₄" to 1¹/₄".

(b) Available in sizes from ¹/₈" to ³/₄".

(c) Available square, or skewed and in a variety of sizes.

(d) Available in differing profiles, ¹/₈" to ³/₈" wide.

Available in sizes from ¹/₄" to ³/₄".

Sizes range from 'miniature' section, to massive heavy duty 1¹/₂" x ³/₈" bar. Numerous profiles available.

# SELECTION AND PURCHASE OF TOOLS

Woodturners in the UK are extremely fortunate in the choice and quality of turning tools available to them. Manufacturers such as Ashley Iles, Coronet, Robert Sorby and Henry Taylor enjoy a world-wide reputation for producing quality woodturning tools. I am certain that anyone who purchases a set of tools bearing any of these brands would not be disappointed. In order to make your choice, spend time in the tool shops, comparing and handling each tool until you are satisfied that a particular tool feels right for *you*. To aid you, here are a few general comments regarding choice.

Some of the most attractive tools on the market are the handled Sorby brand. The handles, which are shaped as handles for woodturning tools should be, are made from beautiful hand-polished ash. Each one comes in its own individual sleeve, which can be used to hang up the tool.

Sorby also market a range of over 60 high-speed steel turning tools fitted with Mexican rosewood handles. While they are more expensive, they do look superb.

I have used Robert Sorby woodturning and general woodworking tools for many years and I have never been disappointed in their quality.

Ashley Iles are world famous for the manufacture of high-quality woodcarving and woodturning tools. The beechwood-handled tools are not so attractive as others, but the handles are adequate and well shaped. Their skew chisels have edges which are slightly radiused, a feature which greatly assists in smooth traversing when planing and rolling beads.

To my knowledge Iles is the only manufacturer producing a 1″ roughing out gouge, which I consider to be the best and most useful size for the beginner (or for anyone who is purchasing only one size).

Coronet, manufacturers of woodturning lathes for over 40 years, have now also entered the woodturning tools market. Visually, their tools also rate very highly. They are available in both carbon and HSS (high speed steel), the former fitted with polished natural beech handles, while the HSS have rosewood-stained beech handles. The general 'feel' and 'balance' of the HSS range, which I have used, seem to be just about ideal, and their 1¼″ roughing out gouge is an absolute joy to use on heavy duty turning.

Henry Taylor tools are also renowned for their superb quality. The design of some of their tools was influenced by the late Peter Child –. an acclaimed and accomplished woodturner – and his designer/engineer son Roy, which is recommendation in itself.

The Superflute bowl gouge designed by the Childs is probably the best-known bowl gouge on the market and for extra large bowls it remains unsurpassed in my opinion.

# CARBON STEEL OR HIGH SPEED STEEL?

In addition to deciding what brand of tool to buy, the would-be purchaser has also to decide whether to purchase carbon steel or high speed steel (HSS) tools.

Without doubt, HSS tools are the better of the two types.

High speed steel tools stay sharp much longer than carbon steel tools. The cutting edge will last up to six times longer, which means of course that the tool itself should have a proportionately longer life. Therefore the initial extra cost is really more economical in the long term.

This extra tool-edge life is not because HSS is necessarily harder, but because it stands up to abrasion and friction better than carbon steel.

In addition to the long-term economical benefits, considerably less time is spent at the grindstone. Perhaps of more importance, the accidental drawing of the temper on HSS during grinding is significantly reduced, if not eliminated.

Unless a very gentle touch is used when grinding carbon steel tools, the tool edge is 'blued' with the attendant 'drawing of the temper'. Beginners are very prone to do just that with carbon steel tools and it all adds up to unnecessary frustration.

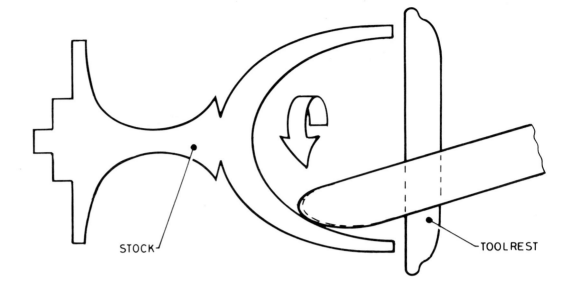

Fig 3.12 The ³⁄₄″ round nose scraper in use.

STOCK

TOOL REST

# THE FIRST SET OF TOOLS

Finally, we come to advice on what tools a beginner should buy.

**Roughing Out Gouge** Either the 1″ or 1¼″ for rapid removal of stock, particularly from square to round, fashioning long slow hollows and rounds, and for other functions which are described later.

**Parallel Parting Tool** ¼″ size. In addition to parting off and sizing cuts, it can be used extensively for rolling fine beads and also for feathering cuts.

**Skew Chisel** 1″ size. For general planing and tapering, the oval section skew manufactured by Robert Sorby is unsurpassed and the easiest for a novice to use. The same size manufactured by Iles, with its radiused edges, is almost as suitable.

**Skew Chisel** ½″ size. For fine V cutting, rolling beads and general 'tidying up', this size is most useful. I prefer not to use the oval section variety for this type of work, so it is a matter of choosing the brand that suits you best.

**Spindle Gouge** ½″ size. Spindle gouges are the 'master' tools in turnery and this size together with:

**Spindle Gouge** ³⁄₈″ size, will enable the experienced turner to fashion any shape or profile. Choose your spindle gouges by handling them and pick those which appeal to you personally. I have spindle gouges from all the above manufacturers and they all perform to my complete satisfaction.

In addition to the six tools listed above, which are primarily intended for between centres turning, I suggest that the initial set of tools should also include four tools to enable the beginner to undertake a certain amount of faceplate work.

**Bowl Gouge** ³⁄₈″ size, this being quite suitable for bowls up to a diameter of approximately 10″.

**Square Ended Scraper** 1″ size for flattening and smoothing convex surfaces.

**Round Nose Scraper** ³⁄₄″ size, for cleaning up the inside of hollow ware such as goblets, vases, egg cups and of course the inside of bowls or any concave surface. For such work, the tool will require profiling as shown in Fig 3.10. An example of this tool in use is shown in Fig 3.12.

**Domed Scraper** 1″ size, for cleaning up the inside of bowls, etc.

As you progress in your turning and your projects become more and more ambitious, you may wish to buy additional tools. Do remember, though, that managing with as few tools as possible teaches you to use them to their full potential. It may surprise you to know that in the course of a day's commercial repetition turning, I rarely use more than five tools.

# CARE OF WOODTURNING TOOLS

Having invested in a good set of tools, it makes sense that everything possible should be done to keep them in good order. First of all, a tool rack is essential so that tools can be conveniently stacked, and to prevent the cutting edges becoming damaged.

An occasional rub with an oily rag will preserve the 'new look' and prevent rust forming. A trick used by some woodturners is to leave the tools under a pile of shavings overnight. Any moisture in the workshop is then absorbed by the shavings. Make sure the shavings are dry and not the product of green turning.

The shavings trick does work but I shall not admit to using it myself. My workshop insurance policy stipulates that I must clean the workshop of shavings at the end of each working day, which I do of course!

# SUMMARY OF CHAPTER

**1** Buy good-quality tools. They will make the learning process that much easier. You will also avoid the constant irritations and frustrations you will surely experience if you buy the cheap varieties.

**2** Buy high speed steel tools. The initial outlay will be nearly double, but the advantages are many.

**3** Take care to store your tools properly so as to avoid damaging the cutting edges – a tool rack is essential.

**4** An occasional wipe with an oily rag will prevent them rusting over.

# Chapter 4

## ON SHARPENING

If it were possible to assemble 100 novice woodturners under the same roof and pose the question, 'What is the greatest single problem you are encountering in your turning?', over 80 per cent would reply: 'Sharpening the tools correctly.'

This is the conclusion I have drawn from research I have carried out, and from talking to hundreds of aspiring woodturners I have met while teaching and demonstrating. It is an irrefutable fact that to be capable of successful and therefore satisfying turning, any turner must use tools which have been ground accurately and to an acceptable degree of sharpness.

When individuals book courses with me, I always ask whether they possess any woodturning tools. If they do, I invite them to bring them along when they come on the course so that I can assess their tool sharpening ability. Unfortunately, it is my experience that the general standard of tool sharpening is extremely low. The overwhelming majority of tools brought for me to assess 'would'na cut butter,' as the old miners in my part of the world would say. When I demonstrate to the owners that I can only bludgeon the wood into some kind of shape, it convinces them of their inability to achieve worthwhile results using tools in such condition.

To borrow a phrase from Margaret Thatcher, tools such as those shown in Fig 4.1(a) *are not for turning.* Fig 4.1(b) shows what they should look like.

Immediately following the 'bludgeoning' demon-

**Fig 4.1 (a) A set of totally unsuitable tools.**

1 2 3 4 5 6 7

1 Used as a roughing out gouge. This tool is too flat in section for such use. The cutting edge is concaved which would result in the protruding 'wings' engaging the wood before the centre of the tool, causing it to twist and dig-in.

2 File adapted for use as a scraper. The grinding angle is too acute (long) and it would rapidly overheat. It is too thin in section for so long a blade and could 'shatter' in use.

3 Spindle gouge. The edge has been ground to a point rather than to a flowing 'fingernail' profile and with too obtuse (short) a bevel.

4 Parting tool. Bevel has been ground to a convex shape which will cause it to dig-in.

5 Another parting tool. Bevel is far too acute making the edge extremely fragile and the tool unpredictable in use.

6 Skew chisel. Adapted from a file. Too obtuse a bevel and multi-faceted. Insufficient file tang driven into the 'handle'.

7 Hooked tool. Claimed by the owner to 'come in handy' for some turning jobs. I can't imagine what!

stration, I give a further quick demonstration using correctly prepared tools, just to emphasize the difference in the *sound* that sharp tools make and the *results* they will produce.

The standard of the tools used in some schools, colleges and further education establishments also causes me concern. This really has to be an indictment of the teacher who, through ignorance or folly, allows turning tools in such poor condition to be used.

I recall going to an open day at such an establishment, and not unnaturally I was drawn to the woodwork section where a boy was demonstrating 'woodturning'. As usual there was a group of interested onlookers, including parents and the teacher.

What I beheld was nothing short of frightening. The pupil had a piece of 3" square stock, about 18" long, mounted between centres and was 'assailing' it with what was obviously a very blunt round nose scraper. He was exerting so much force that the tool was overheating and smoking, but more alarmingly, on two occasions the wood flew off the lathe.

The teacher remained impassive and apparently unconcerned, so I could only assume that what I had just witnessed was the norm. Before beating a retreat to safer confines, I did manage a look at the results of the 'turning' and I can honestly say that better results are achieved by beavers on logs.

I mention this incident for no other reason than to convince the reader that using tools which are blunt, or using them for the wrong purpose, *can be dangerous.*

# EQUIPMENT FOR SHARPENING

There are several types of grinders on the market, including dry grinders, wetstone grinders and combinations of the two. Personally, I prefer and use the double-ended 'dry' bench variety, as do most of the professional turners I know.

Buy the best grinder you can afford, made by a reputable manufacturer. My grinder is equipped with two 7" diameter wheels which are ¾" wide, one

**Fig 4.1 (b) Good, sharp tools!**

being a fine white stone for general sharpening, the other a coarser grey stone for heavier grinding and reshaping.

Avoid grinders with wheel diameters of less than 5". They will impart too much of a hollow ground effect to the tools, particularly the chisels and the 'parters'. This can result in the tool becoming too fragile behind the cutting edge and lead to unpredictable tool behaviour and consequent loss of control.

Avoid also grinders with narrow faced wheels. I consider that anything less than ¾" wide is unsuitable, as they do make the grinding of wider tools more difficult.

Remember that a grindstone is a cutting tool and consequently needs to be kept in good order to retain an efficient cutting action. Continued grinding results in the face of the stone becoming impregnated with metal particles or 'glaze'. If allowed to remain, it will impair the cutting action of the stone, and more force will have to be exerted to complete the grinding.

Extra force results in a greater degree of friction, which in turn generates more heat leading to the tool edge being 'blued', which in the case of carbon steel tools renders them useless by 'drawing the temper'.

If you use the wheels for grinding softer metals such as copper or aluminium, they will rapidly clog up. It makes sense, therefore, to avoid these metals.

The faces of the wheels can be kept in good order

by 'dressing' them with one of the proprietory products available on the market. The most expensive is the diamond dresser. The 'star wheel' type of dresser is a great deal cheaper. However, in my opinion this is one of the rare occasions where buying cheapest is the best, for you can buy a 'devil stone' for a small sum. These are perfectly adequate to maintain the quality of the cutting edge on the face of the wheels.

# SITING AND MOUNTING THE GRINDER

Everything possible must be done to encourage the turner to keep his tools sharp. The grinder must be sited adjacent to the lathe and not a 'route march' away. Similarly, the turner must be able to adopt a comfortable posture when grinding. Accordingly, the centre of the wheels needs to be approximately in line with the centre of his chest. This is particularly important if you are going to adopt the method of tool grinding that I advocate.

# SAFETY CONSIDERATIONS WITH THE GRINDSTONE

Some form of eye protection is absolutely essential when using the grinder. While most manufacturers fix transparent visors over the wheels, these are not totally adequate and must be supplemented by wearing goggles to prevent particles of stone or metal getting into the eyes. There are several types on the market, so choose a pair which are comfortable to wear and store them in a box to keep them dust free.

As part of my maintenance schedule, I remove the wheels from the grinder and do a test to ensure they are still sound and free from cracks. Simply hold the

stone with a length of dowel passed through the centre hole and give the stone a positive flick with a finger on the other hand. If the stone is sound, a distinct high-pitched 'ping' should be heard (see Fig 4.2).

If there is any doubt in your mind about the stone being sound, discard it and buy another. Unsound stones can be *extremely dangerous* if they shatter in use. Workmen have been seriously injured and indeed killed by the shrapnel-like effect of an exploding stone.

Similarly, the mounting of an unenclosed stone on the outboard of the lathe is not only extremely dangerous, but also very stupid and irresponsible. Also, the practice of grinding on the sides of the stones should be avoided. This can have the effect of weakening the stone and could result in it distintegrating.

**Fig 4.2 Testing the grindstone. A wheel in good condition gives a distinctly clear ring when flicked with a finger.**

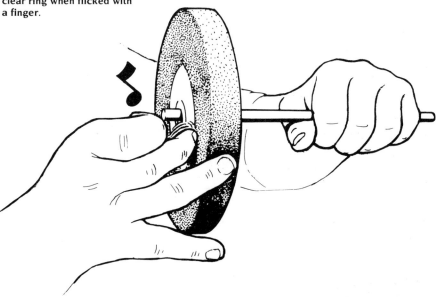

# GRINDING ANGLES

If it were possible to examine and compare sets of turning tools belonging to half a dozen professional turners, it would be evident that hardly any two use the same grinding angles.

Experience would have taught them to grind the angles *best suited to them*, taking into account the type of work they generally undertake and the hardness or softness of the wood they mainly work with.

The longer or more acute the bevel which is ground on a tool, the sharper the edge achieved. There will obviously be less resistance to the tool being pushed into the wood but the edge will be fragile and prone to overheating and crumbling.

Conversely, too short a bevel or obtuse angle on the cutting tools means there will be more resistance to them being pushed into the wood. Accordingly, we are looking for a compromise so the tools will not only cut efficiently and without undue effort, but also stand up to their intended use and provide a reasonable 'tool-edge life'.

As will be explained in some detail later in the book, one of the laws of woodturning is that 'the bevel or grinding angle must rub the wood behind the cut'.

Now if the grinding angle is too acute, the tool, in order to achieve the 'bevel rubbing' mode, will need to be presented with the handle well down, not only in an uncomfortable position but also probably fouling the lathe bed or bench.

Conversely, if a short, obtuse angle is ground on the tool, it will need to be presented almost horizontally, and as the cut proceeds the tool will probably have to be raised to a most uncomfortable position (Fig 4.3).

As I undertake a great deal of commercial softwood turning, I keep a special set of gouges and chisels for this work, all ground with longer than average bevels. Paradoxically, turnings in softwood require sharper tools than hardwood turnings if an acceptable finish is to be achieved. Using other than very sharp tools on softwood will tear the fibres severely, but the effect of such tools used on hard, close-grained timbers would not be so pronounced.

The hobby turner will have no need to go to such expense. He will manage quite adequately with one set of tools ground to an 'average angle'.

What then is the 'average angle'? Taking into account what I have said, I recommend the following approximate angles:

Roughing out gouges – 45°

Spindle gouges – 35°

Chisels and parting tools – 25°

Bowl gouges – 55°

Scrapers – 80°

By all means experiment with different angles, and having found the angles which suit you, it makes sense to keep a note of them.

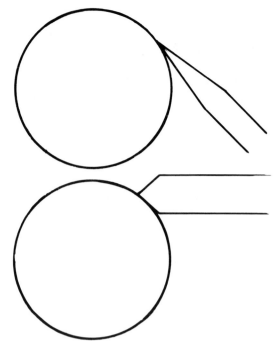

**Fig 4.3 How acute and obtuse bevels affect tool presentation. If the bevel is too long the tool handle will be uncomfortably low. If the bevel is too short the tool handle will be uncomfortably high when turning small stock.**

This can be done by drawing the optimum angles on a piece of stiff card or thin plywood and checking the tools from time to time by simply laying them on the 'datum line' and comparing (Fig 4.4).

My final words on grinding angles are these. If you find the tool is not performing as well as it did when you first bought it, it generally means you have allowed the grinding angle to become too obtuse or too short. Try lengthening the bevel and I shall be surprised if it does not prove more satisfactory in use.

**Fig 4.4 A grinding angle template for the angles that suit you.**

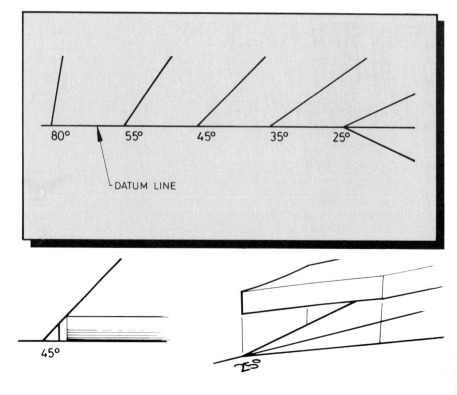

80°  55°  45°  35°  25°

DATUM LINE

45°

25°

# METHODS OF TOOL GRINDING

What is the best method of tool grinding? I was trained to use the 'free-hand method', which most professional turners use and recommend. With this method the tool is offered up to the stone on the heel of the bevel. The back end is then lifted until the grinding sparks just start to come over the top of the tool, indicating that the tool is being ground right up to the edge (see Fig 4.5).

At the beginning of the chapter I drew attention to the fact that the greatest single problem the majority of novice woodturners encounter is tool sharpening. The reason is simple — they use the free-hand method of grinding. I am convinced that more beginners to the craft give up woodturning because of sharpening problems than for any other reason.

When I began teaching the craft, and being aware of such problems, I decided to simplify the sharpening process for two very good reasons:

**1** The absolute need to have *one* continuous angle ground on the tools. The reason will be explained in Chapter 5 on the Laws of Woodturning.

**Fig 4.5 Freehand grinding. The tool is presented so that the heel engages the grinding wheel first. Sparks will flow beneath the bevel. The handle of the tool is gradually raised until the sparks flow over the top of the tool.**

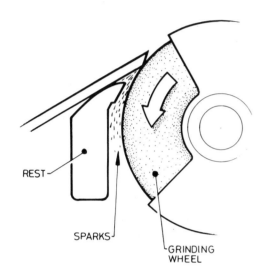

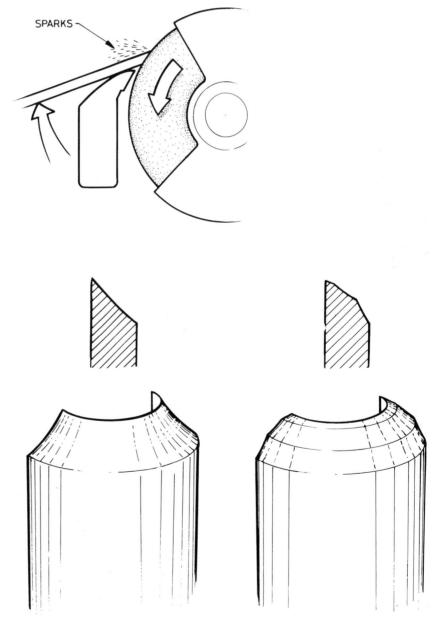

If anyone tries to persuade you that this method is easy, don't you believe them! To be able to 'free-hand' grind to an acceptable standard takes considerable practice and no little time, particularly on the larger gouges and scrapers which require substantial rolling and swinging movements. It is not easy to avoid a multi-faceted or convex bevel, as opposed to the desired single-facet, concave bevel (see Fig. 4.6).

**Fig 4.6 Correct and incorrect grinding. On the left is what we are trying to achieve: a single-facet concave bevel. On the right is what we are trying to avoid: a multi-facet convex bevel.**

**2** It is of paramount importance for beginners to enjoy a certain amount of success, in order to motivate them and to maintain desirable degrees of interest and enthusiasm.

If they do not have success with their tool grinding, they most certainly will not have success with the subsequent turning. Interest and enthusiasm will dwindle, sharpening will be looked upon as a chore and the chances are that they will become disillusioned and give up. Even if they carry on, they will never make good woodturners using badly prepared tools.

Taking all this into consideration, I strongly recommend that not only beginners but also any turner who is experiencing difficulty with sharpening, should adopt the 'jigged' method of sharpening.

Most grinders are supplied with adjustable platforms or 'jigs', if you like, but for the purposes of 'jigging' for turning tools they are not suitable. Incidentally, if you do adopt this method, the existing slotted supports for the platforms will need to be sawn off with a hacksaw (see Fig 4.7).

The slots in the baseboard should be in line with the two grinding wheels to facilitate use on both. The four bolts securing the grinder to the baseboard need to be countersunk flush with the underside to prevent rocking.

Similarly, the two slots in the baseboard should be routed out (alternatively, use tenon saw and joiner's chisel) to a depth and width to accommodate

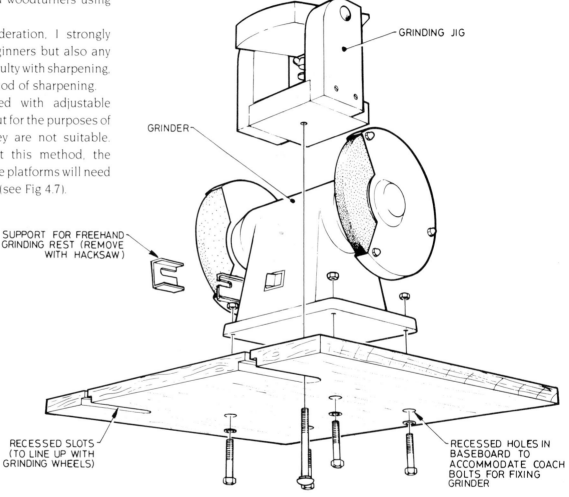

**Fig 4.7 Exploded view of the grinder and jig.**

SUPPORT FOR FREEHAND GRINDING REST (REMOVE WITH HACKSAW)

GRINDING JIG

GRINDER

RECESSED SLOTS (TO LINE UP WITH GRINDING WHEELS)

RECESSED HOLES IN BASEBOARD TO ACCOMMODATE COACH BOLTS FOR FIXING GRINDER

My particular method is to make use of a purpose-built wooden jig, which is easy to make, simple to use and will ensure *accurate grinding* after very little practice. The method is so simple, I rarely free-hand grind these days. What is more, despite all the years of practice I have had free-hand, I can grind the tools more accurately with the jig.

Basically the arrangement, as can be seen from Fig 4.7, consists of a baseboard on to which both the grinder and the jig are bolted. This makes it portable and capable of being G-clamped to any flat surface.

the bolt heads. This will enable the jig to be easily moved from stone to stone.

The actual jig platform on which the tools are placed needs to be no less than 3½" wide. The need for this width will become apparent when you grind tools like the large section round and domed scrapers which require substantial swinging movements (Fig 4.8).

The reason for this platform being slotted out – use brace and bit and square out with chisels – will also become obvious in use. If it was not, you would have difficulty in adjusting to the various angles without the platform fouling the grinding stone.

Make sure you use wing nuts on the bolts securing the jig to the baseboard and the one passing through the platform. They are much more convenient to use and more than adequate tension can be applied by finger pressure.

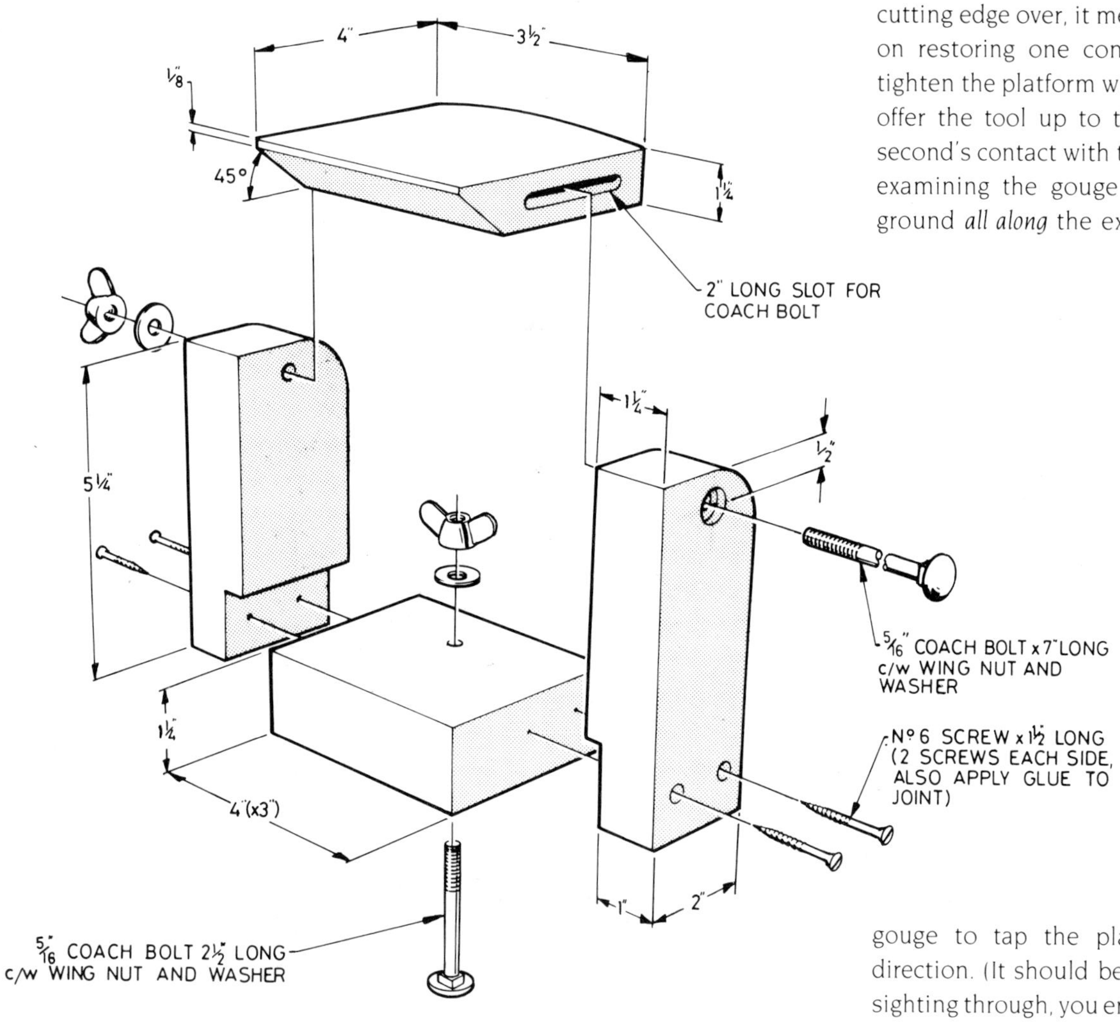

4"  3½"

1/8"

45°

1¼"

2" LONG SLOT FOR COACH BOLT

5¼"

1¼"

½"

Fig 4.8 The construction of the grinding jig showing dimensions.

5/16" COACH BOLT x 7" LONG c/w WING NUT AND WASHER

N° 6 SCREW x 1½" LONG (2 SCREWS EACH SIDE, ALSO APPLY GLUE TO JOINT)

1½"

4"(x3")

1"  2"

5/16" COACH BOLT 2½" LONG c/w WING NUT AND WASHER

# HOW TO USE THE JIG

At first, I suggest the correct angles are approximately determined with the grinding wheels stationary. (After very little practice, you will find you are able to adjust the jig with the grinder

running, which of course speeds up the process.)

Take a roughing out gouge and lay it on the jig. Slacken the wing nut on the platform and adjust to the approximate angle by 'sighting through' from one side. (Now it becomes obvious why the centre of the grinder needs to be high enough to line up with the centre of your chest – too low a position and you could finish up being wry-necked, Fig 4.9(a).)

If anything, in the sighting through process, err on the side of the heel of the bevel. If you 'dub' the cutting edge over, it means unnecessary time spent on restoring one continuous angle. Now lightly tighten the platform wing nut, start the grinder and offer the tool up to the stone *very gently*. Only a second's contact with the stone is necessary before examining the gouge to ascertain if it is being ground *all along* the existing bevel. If not, use the

gouge to tap the platform in the appropriate direction. (It should be on the front edge if, when sighting through, you erred on the heel of the bevel.)

Repeat the process until the new, shiny grind can be seen all along the bevel. Now nip the wing nut and complete the grinding (Fig 4.9 (b) and Fig 4.10).

If all this sounds difficult and complicated, I can assure you that it is not. After a few attempts, you will be able to set the platform to follow the existing bevel in seconds.

To make a *precision* grind, it merely remains for the tool to be kept flat on the platform and rolled from side to side. I use the fingers of my right hand to both roll the tool and apply a gentle forward

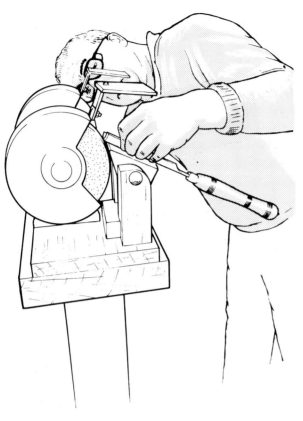

Fig 4.9 (a) 'Sighting through' of the grinding angle.

pressure to maintain tool contact with the stone. I use the fingers of the left hand to keep the tool perfectly flat on the platform and to assist in the rolling movements also.

Do not 'dwell' either at the beginning or the end of the roll, or you run the risk of 'bluing' the tool edge. Keep a pot of water adjacent to the grinder and dip the tool into it frequently during the learning stages. Constant practice develops the desired gentle touch and then you will have no need to dip the tools in the water.

Very little metal needs to be removed to restore an acceptable degree of sharpness to the tool edge, and you will find just a few rolls of the tool is sufficient. This, combined with the gentle touch, means that there is little chance of the tool edge over-heating. A good test is to grasp the tool edge in the palm of the hand immediately after grinding. It should not feel uncomfortably hot. If it does, *drop it quickly*, taking care to miss your feet!

I will not go through the method of sharpening every type of tool in this chapter. Individual tools are dealt with in Chapter 6, Turning Between Centres, and Chapter 7, Faceplate Turning.

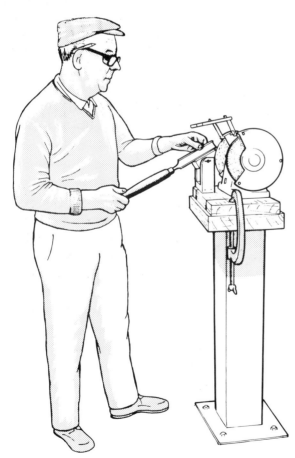

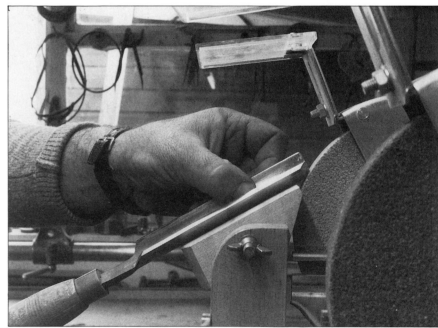

Fig 4.9 (b) The grinding jig in use.

Fig 4.10 The requirements for tool grinding.

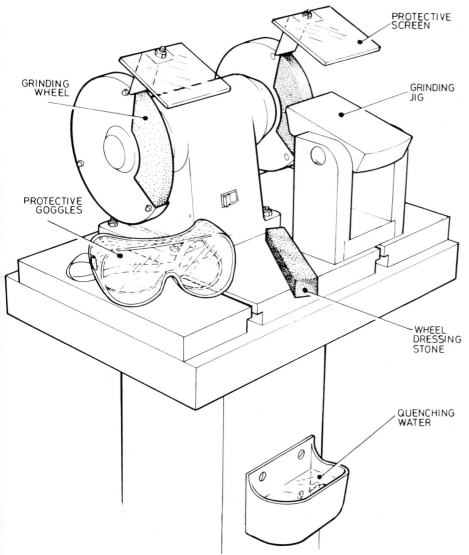

- PROTECTIVE SCREEN
- GRINDING WHEEL
- GRINDING JIG
- PROTECTIVE GOGGLES
- WHEEL DRESSING STONE
- QUENCHING WATER

# ACCEPTABLE DEGREE OF SHARPNESS

This could be defined as: 'Preparing the tool edge to a degree of sharpness which will, in skilled hands, produce as good a finish as possible, taking into account the characteristics of the wood.'

As a general rule, this edge can be achieved direct from the grinder, without recourse to oil-stones. This is the opinion of myself and a number of professional turners. However, a sharper edge can be achieved by honing the edge on an oil-stone. The question is: 'Is it necessary?'

Other than for softwoods, I don't think it is. If you decide to hone, extreme care must be taken not to create a multi-faceted tool, which can cause the tool to 'dig-in'.

To avoid spending a disproportionate time on sharpening, I suggest you first of all try the tools straight off the grinder. I should be surprised if you were not satisfied with the results. Fig 4.10 illustrates a typical grinding set-up and the required ancillary equipment.

# SUMMARY OF CHAPTER

**1** Before successful and enjoyable woodturning can be achieved, there is an absolute requirement for the tools to be accurately ground with *one continuous bevel* and to an *acceptable degree of sharpness.*

**2** Eye protection is essential when using the grinder.

**3** The angles which are used to grind the tools are not critical, but having found the angles that suit you, make a note of these on a template.

**4** Making use of a grinding jig ensures accurate grinding, the jig being easy to make and simple to use.

# Chapter 5

## LAWS OF WOODTURNING

When it comes to actually using your tools to shape the wood in woodturning, there are certain rules, or as I prefer to call them, 'laws', which need to be complied with in the interests of safety, tool control and quality of finish. Just as you may expect punishment if you offend the criminal law, you will certainly receive punishment in the form of pain if you offend these 'Laws of Woodturning'!

Drawing on my own and other turners' experience, I have always been reluctant to make definitions relating to woodturning 'laws' and 'procedures', because you can be assured that someone, somewhere, is doing exactly opposite to what you are preaching.

For instance, I was demonstrating at a local woodworking show when I was approached by a man who had brought along some of his work for me to assess. There were items of both spindle and faceplate work and the standard, taking into account the short time he had been turning, was quite good.

He went on to say that he had not read any books on the subject, neither had he ever seen anyone else demonstrate the craft. Then in all sincerity, and to my utter amazement, he enquired if it was usual for turners to stand at the side of the lathe on which I was standing, because he always stood at the back of the lathe!

Nevertheless, being well aware that there are loopholes in every law, and that in stating or defining laws, I am likely to be in conflict with other turners, I put forward and define what I consider to be the 'Laws of Woodturning'.

**Law 1** The speed of the lathe must be compatible with the size, weight and length of wood to be turned.

**Law 2** The tool must be on the rest *before* the whirling timber is engaged, and must remain so whenever the tool is in contact with the wood.

**Law 3** The bevel (grinding angle) of the cutting tools must rub the wood behind the cut.

**Law 4** The only part of the tool that should be in contact with the wood is that part of the tool that is receiving *direct support* from the toolrest.

**Law 5** Always cut 'downhill' or with the grain.

**Law 6** Scrapers must be kept perfectly flat (in section) on the toolrest and presented in the 'trailing mode', i.e. with the tool handle higher than the tool edge.

# Law 1

**The speed of the lathe must be compatible with the size, weight and length of wood to be turned**

Considerable downward forces can be encountered in woodturning, such forces increasing in proportion to increased speeds and the size, weight or imbalance of the timber being turned.

The inherent *dangers* in mounting large pieces of 'out of balance' stock in the lathe cannot be overstressed. Perhaps relating two separate incidents will serve to illustrate and highlight such dangers.

The first incident involved an acquaintance who, at the time of the mishap, had not acquired much turning experience. Thinking that large-bowl turning was the thing for him, he decided to tackle an 18″ x 4″ disc of imbalanced elm.

He neglected to adjust the lathe to its slowest speed, but started the machine up while it was set to run at its fastest speed about – 2000 rpm.

The inevitable happened: the wood came loose on its mounting and flew from the lathe with considerable force, smashing into his face. He sustained serious facial injuries and his nose was shattered. He still bears the scars.

The second incident happened to me personally and was really caused by carelessness. Again it highlights the absolute requirement to comply with Law 1 *before* the lathe is switched on.

I had been engaged in turning some newel posts in 5″ square stock and exceeding 5′ in length. Shortly before lunchtime and just as I was removing a completed newel from the lathe, one of the farm labourers came into the workshop and asked me to turn a bung for a device on a farming implement. I adjusted the lathe from the slow, safe speed that I had been using for turning the newels to the top speed of 2000 rpm for the small diameter bung. I completed this 'free' job and went for lunch.

You can no doubt guess what happened when I returned to continue with the newel posts. I neglected to adjust the lathe back down to the slower, safe speed. Fortunately for me, however, I was standing to one side and out of the 'firing line' when I pressed the start button.

41

There followed a terrifying and nerve-shattering noise, the whole of the substantial lathe mounting started to vibrate severely, and before I could press the stop button, the wood flew out of the lathe sending bottles of polish and sealer stacked on an adjacent bench to all corners of the workshop.

Obviously, I could have been seriously injured. It is now a habit of mine to stand out of the 'firing line' when I press the start button. I strongly recommend you do so also.

What then can be considered safe turning speeds?

The general rule is that the larger, heavier or longer the stock, the slower the lathe speed that should be set.

If in doubt, always err on the side of safety, that is, on a slower speed than you think it should be, particularly when using imbalanced stock. It is no trouble to stop the lathe and increase the speed once you have reduced the timber to a cylinder and thus to balance.

This is common practice anyway, because too slow a speed makes it extremely difficult to get an acceptable finish and invariably results in a 'thread' effect, particularly if the tool is traversed other than very slowly.

So far as the length of timber is concerned, it will become evident that fast lathe speeds and long pieces of timber do not go together. Longer lengths usually mean increased weights anyway, but even if the stock is not particularly heavy, e.g. long slender work, the tendency for it to 'whip' increases as the lathe speed is increased.

Taking all these things into consideration, I put forward the following guide to safe lathe speeds. But remember that such speeds can only be approximate because of the differing range of speeds available from lathe to lathe.

### Between centres turning

| Stock size | Up to 24″ long | Over 24″ long |
|---|---|---|
| Up to 2½″ square | 2000 rpm | 1500 rpm |
| 2½″ to 4″ | 1500 rpm | 1000 rpm |
| Over 4″ | 1000 rpm | 750 rpm |

### Faceplate turning

| Stock size | Up to 2″ thick | Over 2″ thick |
|---|---|---|
| Up to 8″ dia. | 1000 rpm | 750 rpm |
| 8″ to 12″ dia. | 750 rpm | 750 rpm |
| Over 12″ dia. | Slowest available | Slowest available |

Finally, remember that your personal safety is the most important consideration, so the general rule

of slow speeds for larger and heavier stock must always be in the forefront of your mind.

# Law 2

**The tool must be on the rest before the whirling timber is engaged, and must remain so whenever the tool is in contact with the wood.**

I make no apologies for stating this law, although some observers might claim that it should not be classed as a law or rule, but merely a matter of common sense.

However, I have never yet taught anyone who has not offended this law, even though I had stressed its importance.

In teaching, I rarely allow students to work on stock exceeding 2″ square during the first morning of the course. Thus, if this or any of the other laws are disobeyed, the consequences are less of a shock to the nervous system than if large section stock was being turned. One of my objectives is to instil confidence in the student, and offending the laws on large section timber does not go far in achieving this aim.

I have already mentioned the considerable downward forces which can be encountered in woodturning and these forces are increased as mass (or weight) and velocity are increased.

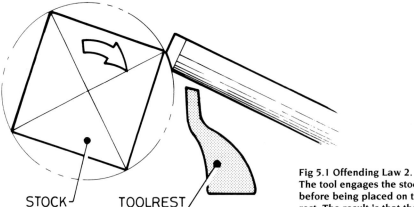

STOCK    TOOLREST

Fig 5.1 Offending Law 2. The tool engages the stock before being placed on the rest. The result is that the tool is smashed on to the rest, tool control is lost and the tool digs into the stock.

If the tool comes into contact with the wood *before* it is in contact with the rest, it will be smacked downwards on to the rest with some force and you may well finish up with bruised fingers and black fingernails. Additionally, the tool may be snatched from your grasp, there will be tearing of wood fibres, and your nerve and courage will be dented (Fig 5.1).

In my experience, beginners are more likely to offend this law in the roughing down of square section stock than during any other operation. The reasons for this are discussed in Chapter 6 on Turning Between Centres.

I have mentioned that there are loopholes in most laws. So far as this particular law is concerned, one is in the use of scrapers on the outside of bowls and discs. Some turners will use 'scraper bars' without bearing them on the toolrest. I have never found any particular advantage in the practice, and I certainly do not recommend that newcomers to the craft try it.

# Law 3

### The bevel (grinding angle) of the cutting tools must rub the wood behind the cut.

Before discussing how to present the cutting tools to the whirling wood in order to achieve the 'bevel rubbing' mode, we should first of all distinguish between cutting tools and scraping tools. This may he helped by stating that there are two distinct methods of shaping or turning the wood to the desired profile.

The first is by use of the cutting tools, these being the gouges, chisels and parting tools, which are presented at a tangent or 'bevel rubbing' angle to the spinning wood (Fig 5.2(a)).

The tools in this category, as described in Chapter 4, On Sharpening, are ground at angles raning from

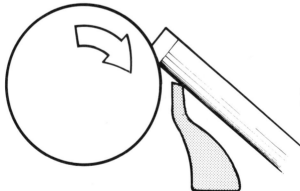

25° to 55°, depending on the type of tool.

Such tools will remove stock from most species of timber at a desired rate, and in skilled hands will give an acceptable finish and retain their cutting edge for a surprisingly long time.

As a general rule, the cutting tools, with the

exception of the bowl gouge, are used only on between centres turning, where the grain runs parallel to the bed of the lathe.

The second method of shaping wood is by the scraping method. You may have read theoretical arguments claiming that a scraping tool *cuts*, and indeed I agree that a sharp scraper will produce cleanly cut shavings on some varieties of timber, even when being used in between centres turning. However, for the purposes of this book and in the interests of clarity, cutting means using the cutting tools and scraping means using the scraping tools.

By referring back to Chapter 4 it will be seen that the scraping tools are ground with a much more obtuse angle (shorter bevel) than the cutting tools.

In the same chapter it was also explained that the shorter the bevel, the greater the resistance to the tool being pushed into the wood.

In theory, scraping tools, with their short bevels, could be presented in the bevel rubbing mode. However, the resistance to the short bevel would be so pronounced that the operator would have great difficulty in preventing the tool succumbing to the downward forces and the resultant heavy 'catch' or dig-in.

For this very good reason, scrapers, as indicated in Law 6 below, must always be used in the 'trailing mode', which means that the tool should not be used on the bevel, but must point slightly down (Fig 5.2(b)).

Now a scraping action with any tool generates

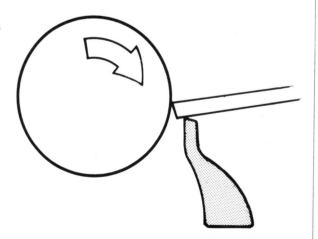

**Fig 5.2(a) The cutting tool is presented at a tangent to the revolving cylinder of wood.**

**Fig 5.2(b) The scraper tool is presented to the wood in trailing mode.**

considerably more friction and heat to the tool edge, which of course means the tool may rapidly overheat. This is why scrapers are ground with an obtuse angle so the heat can be absorbed and give acceptable 'tool edge life'.

Applying the same logic, if cutting tools, with their longer bevels, are used scraper fashion, the edge will rapidly overheat, having the effect of both softening and dulling the tool edge extremely quickly.

This is why accomplished turners, using the cutting tools as they should be used, spend less time at the grindstone than the less skilled turner, whose part scraping, part cutting technique necessitates more frequent visits to the grinder.

Hopefully, by now I have convinced you that the gouges and chisels (parting tools are really chisels) should be used in the bevel rubbing mode, and the scrapers should be used in the trailing mode.

I dismiss those who say that there is no craftsmanship in using scrapers, and I will discuss this further in Chapter 7, Faceplate Turning.

### How to Achieve the Bevel Rubbing Mode

I like to compare this technique with 'clutch control' when driving a motor car.

In driving, the clutch must be raised slowly and smoothly to avoid 'biting' or engaging too quickly. The consequence of too quick a bite is the embarrassing and sometimes nerve-racking 'kangarooing' known to us all.

To achieve a smooth 'takeaway' with the cutting tools, they must first of all be presented to the whirling wood so that they will not cut at all, or at what I like to call *the safe angle of presentation.*

This is done by placing the tool on the rest with the tool handle well down so only the heel of the bevel is making contact with the wood.

The engaging, biting or cutting is brought about by the smooth drawing down of the tool towards the turner, while at the same time the back end is lifted, (Figs 5.3(a) and 5.3(b)).

This will ensure that you *find the bevel,* a term I shall be using frequently throughout the book. In clutch control, the more you lift your foot, the greater the degree of bite. In tool control, the more you lift your back hand (after having 'found the bevel') the greater the bite, or in other words, the thicker the shaving you will fetch off.

When learning clutch control in a car, the learner driver practises on an up-slope until able, by lifting or depressing the foot, to move slowly forward or remain stationary.

A direct comparison can be made between 'holding the car on the clutch' and bevel rubbing, for

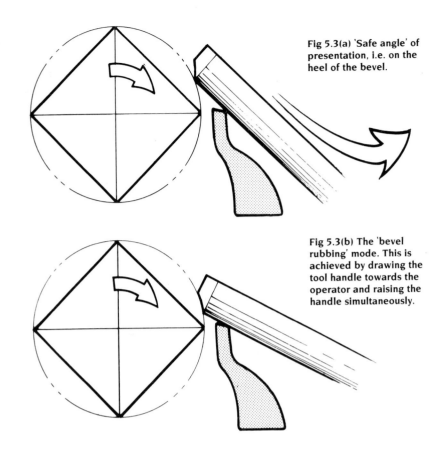

**Fig 5.3(a)** 'Safe angle' of presentation, i.e. on the heel of the bevel.

**Fig 5.3(b)** The 'bevel rubbing' mode. This is achieved by drawing the tool handle towards the operator and raising the handle simultaneously.

when the whole of the bevel is rubbing, it is like holding the car on the clutch, because *nothing is happening.* The car isn't moving; no wood is being removed.

In both cases, all that is needed to make something happen is to lift. Lift the foot on the clutch or lift the back end of the cutting tool: the car moves or, similarly, cutting commences.

Does this appear to be a paradox? Firstly I'm saying the bevel must rub, then I'm saying if the whole of the bevel is rubbing, nothing is happening.

The truth of the matter is that *behind the cut* the bevel must be rubbing and a frequent comment I make to students who are struggling to make balanced shapes is, 'put the bevel where you have just cut'.

Also, remember with scrapers that the shaving thickness is dictated by the amount of forward pressure applied to the tool. With the cutting tools, the amount of forward pressure does not affect the shaving thickness in the slightest if the correct technique is used. Try it, by first of all 'finding the bevel' with a roughing out gouge, lifting the back end of the tool to take a fine shaving and then, while traversing the tool along the rest, applying as much forward pressure as you like. The shaving thickness remains constant because of the bevel rubbing on the wood behind the cut, supporting the cutting edge.

The only thing which can affect the thickness of shaving is *the lifting of the back hand*, but despite the thickness of the shaving, the bevel of the tool must rub the wood behind the cut.

If the tool edge is not receiving such support, it is free to bury itself into the wood. This is likely to happen if you present a cutting tool in a scraping mode because it will be impossible for the bevel to support the cut.

In the chapter 'On Sharpening', the importance of grinding the tools with one continuous bevel was emphasized. The reasons should now be obvious because if you use a multi-faceted tool, it will not take a shaving until it is lifted off the bevel nearest to the cutting edge. This means the other 'bevels' cannot possibly support the cut (Fig 5.4).

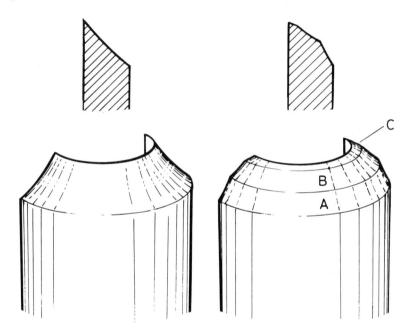

**Fig 5.4 Correct and incorrect grinding. On the left is the single-facet concave bevel which would provide adequate bevel rubbing potential. In the example on the right it would be impossible for the bevels marked A and B to give support to the cutting edge. The only part of the bevel that could possibly rub behind the cut is C, which is inadequate. A rounded or convex bevel would be similarly inadequate.**

Similarly, a tool ground to a rounded or convex profile will likewise give no support to the cutting edge.

## Other Advantages of Bevel Rubbing

The ability to make the bevel rub behind the cut also helps to provide flowing, balanced shapes in your turning.

Additionally, bevel rubbing imparts a burnishing effect on the wood, making it smooth and shiny. This manifestation is one of the hallmarks of the skilled turner.

If you dobt this, take a roughing out gouge and reduce a piece of 2″ square pine to a cylinder, leaving as good a finish as your level of skill allows.

Now drop the back end of the tool until it just stops cutting (remember holding the car on the clutch?) and apply a moderate or, if you like, a positive forward pressure as you traverse the tool along the rest. Now see the wood take on a burnished, shiny look!

This is what you should be aiming for in the use of all your cutting tools, and when you can consistently achieve it, you have progressed a long way down the path to being an accomplished woodturner.

# Law 4

**The only part of the tool that should be in contact with the wood is that part of the tool that is receiving direct support from the toolrest.**

Failure to obey this law will nearly always result in a catch or dig-in.

Let me then explain this and make it as simple as possible to understand. I have already mentioned the downward forces encountered in woodturning, such forces increasing as the mass (weight of timber) and velocity (speed of lathe) are increased.

To counteract these forces, it has been stressed that the tool must be on the rest during the cutting process (Law 2).

Notwithstanding your obedience to Law 2, a dig-in will almost certainly occur if the downward forces are applied to a part of the tool edge not receiving *direct support* from the toolrest.

The principle of a child's seesaw provides an adequate analogy. If the seesaw was perfectly balanced on its centre pivot or support, it would remain perfectly parallel to the ground. If downward force is applied where the seesaw is balanced – that is, over the centre support – the seesaw will remain in the same position. Applying downward force either side of the centre support will tip the seesaw in the same direction. The further away from the centre support the downward force is applied, the faster the 'supported' end smacks down on the ground (Fig 5.5).

Apply the same principle to using a roughing out gouge. If the tool is being used on its back, the *only* part of the tool edge receiving *direct support* is the corresponding centre of the gouge.

**Fig 5.6 (left) Supporting the tool edge. The cut should be made with the portion of the tool that is supported on the rest. When the cut is made with a portion of the tool not supported on the rest . . .**

**. . . the stock will force the tool to rotate until that portion of the tool finds support. Damage may occur to both the operator and the stock!**

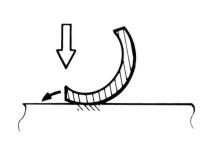

TOOLRES

AREA OF SUPPORT

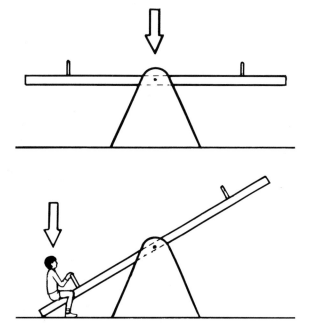

**Fig 5.5 The seesaw principle. A load applied to the centre of the seesaw (top) would not affect equilibrium. A load applied off-centre (below) without support would affect equilibrium.**

Just like the seesaw, if the downward forces are allowed to contact either side of the centre of the tool, it will be smacked downwards on to the rest. Tool control will be lost and the tool will almost certainly bury itself into the wood (Fig 5.6).

A practical example of how this law can be offended is shown very clearly in Figs 5.7 to 5.10.

The example shows a length of wood being turned to a cylinder, but with a pummel or square end being left on, typical of table and chair legs, etc. allowing them to be mortised to receive the cross rails.

Fig 5.7 shows the gouge being used on its back with the shaving coming from the corresponding

part of the tool receiving direct support from the toolrest.

Fig 5.8 shows the gouge position altered in that it has been rolled right over on its edge to allow it to be cut right up to the square section without fouling it. Law 4 is not being offended because the shaving is coming from the part of the tool receiving direct support from the toolrest.

If you study Figs 5.9 and 5.10 you will see the consequences of failing to roll the gouge over on to its edge. The tool is receiving support only in its centre, but the leading 'wing' of the gouge (*unsupported*) has been allowed to engage the square section. Just like the child's seesaw, the downward forces on an unsupported section will smash the tool down on the rest, resulting in the heavy 'catch' shown in Fig 5.10.

This particular law will be enlarged upon when I come to describe the functions of the various cutting tools in Chapter 6, Turning Between Centres.

**Fig 5.7 Using the supported tool.**

**Fig 5.9 Using part of the tool unsupported by the toolrest.**

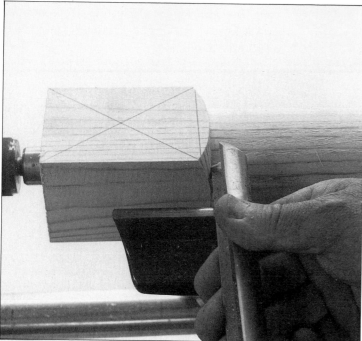

**Fig 5.8 Using the supported tool.**

**Fig 5.10 The consequences of using an unsupported tool – the dig-in.**

# Law 5

**Always cut 'downhill', or with the grain.**

In all branches of woodworking, from carpentry to carving, from joinery to cabinetmaking, smoother and easier cuts are achieved by 'working with the grain'. Woodturning is no exception.

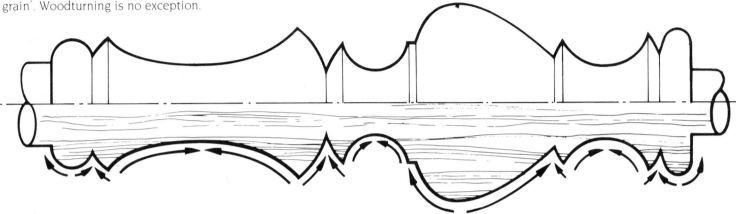

Fig 5.11 Law 5: Cutting with the grain. The arrows indicate the direction of cutting 'downhill' or 'with the grain' in between centres turning.

On spindle turning or working between centres, cutting with the grain invariably means cutting from larger to smaller diameters, hence the saying, 'cutting downhill' (Fig 5.11).

On faceplace turnings, cutting from larger to smaller diameters does not necessarily mean you are cutting with the grain. This will be explained later in the book when I deal with bowl turning.

Perhaps the easiest way of appreciating this law is to try this exercise. Take any piece of timber in which the grain is clearly not parallel to the surface of the wood. By making use of a hand plane we can see the effects of planing with the grain and against the grain. The former will produce a clean, smooth surface, but the latter results in a rough, torn surface (Figs 5.12(a) and (b)).

Fig 5.12(a) Planing downhill (with the grain) produces a clean smooth surface.

Fig 5.12(b) Planing uphill (against the grain) produces a rough broken surface.

Another less appreciated consequence of cutting uphill is that you are in danger of offending Law 4, particularly when cutting hollows or coves with the spindle gouges. I will expand on this when describing the use and functions of the gouges in Chapter 6, Turning Between Centres. Suffice at this stage to repeat that disobedience to Law 4 nearly always results in a dig-in.

# Law 6

**Scrapers must be kept perfectly flat (in section) on the toolrest and presented in the 'trailing mode', i.e. with the tool handle higher than the tool edge.**

Appreciating and understanding the foregoing laws really makes this easy to understand.

I have discussed at some length under Law 3 the reason why scrapers, because of their obtuse or short grinding angle, must not be presented in the bevel rubbing mode as the resistance to the tool would be so great that a dig-in would most certainly ensue.

Accordingly, these tools must point slightly down (bevel underneath) so that only the extreme edge of the tool is in contact with the wood (Fig 5.2(a) and (b)).

It is equally important for the scrapers to be kept perfectly flat on the toolrest. If you do not do this, and allow the corresponding part of the tool to that *not in contact* with the toolrest to touch the wood, you will be offending Law 6 and Law 4 as well (Fig 5.13). The result will be a dig-in which will probably live in the memory.

I strongly recommend you regularly review this chapter until you fully understand the six laws.

Bad and unsafe habits can creep up on you, so in the interests of safety, particularly in the learning stages, take your time, have regard to these laws, and *relax*.

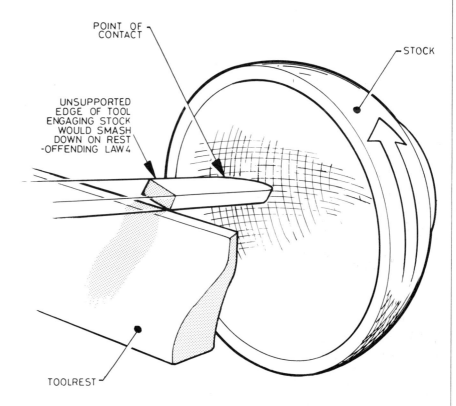

**Fig. 5.13 Offending Laws 6 and 4.**

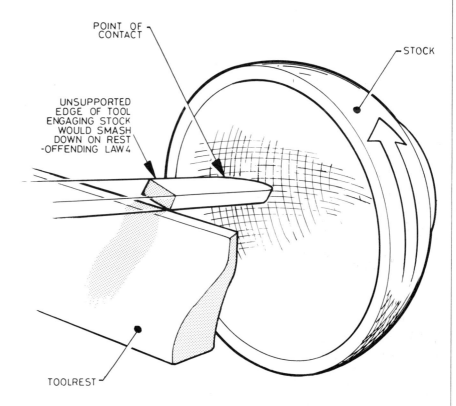

# SUMMARY OF CHAPTER

**1** A thorough understanding of the laws will ensure that when things go wrong, you will be able to identify the reason and thus avoid a repetition.

**2** Such an understanding will also help you to grasp not only 'how' a tool is used, but also 'why' it is used in a certain manner.

**3** Compliance with the laws makes it most unlikely that you will sustain any serious injury.

**4** Control of the cutting tools is determined to a great extent by bevel rubbing. Remember therefore to practise clutch control and to master it, not only on straight cylinders, but also in hollows and around convex shapes.

# Chapter 6

## TURNING BETWEEN CENTRES

It is now time to decide which category of woodturning we ought to begin with. Would it be better to start with faceplate work, or turning between centres?

The majority of people to whom I give instruction are under the impression that a turner's merit is judged by his ability to produce quality faceplate work, such as bowls, platters and vases.

While I agree that a great deal of skill may be required to produce such work, I certainly do not believe *more* skill is called for in faceplate work than in turning between centres.

A good faceplate turner will almost certainly be an accomplished turner between centres, but conversely, a turner who is accomplished in spindle work will also be quite capable of producing quality faceplate work.

Taking this a stage further, it is quite possible for the *mediocre* faceplate turner to produce attractive artifacts, but cloak the fact that they may have been made using methods that are *crude, uncraftsmanlike, dangerous, dusty and slow.*

For example, a turner may make bowls which are of an acceptable standard and which sell. However, his knowledge of the correct function and use of the bowl gouge may be minimal as he relies to a great extent on scrapers to shape the bowls, and to a greater extent on power sanding to arrive at an acceptable finish. Ask the same person to turn a leg for a Windsor chair, where crisp, cleanly cut, traditional profiles are required, and his lack of craftsmanship would quickly become evident.

In other words, it is my view that the mediocre turner can get away with crude, uncraftsmanlike methods on some types of faceplate work, but he will most certainly be exposed for what he is when using other than correct cutting techniques on between centres work.

Another good reason for starting your education on spindle turning is that, generally speaking, larger pieces of wood are used in faceplate work, which means increased downward forces will be encountered see page 41.

Gouges and scrapers presented incorrectly to large chunks of wood whirling round on the faceplate can be dangerous, and the severity of the resultant dig-ins or catches can be alarming. Such experiences will make the operator nervous and tense, almost certainly denting his confidence for some considerable time.

It is vital that the learning process should be as calm, unhurried and tension-free as possible, and therefore I am firmly of the opinion that 'early learning' should be restricted to between centres turning with pieces of wood that are neither too long nor too large in section.

Accordingly, for our initial exercise we will make use of a piece of Scots pine about 13" long and 2" square. I have chosen this length for demonstration as one of my toolrests is 15" long and consequently the need to keep moving the toolrest is avoided.

We will go through my usual order of working, (see below), examining each step in detail.

1 Rough down to a cylinder.

2 Mark out the wood with template and pencil to indicate the positions of the various design features and key diameters.

3 'Size in' in these marked places with the parting tool, making use of calipers, verniers, etc. to establish the correct diameters (more of this later).

4 Cut in the required shapes with the spindle gouges and chisels, blending in the profiles to the predetermined depths.

# PREPARATION OF THE TIMBER

You may have read elsewhere that stock to be mounted between centres should be reduced to an octagonal shape, in the interests of safety. Not only is this procedure time consuming, it is totally unnecessary!

If this work is done with a hand plane, it will take some considerable time. If the turner makes use of a power planer or saw, it will be more dangerous than turning it to a cylinder on the lathe!

# CENTRING THE WORKPIECE

After a little experience you will be able to guess the centre of a piece of square stock well enough for practice purposes, but initially it is best to draw diagonals on the ends of the stock. (In many instances, it is important to be as accurate as

**Fig 6.1 Use a mallet or block of wood for this job.**

**Fig 6.2 Applying the 'test of tightness'.**

possible in determining centres, for example when squares or 'pummels' are being left on the workpiece as with table or chair legs.)

Take a pointed awl and make small locating holes at both ends. Place your drive centre in one of these holes and give it a sharp rap with a mallet or lump of wood, preferably with the workpiece over the bench leg or something solid. Avoid the use of hammers or you may 'burr' over the end of the drive, thus preventing it homing in properly in the mandrel morse taper. See Fig 6.1.

# MOUNTING THE STOCK

Insert the drive centre into the headstock mandrel and place the wood up to it, ensuring the indentations you have just made receive the driving spurs. Your other hand serves to keep the wood pulled up to the drive while you position the tailstock to within about ½" of the other end.

Next, lock the tailstock in position and advance the tailstock barrel with the handwheel until the revolving centre engages the hole made in the centre of the end of the wood.

# DETERMINING CORRECT TAILSTOCK PRESSURE

The tailstock should apply only sufficient pressure to efficiently drive the wood. Do not over-tighten the workpiece as this can have the effect of damaging the headstock bearings if done repeatedly. I recommend the following simple method.

Place your left hand on either the drive belt or pulleys and with your right hand try to revolve the wood. If you can feel movement on the drive spurs, tighten a little more until all the play is taken up (I call this *the test of tightness*, see Fig 6.2.) The power to the lathe should be isolated during this procedure.

# POSITIONING THE TOOLREST

The general rule is that the height of the toolrest is not critical in between centres turning. Fix it at approximately 'centre height', i.e. with the top edge of the rest in line with the centre of the wood. This will be fine. (There are occasions when the rest height is critical, and these are dealt with in Chapter 7.)

My method of determining both the height of the rest and the safe distance from the workpiece is to revolve the wood by hand until the diagonals are parallel to the bench top. I then position the rest in line with the nearest corner leaving no less than a ¼" gap for the roughing down process (Fig 6.3).

If the toolrest is not long enough to span the length of the workpiece, it is important to position it so that no less than ¾" is protruding by the end of the wood where you are working.

Why? Assume your toolrest is positioned just short of, or in line with, the end of the workpiece. In attempting to cut to the end of the wood, you would probably drop the tool off the end of the rest and the downward forces would almost certainly twist the tool in your hand and trap one or more fingers. I have seen more than one black fingernail as a result of people disregarding this advice.

# HOLDING THE TOOLS

Some teachers and books use the word 'grip' when describing the application of the hands to the tools. I prefer to use the word 'hold', as grip implies a high degree of tightness and strength. A secure 'hold' is needed, but not the vice-like grip which most novices tend to use.

While at first a certain amount of tension and apprehension is understandable, flowing, fluid tool manipulation can only be achieved by a relaxed approach and the absence of tension, not only in the hands and wrists but in the whole body.

There are basically only two methods of holding the tools:

**Fig 6.3 Positioning the toolrest.**

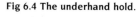

**Fig 6.4 The underhand hold.**

## 1 The Underhand Hold

This is the hold I use for the majority of my between centres turning.

As shown in Fig 6.4, the thumb of the hand nearest the toolrest (be it right or left hand) is placed on top of the tool while the fingers cradle it from underneath.

The thumb serves to keep the tool pressed down on the rest (thus avoiding offending Law 2) and the index finger *lightly* presses against the toolrest. This

assists balance and facilitates the cutting of straight lines in the roughing down process in much the same way as the carpenter draws parallel lines on a board with a pencil, Fig 6.5.

This same hand, particularly the thumb and index finger, provides fine control and flexibility on spindle turning where intricate shapes and positive entry are often called for.

The 'back' hand cups the tool handle in a position that is comfortable and where the tool is balanced when placed on the rest. Positioning this hand too far back results in exaggerated and tiring movements.

The 'back' hand is also the 'dominant' hand, determining the thickness of the shaving by virtue of lifting or lowering. It also dominates the swinging and rolling movements called for in many techniques. Fig 6.4 shows the 'underhand' hold.

### 2 The Overhand Hold

This is the hold I use for the greater part of my faceplate turning.

The back hand holds the tool in exactly the same way, but the front hand is positioned with the

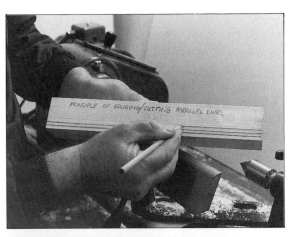

Fig 6.5 Principle of gauging/cutting parallel lines.

Fig 6.6 The overhand hold.

Fig 6.7 A comfortable posture: weight has just been transferred from the left leg to the right leg as the cut proceeds from left to right.

fingers overlapping the tool from the top with the outside of the palm resting on the toolrest, thus assisting balance and control, Fig 6.6.

Because this hold is used primarily on faceplate work, it will be dealt with in greater detail in the next chapter.

# STANCE, BALANCE AND MOVEMENT

Positioning of the feet, balance, weight transference and movement are of vital importance in woodturning.

Your stance should feel comfortable, with your feet sufficiently parted to afford optimum balance and therefore movement. In long traversing cuts (e.g. when roughing down) or when substantial swinging movements are called for (e.g. when shaping a bowl) widen your stance to enable you to sway from side to side without losing balance.

Both elbows should be tucked into your body, enabling your hips, legs and shoulders to play their part in assisting the hands, wrists and forearms. This provides for greater control and is certainly less tiring.

Balance and movement can be assisted in some operations by leaning on part of the lathe structure or the lathe bench. It is amazing what assistance to balance is afforded by the index finger of the front hand being pressed up to the toolrest.

Most beginners are far too stiff and restrictive in their movements around the lathe, probably because they are apprehensive at the sight of a piece of wood whirling round at 2000 rpm, but it is essential to learn to relax and be fluid in your movement. Fig 6.7 shows a correct, relaxed stance.

# THE TIME HAS COME

Before you press the button, let me remind you of the *very important* safety considerations. Impress upon your mind the word SAFER, from which we can develop the most useful mnemonic:

**S** for Speed – is it compatible with the size of wood to be turned?

**A** for Aside – stand out of the 'firing line'.

**F** for Fastened – are all locking handles secure?

**E** for Eye protection.

**R** for Revolve the wood 'freehand' to ensure it spins freely.

(Why not write down the above mnemonic on a piece of card or plywood and put it close to the lathe to act as an aide memoire – *remember*: safety must be number one priority.)

The tool that you will invariably pick up first for between centres turning, and certainly for reducing a piece of square stock to a cylinder, is the:

# ROUGHING OUT GOUGE

Start the lathe and take hold of the tool as described above. The first cut will start about 2″ in from one end of the piece of wood and in this exercise start at the right end as you view it. (There are two very good reasons for starting the cut this distance from the end, see page 56.)

### Technique

**1** The tool must be on the rest *before* the wood is engaged (Law 2, page 42).

**2** Present the tool with the handle well down so that the tool will *not* cut (Safe Angle of Presentation, Fig 5.3(a)), with the heel of the bevel rubbing the wood.

**3** Remember how 'clutch control' was achieved to provide a nice smooth take away by finding the bevel? (Law 3, page 44.) To refresh your memory, this is brought about by drawing down the tool towards your body and simultaneously lifting the back end. The tool will now start to cut, the thickness of the shaving (and we do not want too much removed at one pass) being determined by how much the back hand is raised. (Refer back to Figs 5.2(a), 5.3(a), 5.3(b) in Chapter 5 on the Laws of Woodturning.)

**4** Now incline the tool approximately 25° in the intended direction of traverse and roll it slightly in the same direction. This angling induces a slicing, paring action and it is important to maintain this same angle to ensure a parallel cut. This is best achieved by body movement and not movement by the hands and arms.

**5** Commence subsequent cuts behind the high spot you have created and with the shaving coming from below the centre of the tool, that is, where it is receiving direct support. Make sure you traverse by the end of the workpiece or you will create an 'uphill' situation (Fig 6.8).

**6** When the end of the wood is reached, *do not* lift the tool off the rest to return it to where you intend starting your next cut. If you do, you will run the risk of engaging the wood *before* engaging the toolrest, (offending Law 2). The consequence of this is a dig-in.

Draw the gouge back slightly towards your body

and slide it back on the rest to the required entry point. This is the reason why the toolrest should not be positioned less than ¼" away from the square stock in the roughing down operation.

With experience, you will be able to detect by sound when you have turned the wood to a cylinder. It is also quite safe to cup the back of the whirling wood with your fingers, to feel for roundness. Do not *ever*, in any operation, touch the *front* of the whirling workpiece or you may get your fingers wedged between the wood and the toolrest, resulting in a nasty accident (Fig 6.9).

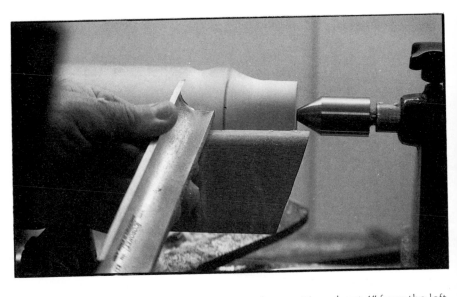

**Fig 6.8 Cut commencing behind the high spot.**

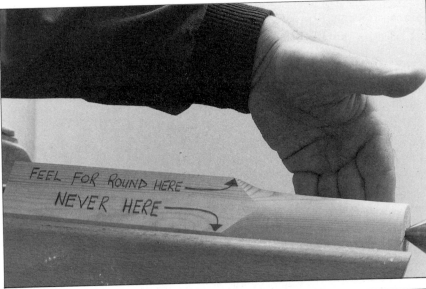

**Fig 6.9 Feeling for roundness at the back of the workpiece.**

**Fig 6.10 The order of cutting on square stock.**

**7** When you reach a position about 4" from the left end of the workpiece, reverse the process and cut towards the headstock until the cylinder is parallel along its full length (Fig 6.10 shows the order of cutting).

**8** Do not allow a large gap to appear between the wood and the toolrest. As soon as the stock has been reduced to a cylinder, stop the lathe and move the rest inwards to leave approximately ¼" gap.

To ensure that you are bevel rubbing correctly, I suggest that you occasionally lower your back hand and 'hold it on the clutch', and then by gently raising the back hand, bring the cut back on.

Most beginners do not exert enough forward pressure on the tool, probably because they mistakenly think this will cause the tool to dig-in. When it is realized that the bevel of the tool prevents this from happening, then the desired moderate forward pressure is applied.

Normally, within a few minutes of acquiring the basic technique, the beginner visibly becomes more relaxed. As a means of further increasing confidence, I recommend that this first exercise be repeated on three or four more pieces of wood, reducing each one to a straight cylinder of approximately 1" diameter.

## Supporting Technique

It will be noticed that if the diameter of the wood is reduced to much below 1", it begins to 'whip', accompanied by a tell-tale sound. This is a problem encountered in many spindle work projects and the 'whip' increases as diameter is reduced.

It is therefore necessary to 'steady' the work, and

on pieces of up to 18" long, the beginner will have little difficulty in steadying the workpiece with his front hand. The fingers on this hand 'cup' the whirling wood, and the thumb, placed on top of the tool, serves to keep it in contact with the rest.

The back hand should be positioned so as to hold the gouge where it is balanced, i.e. well forward on the handle, adjacent to the ferrule.

Exert only an equal and opposite steadying pressure, which in the case of small diameter work should be light.

Excessive steadying pressure may result in the flesh over-heating and, in extreme cases, smoking. If it does, let go and start again, making use of something to absorb the heat, such as a pad of leather or a handful of shavings (Fig 6.11).

## Mechanical Steadies

There are several types of mechanical steady, both manufactured and home made, which can be employed for long, slender turnings, and these are described on page 104.

## Other Uses

The roughing out gouge is really inappropriately named. Although its basic function is to rough down, it can be used for many other operations. In skilled hands, and with a sharp edge taking fine cuts, it is possible to obtain a finish on the wood almost equal to that obtained by the skew chisel. The novice will improve his skill with this tool if he regularly attempts:

**Hollows** It is important to understand that no gouge can cut a hollow or concave shape 'quicker' than the radius of the tool. It follows, therefore, that the roughing out gouge will only cut fairly 'slow' shapes, be it hollows or rounds.

**Rounding over** Because this tool is ground square across, it is not possible to fashion other than a 'slow' rounding over profile, as the wings of the gouge prevent it.

## Exercise

Reduce your piece of wood to a parallel cylinder. Set it out, lathe running, with the aid of a ruler and pencil into approximately 2" spaces. Make sure the toolrest is close in to the work while marking.

The object of this exercise is to form hollows in alternate spaces, and practise cutting rounds on the others. Start with the hollows by presenting the gouge approximately in the centre and push it into the wood with a slight scooping action, and at right angles to the workpiece. Gradually widen the hollow out to your pencil lines by taking cuts from either side, taking care to stop the cut at the bottom of the hollow. Don't cut uphill and thus offend Law 5 (page 48). Complete all the hollowing (Fig 6.12).

**Fig 6.11 Preventing 'whip' with the supporting technique.**

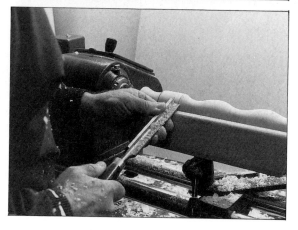

**Fig 6.12 Forming hollows with the roughing out gouge.**

**Fig 6.13 Forming rounds with the roughing out gouge.**

Now for the rounding over. As a profile is being fashioned exactly opposite to a hollow, the tool must be used in an exactly opposite manner, that is with a slight rolling action. Commence the cut close to the corner of a flat and roll the tool gently towards the hollow. To blend the rounding over in to the hollow, final cuts will necessitate a rolling action followed by a slight scooping action (Fig 6.13).

Finally, before passing on to the next tool, I think that a technique to deflect the shavings (perhaps more accurately described as 'chippings' until the wood is cylindrical) away from the turner's face is well worth mentioning.

Fig 6.14 shows this technique, which entails the fingers of the front hand being positioned to divert the shavings, and the thumb again serving to keep the gouge in contact with the toolrest.

I have advised starting the cut approximately 2" from the end in the roughing down of square section stock. This is basically in the interests of safety. If there are any shakes or 'pith' close to any of the square corners, you may well get long flying splinters of wood. If, however, you start the cut 2" from the end and work towards this open end, the length of the splinter is limited to the same length. Additionally, you will encounter less resistance to the tool because subsequent cuts will be slightly 'downhill'.

### Sharpening

The roughing out gouge should be ground square across with a bevel of approximately 45°. The method of sharpening by means of the grinding jig is explained in Chapter 4, On Sharpening.

# PARTING TOOL

Having attained a certain amount of skill and familiarity with the roughing out gouge, it is time to turn attention to the parting tool, which is the tool I would be most likely to use next during the course of my everyday turning between centres. From my order of working, page 51, it will be appreciated that the parting tool is used more in the role described in step 3 than in actually 'parting off'.

Additionally it can be used for several other purposes and its versatility is often not recognized by a good many turners. After all, the ¼" parallel parting tool which I recommend as part of your first set of tools is really a chisel and a chisel can perform many functions.

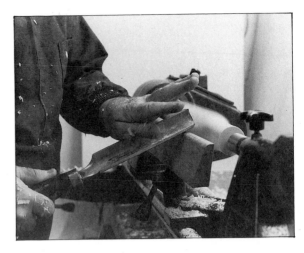

Fig 6.14 Deflecting shavings away from the face with the fingers.

### Technique: Normal Two-Hand Hold

As with all cutting tools, the parting tool should be used wherever possible in the bevel rubbing mode, (Law 3, page 43).

It will be found, however, that when this tool is presented to the stock in this mode, it will more than likely 'fray' the sides of the intended groove as it enters the wood. This fraying, or slight spelching, is more pronounced on softwoods and coarse-grained hardwoods (Fig 6.15).

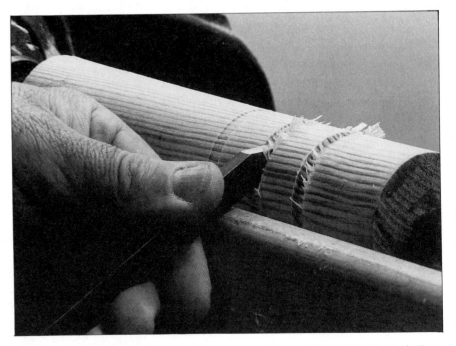

This problem is exacerbated if the tool has been sharpened so that the cutting edge is other than dead square across, i.e. slightly domed. Some turners intentionally grind a slight concaved edge on the tool so that the extreme tips 'scribe' the wood first to avoid the fraying.

Fig 6.15 The 'fraying' effect when the cut with the parting tool is begun in the bevel rubbing mode.

I prefer to keep my parting tools ground square across, because I think they lose their versatility if ground otherwise.

The problem can be overcome (if it matters, and on many projects it does not) by *initially* presenting the tool horizontally (scraping mode) and entering the wood to a depth just sufficient to get through the first fibres (Fig 6.16).

Do *not* continue the cut with this scraping mode. The abrasive action will quickly dull the sharpest of tools and undue force will be required to push it forward.

Instead, lower the handle and 'find the bevel'. The cut is then brought on and continued by lifting the back hand until the desired diameter has been reached.

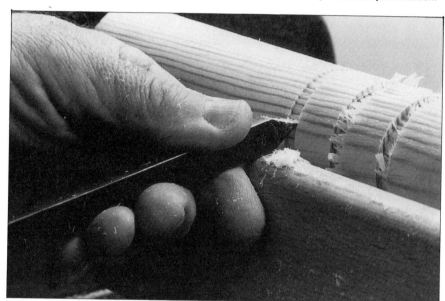

Fig 6.16 Fraying prevented by horizontal presentation.

### Technique: One-Hand Hold

When making use of calipers or any device to size in, obviously the parting tool must be held in one hand.

I take hold of the tool well up the handle, finger and thumb in line with the ferrule. The tool handle rests on my wrist and forearm for greater stability and control. (Sizing cuts should be *started* with both hands holding the tool, the front hand being released to pick up the calipers when approaching the desired diameter.)

Complete the cut as before by merely lifting the back hand (Fig 6.17).

### Cautionary Notes

**1** The parallel parting tool must be kept at right angles to the work or the tool will quickly bind.

**2** Even when the tool is kept at right angles, it is advisable not to go below a depth of ½" without withdrawing the tool and widening out the groove in the 'waste wood' side.

**3** When using verniers to size in, do not hold them on the points. If they 'jump' or bind, they could stick in your flesh.

**4** When you reach the required depth, place the vernier on the bench and withdraw the tool with two hands in the same plane as you finished the cut. Do *not* lift the tool out of the groove you have just cut or you will leave the toolrest and most likely foul the side of the groove, causing a dig-in.

**5** Ensure that the tool is kept perfectly flat on its edge when parting or sizing. The full width of the tool is being used and therefore the full width must be supported by the toolrest (Law 4).

### Parting Off

A typical example of when this is done is shown in Fig 6.18. Here, a clock finial has been turned on a

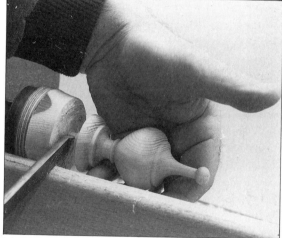

Fig 6.17 Sizing in with the vernier one-handed tool hold.

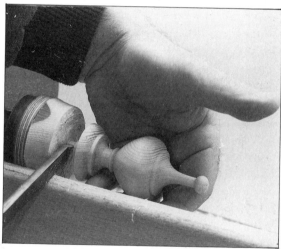

Fig 6.18 'Cradling' a clock finial just before parting off.

screwchuck, and the dowel at the headstock end is about to be parted off. The left hand is shown 'catching' the finial as it is cut off. As the parting cut nears completion, only gentle pressure should be applied to the cut.

## Other Uses

The tool's versatility includes the following operations:

**Feathering cuts** A parting tool entered at right angles to the work will cut directly across the grain and the completed shoulder, fillet or trench is consequently rough.

This can be remedied by a 'feathering cut'. The tool is tipped *very slightly* in the direction of traverse, allowing the leading tip to gently 'feather' under the fibres as it moves along the grain in either direction. The roughness will be transformed to a nice smooth finish.

**Beading (rounding over)** The parallel parting tool is particularly useful for the forming of small beads, although I use it extensively for rolling beads of all sizes.

Here's how it is done, and the exercise will provide practice for using the tool in the ways described above.

Prepare a piece of Scots pine as before, roughing it down to a true cylinder. Mark it out with ruler and pencil, lathe running, with alternate ¾" and ½" spaces. The ¾" spaces are for the trenches and the ½" spaces will form our beads. Size-in on either side of all the beads to a depth of about ¼", making use of the vernier. Remove the waste wood between these sizing cuts, using *both* hands on the tool. You will see that the bottom of the trench is quite rough, so practise the feathering cut to smooth it off (Fig 6.19).

To cut the beads, the tool is presented to the work at right angles and in the bevel rubbing mode. Now feather the right-hand tip of the tool under the wood about ⅛" in from the right-hand side of the bead. The tool is then lifted *and* rolled in a nice smooth action, ensuring that only the leading tip of the tool is in contact with the wood. Repeat the process until the centre of the bead is reached. The left-hand side is then cut in the same manner, reversing the whole process (Fig 6.20).

For successful, balanced bead cutting with the parting tool, movements must be smooth, unhurried and tension free. It is courting disaster to try to take

**Fig 6.19 Feathering cut with the parting tool.**

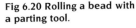

**Fig 6.20 Rolling a bead with a parting tool.**

too much wood in one pass, this being the reason why the cut is started near to the corner of the bead. The most common reason for getting a 'catch' is when the trailing edge of the tool is allowed to touch the wood (using unsupported tool – Law 4). This should not happen if you remember to keep the tool *rolling* as you lift.

## Sharpening

As outlined in Chapter 4, On Sharpening, the tool is ground square across with a bevel of approximately 25° either side.

Sharpening this tool by making use of the jig is very simple. Fix the adjustable jig platform as

explained, lay the tool on its edge and apply the 'gentle touch' to grind right up to the tool edge. Now turn the tool over and repeat the process. You should finish up with a precision ground tool (Fig 6.21).

**Fig 6.21 A method of grinding the parting tool using the grinding jig.**

# THE 'REAL' SHAPERS

In simplistic terms there are only *three shapes* (and combinations of such) in any design in woodturning, these being straight lines, hollows and rounds (but see below).

Again in simplistic terms, only *four tools* are required in spindle turning to cut such shapes.

Two have already been dealt with, that is the roughing out gouge and the parting tool.

The two remaining tools are what I refer to as the 'real' shapers, namely the skew chisels and the spindle gouges.

Before dealing with these two tools, it is advisable to expand on the more common shapes and profiles that go to make up traditional turned designs.

## Terminology: Shapes and Profiles

Many of these terms are derived from classical Greek and Roman architecture and consist of flowing curves (serpentine lines), concave shapes (hollows or coves), and convex shapes (rounds or beads). These are very often interspersed with fillets or V-cuts.

Fig 6.22 depicts a typical piece of spindle turning which includes some of these traditional profiles.

## Spindle Gouge

The tool most likely to be used following the roughing down process and sizing-in is the spindle gouge. The reason they come in sizes ranging from ⅛" to ¾" is that no gouge will cut a cove 'quicker' than the radius of the tool. It follows that a large wide cove can be shaped with a very narrow gouge, taking repeated cuts, but it is not possible to fashion very narrow coves with a large gouge.

The principles of using *any* size do not vary, however, and proficiency in the use of say the ⅜" spindle gouge will ensure proficiency in the use of the others.

In skilled hands spindle gouges will fashion almost any profile and also leave a first-class finish on the wood. It is possible to complete virtually the whole of the piece of turning shown in Fig 6.22 using

**Fig 6.22 Traditional turning profiles.**

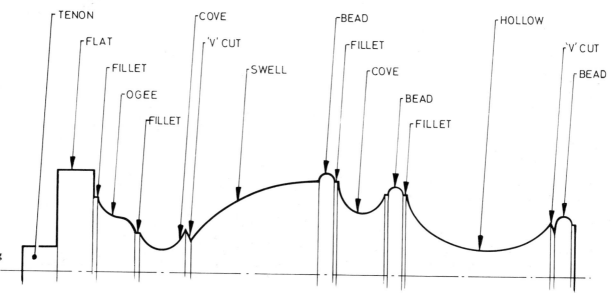

spindle gouges only. (Of course, it would be more convenient and quicker to rough down with the roughing out gouge, size-in with the parting tool and 'clean up' the fillets and intersections with a chisel, but the fact remains that almost all the operations could be carried out with the spindle gouges.)

### Fingernail Profile – and Why?

Advice from all the authorities is to grind the end of the spindle gouge to a nose or 'fingernail' profile. But why must we grind it so?

It is definitely *not* so ground to form coves by presenting it horizontally to the workpiece and *scraping* hollows, as some people imagine. Not only would this tear out the grain, particularly on the extremes of the cove, you also run the risk of a dig-in.

*Why?* The underneath of the gouge is round in section, but you would be using the whole width of the edge as the scrape proceeds. Result — the downward forces on the unsupported sides could twist the tool over, thus digging-in. (The wider the gouge, the more likely this becomes.)

It may be simpler to understand why the fingernail profile is ground if it is explained what would happen if it were *not* ground this way.

Assume the tool was ground square across or only with a very slight nose. Cutting tools must be used in the bevel rubbing mode (Law 3) and because of the reasons described above, you cannot offer the tool up on its back. The tool must be offered up to the work right over on its edge, flute facing the centre of the intended cove.

The action called for to form a cove is a twisting, scooping movement combined with a forwards push. If you were able to get the cut started and then used sufficient force to twist the tool, you would almost immediately be cutting wood with an unsupported tool (Law 4). The tool would eventually succumb to the downward forces and you would have a dig-in.

It is also important that the fingernail profile is one flowing curve. If a pronounced point is ground on it or there are 'high spots', it will prove difficult to use without the cut becoming 'blocked'.

### Method of Grinding

This therefore seems an appropriate point at which to describe how to grind the tool to the desired

**Fig 6.23** Method of grinding the spindle gouge.
**Position 1.** The gouge on its right-hand side.
**Position 2.** The gouge on its back.
**Position 3.** The gouge on its left-hand side.

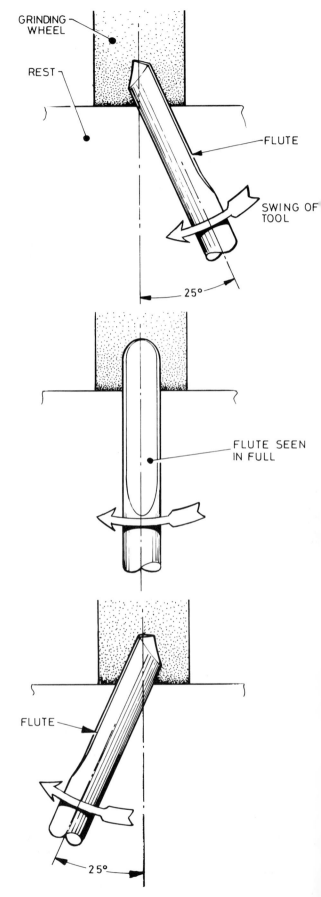

profile. I will not pretend this tool is easy to grind correctly, even with the aid of the grinding jig, but continued practice with the method I recommend will quickly overcome initial shortcomings.

Determine the correct angle on the platform of the grinding jig as described in Chapter 4 (this should be about 35°). To form or maintain a flowing rounded profile, the handle must be swung from side to side. Place the tool on the jig platform on its side and at an angle of about 25°. (The more you increase this angle, the more likely you are to finish up with an undesirable pointed profile.)

Now, as you slowly begin to roll the tool on to its back, swing the handle in a smooth arc so that when the centre of the tool is in contact with the grindstone, the tool handle is dead in line with the face of the stone. Continue both the roll and the swing until you have gone the equivalent 25° the other way, by which time the tool should have also been rolled right over on to its other side. Repeat the process until the desired degree of sharpness has been attained. (The value of the wide platform on the grinding jig now becomes obvious.)

The action sounds much more complicated than it really is, and Fig 6.23 shows the required movements in detail.

## Technique: Cutting Coves

Choose a spindle gouge of a size compatible with the width of cove to be cut. Very narrow coves can be completed with a couple of 'scooping' cuts from either side, but the starting cuts on wider coves will need to be begun just either side of centre and widened with successive cuts.

Use a piece of softwood about 13" long by 2" square. Rough it down to a cylinder and set it out (lathe running and toolrest close in) with a pencil and ruler to give alternate spaces of 1¼" and ¾". (The ¾" spaces will form the coves and the larger spaces will provide for bead and V-cutting practice.)

Offer the gouge up to the workpiece so it is well over on its side, flute facing the intended centre of the cove. To observe the 'law of cutting', the handle should be well down in the bevel rubbing mode and for the initial cuts the gouge should be at right angles to the work.

It is at the stage of entry into the wood that things can go wrong. Unless a *positive* entry is made, the gouge has a tendency to 'skid' sideways, and always in the direction of the bevel, scarring the work. This

irritating lateral skid is caused because the bevel has nothing to bear against until it has started the cut. The problem can be overcome by several methods:

**1** By making slight V-cuts with the skew chisel or parting tool on the marked out coves (several cuts will be necessary on wide coves). The small 'nicks' will give the bevel immediate support and prevent the skid (Fig 6.24).

The coves can now be cut by employing the 'normal hold', that is with the thumb on the top of the gouge and the fingers cradling it underneath as shown in Fig 6.25.

**2** By making a slight adjustment on the front hand hold, so the thumb is pressed down on to the toolrest to act as a stop. This will prevent the skid towards the headstock (Fig 6.26).

To prevent the skid towards the tailstock, swing the same thumb right over the gouge and secure it to the toolrest on the other side (Fig 6.27).

**Fig 6.24 Making V-cuts with the skew to prevent skids.**

**Fig 6.25 Normal hold on spindle gouge.**

**3** Remember how the parting tool was used so it was presented horizontally, scraper fashion, to ensure a clean entry to the wood and prevent fraying (see page 57).

A similar technique can be used with the spindle gouges to effect 'precise point of entry'. Line the *bevel* of the tool up with the *intended* shape of cut (for the final cuts on a well-shaped cove, this means the handle must be inverted towards the centre of the

**Fig 6.26 Hold adjustment number 1 to prevent skid to left.**

**Fig 6.27 Hold adjustment number 2 to prevent skid to right.**

cove). Ensure the gouge is almost horizontal and on its side. Now push forward into the workpiece with the *tip* of the gouge, Fig 6.28. (This is one of the few occasions when I suggest the tip of the gouge should be used.)

As soon as entry is effected, drop the handle from this scraping mode and continue the cut with the

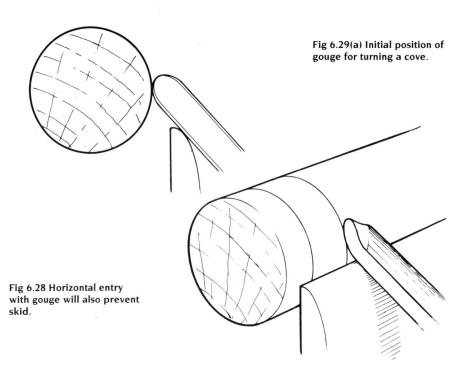

**Fig 6.29(a) Initial position of gouge for turning a cove.**

**Fig 6.28 Horizontal entry with gouge will also prevent skid.**

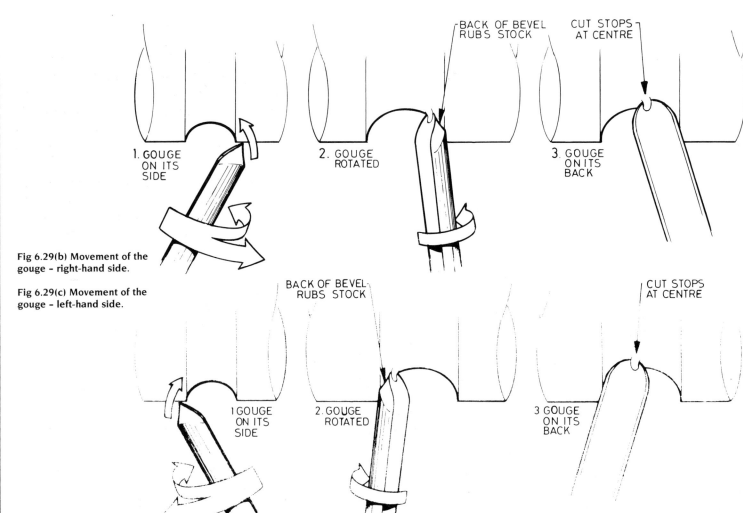

BACK OF BEVEL RUBS STOCK

CUT STOPS AT CENTRE

1. GOUGE ON ITS SIDE

2. GOUGE ROTATED

3. GOUGE ON ITS BACK

**Fig 6.29(b) Movement of the gouge – right-hand side.**

**Fig 6.29(c) Movement of the gouge – left-hand side.**

BACK OF BEVEL RUBS STOCK

CUT STOPS AT CENTRE

1 GOUGE ON ITS SIDE

2. GOUGE ROTATED

3 GOUGE ON ITS BACK

bevel rubbing mode, the tool being rolled and swung down to the bottom of the cove. Do *not* go past half way or not only will you be cutting uphill, you will also be using an unsupported tool which could result in a 'catch'.

## My Method

I use none of the above aids. I present the tool on its side, with handle well down in the bevel rubbing mode, and then I lever upwards, forwards and *positively* into the workpiece. It takes a good deal of practice and confidence, but it is certainly the quickest and best method for me. Fig 6.25 shows the cut about to commence.

Fig 6.29(a) shows the commencement of the cove cutting process and Figs 6.29(b) and 6.29(c) show the necessary rolling and swinging movements from both sides of the cove.

Used in this manner the shaving is coming from where it should do, i.e. below the tip of the' tool, inducing a nice slicing action.

I suggest you try all the above methods and settle for the one that suits *you*. For the purpose of this exercise, I suggest you use a ³⁄₈" spindle gouge and complete the whole of the shaping with it. After cutting all the coves, the next step is:

## V-cuts

Present the tool in the bevel rubbing mode and inclined on its side at an angle of about 25°. The gouge is at right angles to the workpiece and you want to start the cut on the edge of the cove. The handle is then lifted to about the horizontal in a 'guillotine' action, which will shape one side of the V. Now repeat the process (flute of the tool facing the opposite direction) from the other side until the V is formed. To ensure a nice, crisp bottom to the V, *draw* the gouge back towards your body and again use the tip of the gouge, otherwise the side of the gouge will 'scar' the other side of the V.

Proceed now to cut the V-shapes along the full length of the wood. Fig 6.30 shows the position of the gouge to start the cut on the last V.

## Bead Cutting

A bead is the exact opposite profile to a cove and it follows that to produce one an exactly opposite action is required. Again, present the gouge to the wood in the bevel rubbing mode, but this time on its back. Before proceeding with the cut, it is important

**Fig 6.30 Forming a V-cut with the spindle gouge.**

**Fig 6.31 Turning a bead with a spindle gouge.**

that the following facts are firmly ingrained in the mind:

**1** To cut the right side of a bead, the gouge must be rolled, lifted and swung to the right, ensuring that the shaving is coming from *below* the tip of the tool. Unfortunately, the natural action is to swing the handle to the *left*, and a conscious effort must be made to avoid this.

**2** To cut the left side of the bead, the only differences are the tool is both rolled and swung in the opposite direction. If the tool handle is swung in the wrong direction, a pointed bead will result.

Fig 6.31 shows these movements.

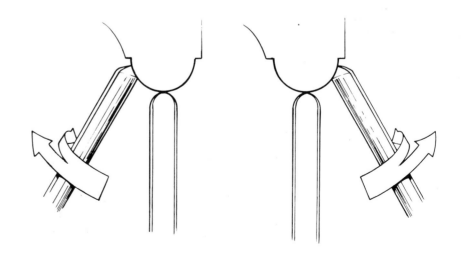

**Fig 6.32 The completed exercise straight off the gouge.**

**Fig 6.33 Section of spindle gouge showing detail of rolling movements. Cutting is safest when shaving appears just below the tip of the gouge.**

**Fig 6.34 The bevel should be lined up with the intended profile and the handle should be swung in the directions indicated.**

On wider beads or convex shapes, in addition to the three movements described, the tool must also be *traversed*.

I suggest you form the right-hand side on all the beads to get into a 'rhythm' and then repeat the process on all the left-hand sides. Do not try to take too much wood in one pass and make the movements slow, smooth and deliberate.

The forming of balanced beads is not easy because you are trying to synchronize three, sometimes four movements. If any one is 'out of time' with the others, the desired smooth, flowing shape will not materialize. Perseverance and patience will bring their rewards, however, so keep trying.

Fig 6.32 shows the completed exercise.

Fig 6.33 shows the position of the gouge (in section) relative to the shape to be cut and also grain direction. Remember the shaving should leave the gouge below the tip or centre of the tool.

Fig 6.34 shows how the bevel of the tool is 'lined up' with the intended profile and also indicates the

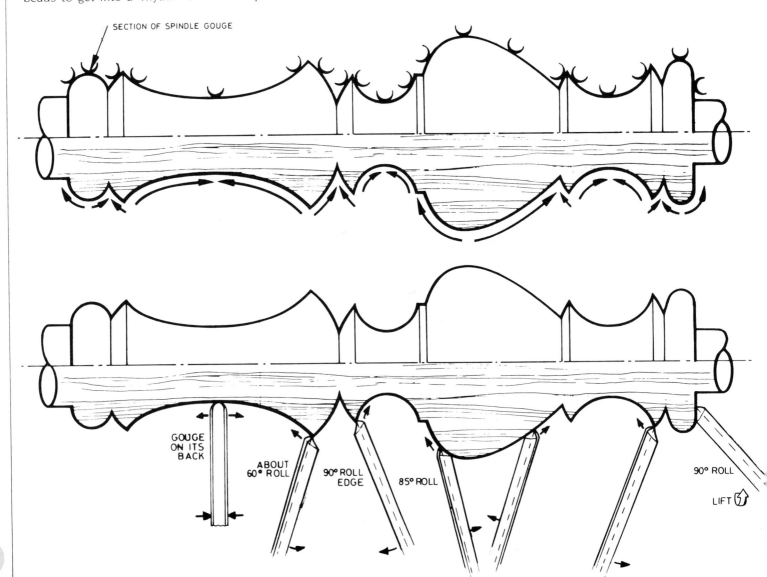

necessary swinging movements. There are other functions the spindle gouge will perform, and these are described on pages 74 and 75.

The limitations of the spindle gouges will be obvious when trying to create nice crisp intersections where the beads and V-cuts merge, and for feathering fillets.

Access to these 'tight' profiles is best achieved with our fourth and last tool, and the one that seems to cause more consternation than any other, namely the skew chisel.

# THE SKEW CHISEL

It is true the skew is peerless in *some* operations (more of this later), but because it is probably the most 'unforgiving' of tools, a lack of knowledge and incorrect technique can result in severe and unwanted 'impressions' being left on both wood and memory. Naturally, subsequent attempts with the tool will be accompanied by even more anxiety, apprehension and tension, and the tool will most likely be held in a powerful grip.

This is a vicious circle, the operator now doing everything he should not be doing, and another dig-in of gigantic proportions results. The skew will probably now be banished to a distant corner of the workshop to gather dust and cobwebs.

I have taught a good few people, and I can say, hand on heart, that with the exception of two or three, I have had no one who has not learned to use the skew safely and satisfactorily. (The few that have failed did so because, having experienced so many heavy 'catches', they found it impossible to relax.)

Another word of encouragement. The skew chisel is not as important as some people would have you believe.

Sure it is versatile, but not so versatile as the spindle gouges. Sure it will leave a super finish, but so will the gouges. Perhaps of greater importance to the beginner is the fact that many operations are a great deal safer when using the gouges.

Where the skew is supreme is in planing of cylinders and 'slow' contours, but even more so (in the case of the ½" skew) for the finishing cuts on fillets, 'tight' detail and intersections.

The skew can be used basically in two modes, that is **1** by making use of part of the long cutting edge for smoothing or planing cuts, and **2** by making use of both the long point (toe) and short point (heel) for such operations as rolling beads, V-cuts, and pummel cutting, and in the case of the ½" skew, cutting those tight details and intersections referred to above.

## Planing or Smoothing Cuts

It is necessary to understand not only how the skew is presented, but also why. When using any woodworking chisel, be it carpenter's, carver's or turner's, removing a shaving from a piece of round section wood is best achieved by using that part of the tool close to the centre. It would not be possible to remove a shaving by using only the points or tips of the tool, this only serving to 'scour' the work.

Let us now apply this principle to a piece of wood mounted in the lathe, the wood having been turned to a cylinder.

Stop the lathe and remove the toolrest. Lay the chisel on the workpiece and you will discover that the only way to get the centre of the chisel to remove a shaving is by presenting it at an angle of approximately 25° in the intended direction of traverse. (Unless it is positioned on the very top of the workpiece and the tool parallel to the lathe bed. This of course would prevent the use of a toolrest, which is not to be recommended!)

By altering this angle of presentation you can dictate at which point the shaving will leave the cutting edge.

Replace the toolrest and offer the tool up to the wood at about the same angle and with the tool *flat* down (in section) on the rest. You will soon realize that with the chisel in this position, it is not possible to get the desired centre portion of the chisel in contact with the wood.

No matter how much you alter the angle of presentation (with the tool still flat on the rest), the only way to get the centre of the chisel to engage the wood is when the *whole width of the cutting edge* contacts the workpiece. The only cut it would be possible to achieve with the tool so presented would be a wide 'parting' or 'peeling' cut, which of course we do not want.

To make the shaving leave the tool from the desired centre portion, it is necessary to tip it so that the long point or toe is clear of the wood. This means of course the area of tool close to the toe is unsupported. If this is allowed to touch 'whirling wood', you will get a nasty dig-in!

I recommend all the above experiments and presentation variations be carried out with the lathe *stationary*, and it does help to get the 'feel' if you can get someone to slowly revolve the work by hand, as I do in teaching.

In addition to understanding this bit of theory, another prerequisite to attaining proficiency with the skew is to make sure you use the type most suited to the task. Without doubt, the most user-friendly skew chisel on the market, for smoothing or planing cuts, is the Sorby oval section variety.

Some of the other manufacturers leave the corners of their chisels square. The tool steel is harder than the mild steel rests and you can find yourself removing shavings from the rest and coming to a halt in the slightest nick in the toolrest.

The Sorby oval skew is a joy to use and it is much easier to acquire that elusive 'feel' by making use of it. The section of the tool is such that when it is tipped sideways, it comes to rest at just about the optimum angle of *tip*. (With some of the other skews, it is possible to tip the tool too far, resulting in bevel contact and control being lost.)

For your first 'practical' with the skew, reduce your cylinder of wood to about 1½" diameter. It does help in the early stages to raise the height of the rest above centre. Now present the tool as described, about 25° and tipped towards its leading edge.

Make sure the handle is well down, feel for the wood and commence slowly traversing and lifting (in that order) until a shaving appears. As with all the cutting tools, the shaving thickness is dictated by the back hand lifting or lowering. Maintain the same angle to the workpiece by imagining you are cutting down a set of tram lines (Fig 6.35).

Repeat the process, keeping your 'north eye' on the danger trailing edge to ensure it is clear of the work. Practise to your heart's content. Testimony to your skill should be evident from the pile of ribbon-like shavings appearing on the bench (Fig 6.36).

As confidence increases, vary the angle of presentation, but beware allowing the 'danger' portion of the tool to contact the workpiece. Practise also forming a taper, cutting from large to small diameter, and up to a square shoulder formed with a parting tool.

As the cut approaches the shoulder, you will need

to alter the angle of presentation, so the extreme leading tip of the chisel is feathered under the wood to facilitate access to the almost 90° intersection (Fig 6.37). (Failure to do this would result in the leading tip fouling the side of the shoulder.)

Those people who are particularly nervous about using the skew chisel for planing cuts can be assured that if you induce the leading tip under the work in the feathering action, it is *virtually impossible* to get a dig-in because you *must* be using a *supported* tool.

The disadvantage is, that unless you take other than a fine shaving, you will have difficulty in traversing the tool (called 'blocking the cut'), but you will not dig-in.

**Fig 6.35 'Planing' on tram lines.**

**Fig 6.36 Shaving coming from the desired centre/heel area.**

**Fig 6.37 The extreme leading tip of the skew is used to feather up to a square shoulder.**

Fig 6.38 The skew is rolled to the right to form a radiused pummel.

Fig 6.39 The roughing out gouge is used right over on its side to cut up to a pummel.

'Traversing in the opposite direction can be achieved by employing the 'same hands' (your stance obviously being to one side), or by swapping hands and working left-handed. I prefer the latter because you are in a position to see the developing profile much more easily than in the former method. Have a go at both – being ambidextrous is a great asset.

## Supporting Technique

As outlined in the section dealing with the roughing out gouge, long slender work needs to be steadied, and the method of achieving this when using the chisels is identical to the method employed when using the gouge.

## Cautionary Notes

**1** Do not attempt to start the plane from a position *outside* the length of the workpiece. It is difficult to find the bevel in fresh air. (Experienced turners do this all the time, but it demands considerable practice of the safer method described to attain the necessary 'feel'.)

**2** In finding the bevel, make sure you are traversing the tool *before* lifting the tool to engage the cut. Control is much easier and safer.

## Shaping

The chisels, particularly the ½" size, can be used extensively for rolling beads, V-cutting, feathering cuts, and smoothing fuller convex and concave surfaces. (I prefer the flat section ½" skew for finer detail cuts, but I radius the edges very lightly on the grinder to facilitate easy movement.)

As mentioned earlier, some of these can be achieved just as well with the spindle gouges, but mastery of the skew is not complete until you can produce the same profiles with it.

## V-Cuts

These can be used as an integral part of a design, or as preliminary cuts when fashioning beads or forming pummels. A pummel is the square section left on a good deal of spindle turning such as table and chair legs, newel posts and balusters.

Accurately centre a piece of 2" square stock and mount it between centres. With the aid of a try square, pencil in pairs of parallel lines about ¼" apart, leaving about 2" space between each pair.

## Cutting Pummels

The wood has been marked out so make use of the toe (long point) of the chisel to first of all form the V and then develop it into a radiused pummel. Present the chisel on its edge with the tool handle only slightly down from the horizontal and at right angles to the workpiece. Aim the toe of the chisel at the right-hand mark, pushing forward and slightly lifting the handle.

Do not try to force the chisel too deep or you will only succeed in overheating the tool edge. Withdraw the chisel and widen the V by taking cuts from alternate sides, progressively inclining the tool so that the tip is 'aimed' at the centre of the V. The radius is formed from the left-hand mark by slightly rolling the tool as you lift in the direction of the intended cylindrical section to your right (Fig 6.38).

The wood to the right of the pummel can now be reduced to a cylinder. Remember to roll the roughing out gouge right over on to its left edge to facilitate cutting right up to the square section, and to prevent a dig-in by fouling the square with an unsupported tool (Fig 6.39).

## Cautionary Notes

**1** Do not attempt to use any part of the cutting edge *other* than the extreme tip (supported tool). If you do, you are *sure* to have a dig-in. When forming a deep V or radiused pummel, it is advisable to tilt the cutting edge of the chisel away from the shoulder *very slightly* to avoid this happening.

**2** If the tool starts bumping about, it is a sure sign that the heel of the bevel is pushing the cutting *tip* off line. Do not try to force the cut deeper, but withdraw the tool and re-present at a slightly shallower angle by lifting the handle.

## Square Shoulder Cutting

Many pummels are designed to finish with a square faced shoulder and these are a little more difficult to cut than a radius. As with all cutting tools, the bevel or grinding angle must be lined up with the intended shape or cut.

Applying this principle to the forming of a square shoulder, it becomes obvious that for the finishing cuts, the grinding angle must be at right angles to the workpiece and *not* the tool. I usually start by making a V-cut to reduce the resistance to the tool before applying the finishing cuts.

When cutting or cleaning square shoulders, particularly deep ones, remember again to tilt the tool very slightly away from the face you are cutting or you will experience a heavy 'catch'. Do not take other than very light cuts. Attempting to take too much wood will result in the tool overheating and the cut becoming 'blocked' (Fig 6.40).

## Bead Cutting

As an exercise, mark out your cylinder with varying widths from say ½" to about 1¼" and make a series of V-cuts to a depth in proportion to the width of the intended bead (all cut with the toe of the skew). (Fig 6.41.)

**Fig 6.40 Cutting a square-shouldered pummel – grinding angle (and not the tool) at right angles to the wood.**

**Fig 6.41 Forming a V-cut with the toe of the skew.**

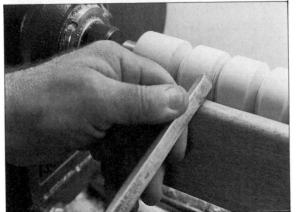

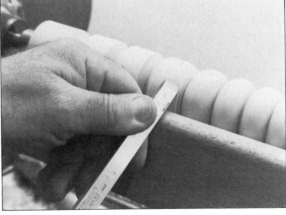

**Fig 6.42 Forming a bead with the toe of the skew.**

Use either the toe or the heel of the chisel to shape the beads. Using the long point is safer, but in my opinion not so good as using the heel, there being very little bevel contact to assist in producing a balanced shape. Additional advantages of using the heel are that the finish is superior, since the bevel is imparting a burnishing effect, and for me it feels less awkward. Try both methods and adopt the one that feels right for you.

Whatever method chosen, you must obey the Laws. First of all, present the tool at the bevel rubbing angle, or on the 'clutch'. The cut is brought on by tilting the blade slightly in the direction of cut while simultaneously lifting. With either toe or heel, the lower hand should control the tempo of the rolling and lifting movements and the thumb and fingers of the front hand serve to keep the bevel pulled on to the wood. The leading tip of the tool is feathering under the wood and it is *only* this tip that should cut. Fig 6.42 shows a bead being formed with the toe of the skew while Fig 6.43 shows the heel being used.

As with the spindle gouges, narrow beads can be completed with just a couple of rolls. On wider beads, the first cuts must be made nearer to the V-cuts or the cut will be 'blocked'.

### Sharpening

Again by using the grinding jig, standard type chisels are very easy to grind accurately. After determining the correct angle, the tool is offered up to the grinder with the *cutting edge* parallel to the face of the stone and flat down on the jig platform. Lateral movements are then necessary to ensure

the full width of the stone is used (Fig 6.44). The oval skew is a little more difficult because it has a tendency to roll, but a little practice keeping it centrally balanced will also ensure accurate grinding.

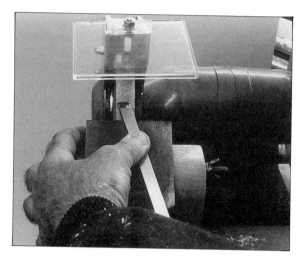

Fig 6.44 The method of grinding the skew.

Fig 6.43 Forming a bead with the heel of the skew.

# WOODSCREW CHUCK TECHNIQUE

In some types of spindle turning, as pointed out in Chapter 3, the workpiece is not always supported by the tailstock.

Examples of this are when hollowware such as egg cups, goblets, ornamental boxes, etc. are turned (the grain of the wood still being longitudinal to the lathe bed), where the tailstock would obviously prevent the hollowing out process.

The woodscrew does not afford the same grip in end grain as it does in side grain. This applies even more so when using softwoods. Therefore everything possible must be done to prevent the workpiece becoming loose on the woodscrew. If it does, you may as well discard it and start again.

Here then is the procedure I adopt, which enables me to turn ornamental goblets in pine up to 8" long.

**1** Centre the workpiece and drill a pilot hole suitable for the screw. I use the appropriate size drill fixed into an old screwdriver handle which is fitted with an adjustable collet, but a Jacobs chuck or a pair of pliers will serve the same purpose (Fig 6.45).

**Fig 6.45 Stock prepared for mounting on the screw chuck.**

**Fig 6.46 Undercutting the open end with the parting tool.**

**2** Mount the stock on the screw and turn to a cylinder with the roughing out gouge.

**3** Take a parting tool and part in at the tailstock end about ⅛" in from the end. Angle the tool inwards a little to create a slightly concaved end (Fig 6.46).

**4** With the toe of a skew chisel, make a shallow cut in the centre of the wood to allow for a pilot hole to be started easily and accurately (Fig 6.47).

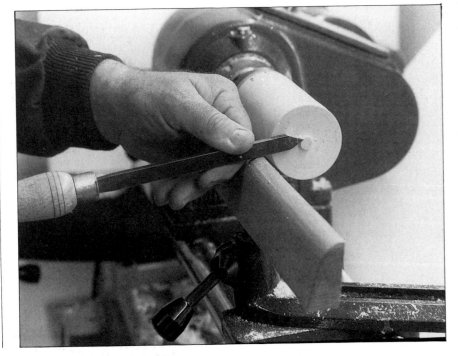

**Fig 6.47 Centre finding with the skew chisel.**

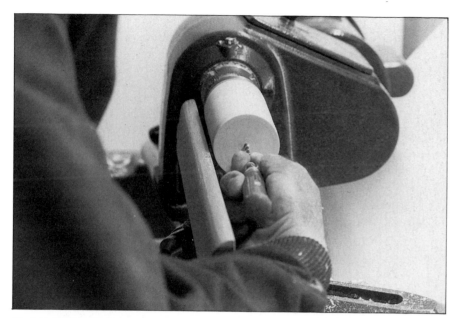

**Fig 6.48 Drilling the pilot hole before reversing ends.**

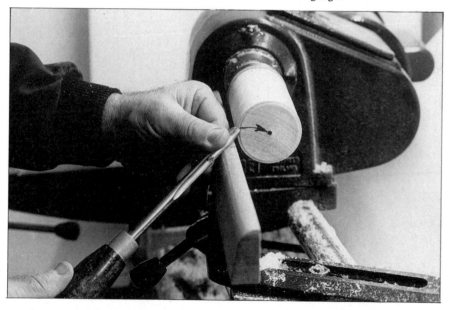

(Where it is necessary to avoid the screw hole, on the now 'open end', the initial turning can be done using drive centre and tailstock. The parting tool, in forming the concaved end, will obviously have to be stopped just short of fouling the tailstock revolving centre.)

**7** It is normal to lose a little centricity in this reversing process, so the first job is to make *light* cuts with the roughing gouge to restore it to a true cylinder.

**Please Note** that to succeed in this type of work, you will need patience, good technique, and to take only *light* cuts with *sharp* tools. Any tool presented at right angles to the workpiece, particularly at the unsupported end, will exert considerable leverage on the fixing. Matters are made worse if the tools are used in other than a bevel rubbing mode, there being much more resistance to a scraping action.

### Hollowing Techniques

Mount a piece of softwood about 5″ long and 2½″ square on the lathe, adopting the 'reversing' procedure described above.

After bringing it to a true cylinder, position the toolrest across the open end at a slight angle. Making use of a ³⁄₈″ spindle gouge presented well over on its side, and the bevel parallel to the end, take a couple of fine arcing cuts from outside to centre (shaving coming from *below* tool tip) which should leave an exceedingly good finish on the end grain (Fig 6.49).

Before deciding on what method of hollowing to employ, and there are several, I think it advisable to reflect on Law 5 which concerns cutting downhill, or with the grain.

Study Fig 6.50 and note that grain direction changes twice on both the inside of the cup and on

**Fig 6.49 Facing up in fine arcing cuts with the spindle gouge.**

**5** Make the pilot hole, lathe running, by pushing the drill forward to the required depth (it is perfectly safe to do this without the support of the toolrest) (Fig 6.48).

**6** Stop the lathe and reverse ends. The concaved face now ensures that when the wood is screwed right up, it is bearing on the outer edge, which prevents 'rocking', thus providing the best possible fixing. (Rarely will you get this secure hold on a surface straight from any type of saw.) Do *not* overtighten or you may strip the threads.

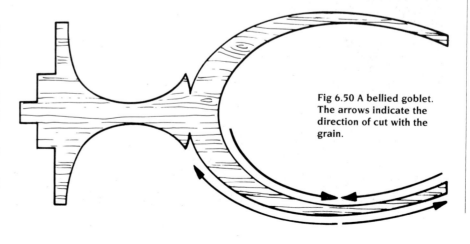

**Fig 6.50 A bellied goblet. The arrows indicate the direction of cut with the grain.**

the outside. It should also be noted that grain direction on the outside is *exactly opposite* to that on the inside.

The rule to remember on this type of work is that on the *inside* of the cup, cutting with the grain is always *from small to large diameter*. On the *outside* of the cup, cutting with the grain is always opposite, that is *from large to small diameter*.

Wherever possible, it is advisable to comply with this Law, particularly on the finishing cuts, or the resulting finish will be less than satisfactory.

**Fig 6.52 The hollowing out operation with the ³⁄₄″ round nose scraper in more detail.**

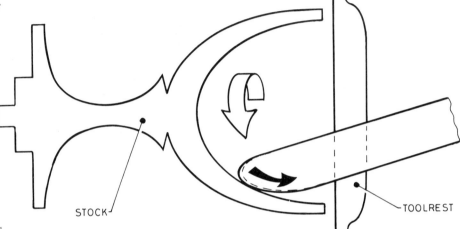

STOCK

TOOLREST

## Hollowing by Scraping

The whole of the hollowing process can be achieved with scrapers alone, and I certainly do not frown on their use in this situation as they perform very well in end grain, if they are sharp. Although not so rapid in removing the stock as in the method to be described, the technique is easy to acquire, so long as the Law applying to scrapers is complied with.

**Fig 6.51 Hollowing out with the ³⁄₄″ scraper.**

To refresh your memory, Law 6 states that 'Scrapers should be kept perfectly flat on the rest and presented in the trailing mode.' The consequences of offending this law can result in a heavy dig-in, and in woodscrew chuck work, the wood could come loose from its fixing.

To get the tool edge to cut at centre height, as it must, the height of the toolrest is important, if Law 6 is to be complied with. Making use of your ³⁄₄″ round nosed scraper, ground as suggested in Chapter 3, start the hollowing in the centre of the workpiece and gradually widen it out until the desired depth and internal profile are arrived at (in this case a simple egg-cup profile). Remember, the final cuts should be from centre to rim so as to cut *with* the grain (Figs 6.51 and 6.52).

## Hollowing by Gouging

Proficiency in the use of a small spindle gouge for hollowing out is something that all woodturners should strive for. Not only is it by far the quickest method, but also the resulting finish will only need a couple of passes with a scraper to achieve the best possible finish.

Use the gouge (in this case a ³⁄₈″ spindle gouge) to good advantage to determine the depth of the cup. I stick a small piece of masking tape on the inside of the flute at the desired place. The toolrest should again be across the end of the workpiece, and the height adjusted so the tip of the gouge is in line with the centre of the wood. The gouge can be made to act just like an auger if it is presented almost on its side (flute facing towards you) and firmly pushed straight into the wood. It sometimes makes matters easier if the tool handle is 'wriggled' from side to side to achieve easy passage down to the required depth (Fig 6.53).

Having established the depth, now gouge out the inside. There are three methods for doing this, but I shall only describe the one I consider to be the easiest.

Drop the height of the toolrest about ¼" and angle the ⅜" spindle gouge slightly upwards and again rolled over well on to its side, flute facing you. Now induce the leading edge of the gouge under the wood to the left of the hole and swing the tool outwards and towards you. In close-grained hardwoods, nice shavings should be brought out. (Don't be disappointed if you get only chippings from softwoods.) (Figs 6.54 and 6.55 show two stages of the hollowing process.)

To ensure a flowing internal profile, it is important that the tool handle should swing in a flowing arc. A series of flowing, swinging cuts should therefore leave you with a smooth, continuous curve. Just a couple of passes with the scraper will remove any undulations.

It does help in the hollowing out process if a gouge with a much shorter bevel, say about 60°, is used, as opposed to the normal angle of 35°. This shorter bevel enables the cutting a 'tighter' curve while maintaining bevel contact.

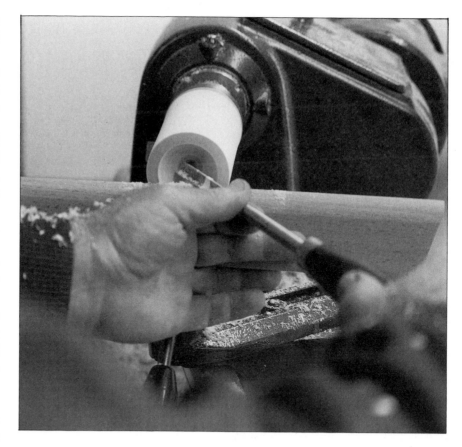

**Fig 6.55 The spindle gouge being swung from centre to rim to complete the hollowing.**

**Fig 6.53 Boring to depth with the taped spindle gouge.**

**Fig 6.54 The early stages of hollowing with the spindle gouge.**

# SUMMARY

**1** Regular practice, using the four basic tools on the three basic profiles, will inevitably lead to rapid improvement.

**2** For the novice woodturner, the Sorby 1" oval section skew chisel is a 'must' for planing straight cylinders and slow contours. Used as described, it will quickly instill confidence.

**3** In bead cutting, the spindle gouge is presented on its back and rolled on to its side.

**4** In cove cutting, the spindle gouge is presented on its side and rolled on to its back.

**5** The ½" skew chisel is indispensable for cutting crisp intersections, fillets and general tidying up.

**6** It is a fundamental principle of woodturning that the bevel or grinding angle is *lined up* with the intended shape to be cut.

**7** Much pleasure can be derived from the making of small section hollow ware on the screw chuck, so ensure you practise your hollowing out techniques frequently.

*Chapter 7*

# FACEPLATE TURNING

As the reader will have gathered from previous chapters, my message is that turning large diameter pieces of wood *can* be dangerous, unless the turner has acquired the fundamentals and fully understands the Laws of Woodturning.

Such understanding and development of technique and confidence can be best and most safely acquired on small section spindle work. Several weeks' concentrated practice in this category of turning should be undertaken *before* tackling bowls, etc.

The alternative is to go on a course with a professional turner. You will probably tackle a medium size bowl on the second day of the course (the first day on some courses), the essential difference being that the teacher is beside you to supervise, prompt and, if necessary, guide the tool movements to avert any potentially dangerous situation. Advice regarding the choice of courses is given later in the book on page 146.

Woodturners and bowl turning go together like eggs and bacon, and in my early days of turning I was always extremely eager to turn bowls of all shapes and sizes, and examples of these are still dotted about the country in relatives' homes. There is something uniquely satisfying about making a nicely designed bowl and the thrill of sending long, rope-like shavings flying across the workshop adds to the satisfaction and fascination.

Certainly, the turning of bowls, vessels and platters must have constituted a substantial amount of ancient turning, arising from the need to utilize one of the planet's most abundant raw materials as a substitute for animal skins, hollow stones, leaves and shells, etc. The first bowls were purely functional, but gradually as tools, equipment and skill improved, so did the form and appeal of turned vessels and platters.

Despite this, for well over two thousand years turnings of this type were designed to be practical, rather than aesthetically decorative or appealing.

However, the last thirty years has seen a resurgence of interest in the craft and gradually there has been a growing tendency to produce artifacts that are first and foremost aesthetically appealing, even at the expense of utilitarianism. I welcome this change in direction, although I have certain reservations about some of these 'modern art' turnings.

Before the newcomer to the craft can even start thinking about design and aesthetic appeal, he must first acquire sufficient knowledge and skills to tackle the basic shapes and profiles confidently. It is of little use being able to *design* anything if you are not capable of then making it.

# GRAIN FORMATION AND TIMBER PREPARATION

In spindle turning, the grain of the wood invariably runs parallel with the lathe bed. In faceplate work, the grain normally runs along the surface of the disc or bowl blank, which means end-grain is encountered twice on every revolution.

The problems of using a hand plane on the end of a piece of wood are familiar. If the edge is planed all along, the wood will split away because the grain at the far end is unsupported. The heavier the shaving, the more the wood is split away (Fig 7.1).

**Fig 7.1 Cutting up to the unsupported edge causes the wood to split.**

**Fig 7.2 A slight chamfer and light cut prevent splitting.**

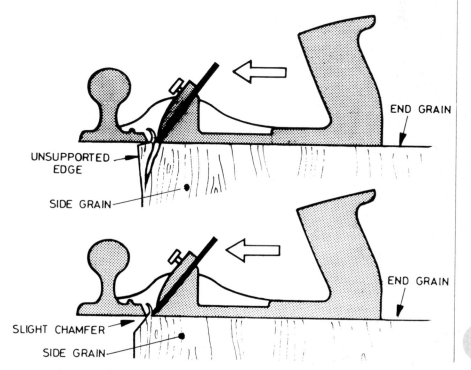

To avoid this, either a slight chamfer is made at the far end and fine cuts taken (Fig 7.2) or you can plane inwards from both ends to the centre (Fig 7.3). Similar techniques must be used on the edges of discs and blanks to prevent the same problem.

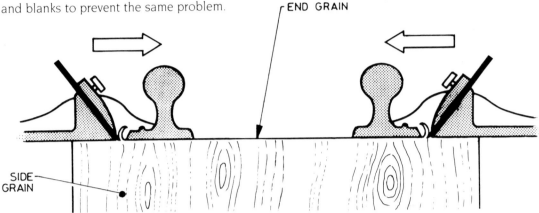

**Fig 7.3 Cutting from both edges to the centre prevents splitting.**

END GRAIN

SIDE GRAIN

One of the Laws of Woodturning is to cut downhill, or with the grain wherever possible. In spindle turning this is always downhill as viewed with the wood in the lathe (Fig 7.4). However, in faceplate turning downhill as viewed with the wood mounted on the lathe is not necessarily cutting with the grain.

**Fig 7.4 Between centres turning: downhill (as viewed) is always with the grain.**

SIDE GRAIN

**Fig 7.5 Turning a disc: downhill (as viewed) with the blank mounted on the lathe, but cutting with the arrow is against the grain.**

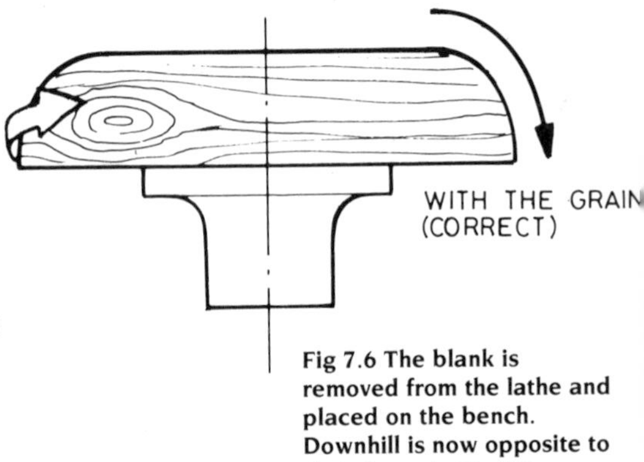

Fig 7.5 shows a blank that has been mounted on the lathe by means of a screw chuck. Viewed from the front, downhill is obviously from the chuck side towards the open end.

Remove the wood from the lathe and lay it flat on the bench as shown in Fig 7.6, and downhill has changed. It is now from the small diameter to the larger. The question is, 'What constitutes cutting with the grain on bowl blanks and discs?' The answer is as follows:

**(a)** Cutting with the grain on the *outside* of a bowl or convex shape is achieved by working from *small* to *large* diameter.

**(b)** Cutting with the grain on the *inside* of a bowl or concave shape is exactly *opposite* and is achieved by working from *large* to *small* diameter.

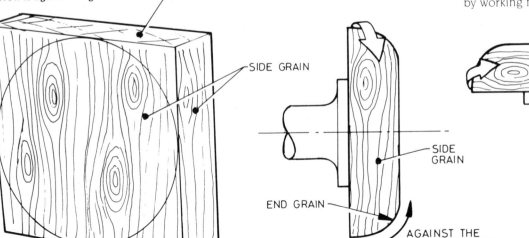

END GRAIN

SIDE GRAIN

SIDE GRAIN

END GRAIN

AGAINST THE GRAIN (WRONG)

WITH THE GRAIN (CORRECT)

**Fig 7.6 The blank is removed from the lathe and placed on the bench. Downhill is now opposite to that shown in Fig 7.5. Cutting with the arrow is with the grain.**

On a simple, conventional-shaped bowl these facts are easily appreciated, but where a full-bellied bowl is being turned, it will be seen that grain direction changes twice on both inside and outside (Fig 7.7).

Next to be considered is whether the timber should be used heart side up or heart side down. In the process of seasoning, timber always shrinks away from the heart, resulting in this side becoming rounded. Thus, if there is any movement and the heart side is at the bottom of the bowl, the bottom will become rounded and consequently the bowl will not sit flat and may well spin or rock on any level surface (Fig 7.8). Traditionally, bowls were always designed so that the heart side was uppermost to avoid this problem (Fig 7.9).

This principle is disregarded by many modern bowl turners because of the popularity of 'natural edge' bowls, or where there is a marked colour contrast between the heartwood and sapwood. Such features can obviously only be incorporated in the design when the principle is waived. (The problem of a 'rounded bottom' is avoided by making the base slightly concaved – Fig 7.10).

## Green or Wet Turning

This is not something new, for after all, the bodgers made virtually all their chair components from green wood. As the wood moved, the joints became tighter, the round mortises shrinking to an oval shape. There has been a revival of this form of turning, particularly in bowl work. Here are some of the advantages of green or wet turning:

**(a)** Green timber is considerably cheaper than seasoned timber.

**(b)** It cuts much more easily than dry timber.

**(c)** The tools stay sharper longer.

**(d)** Seasoning time is reduced considerably if the wet wood is rough turned to a wall thickness of about ¾". Air drying should not take more than about six months and this can be halved if the blanks are stored in 'airing cupboard' conditions. (It is normal and advisable to coat the rough turned blanks with wax to prevent uneven drying, the cause of splitting.)

Turning wet is also very good for the ego. On spindle turning you can expect to see streamers of ribbon-like shavings leaving the tools, and in bowl work the rope-like shavings will quickly cover both bench and floor.

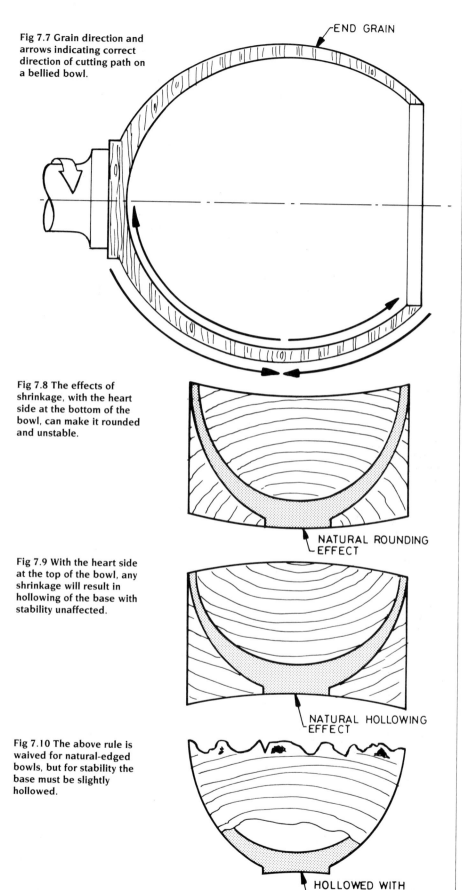

**Fig 7.7 Grain direction and arrows indicating correct direction of cutting path on a bellied bowl.**

END GRAIN

**Fig 7.8 The effects of shrinkage, with the heart side at the bottom of the bowl, can make it rounded and unstable.**

NATURAL ROUNDING EFFECT

**Fig 7.9 With the heart side at the top of the bowl, any shrinkage will result in hollowing of the base with stability unaffected.**

NATURAL HOLLOWING EFFECT

**Fig 7.10 The above rule is waived for natural-edged bowls, but for stability the base must be slightly hollowed.**

HOLLOWED WITH GOUGE TO COUNTER EFFECT OF SHRINKAGE

# METHODS OF FIXING

### Faceplate Only

Traditionally, as the name implies, faceplates were screwed on to a prepared blank and mounted on the lathe. The turning was completed all in one operation without using any re-chucking device. The main disadvantages of this system are: **1** the screw holes in the bottom will be seen, although they can be plugged or covered with baize; **2** the bottom of the bowl is required to be a minimum of ½" thick to accommodate the screws. Invariably, this is too thick and makes the bowl inelegant and bulky.

### Combination or Multi-purpose Chucks

Mention was made of these in Chapter 2. I made the point that these sophisticated chucking devices are not essential in developing basic skills, but they are extremely useful in speeding up and simplifying many projects. In essence, these chucks will grip internally and externally and also, by using the various accessories, can be converted to a woodscrew chuck or pin chuck.

### Faceplate (or Screw Chuck) Combined with Home-made Friction Chuck

This was the method I was brought up with, and making use of it entails the use of either the faceplate or the screw chuck for the initial mounting. After the external shaping has been completed, the bowl is 'reversed' and driven by a 'friction fit' chuck (again secured to either the faceplate or screw chuck), made from a waste piece of wood. Not only does this system avoid unsightly screw holes in the base, it is very satisfying to be able to complete such a project by making use of a device that itself needs careful preparation to make it function efficiently.

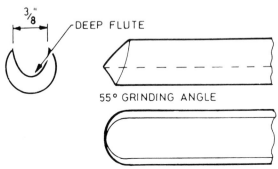

Fig 7.11 Suggested bowl gouge profile and grinding angle.

# TOOLS FOR BOWL WORK

### Bowl Gouge

Your recommended beginner's set includes a ⅜" bowl gouge, a tool that will be quite adequate to complete virtually all the shaping on bowls up to about 10" diameter and 3" deep. For bowls larger than this (and beginners are advised not to tackle such), the heftier ½" size is recommended. It is as well to know bowl gouges are measured across the *inside* of the flute; thus the ⅜" bowl gouge is made from ½" round bar and the ½" gouge is made from ⅝" bar.

Some turners, including myself, use spindle gouges on faceplate work of all kinds, particularly for finishing cuts and the forming of decorative detail. The novice would be best advised to stick with the bowl gouge (its deep U-section making it much easier to control on this type of work) and scrapers.

Roughing out gouges must *not* be used on faceplate work. They should be restricted to use on between centres turning. Some bowl turners do use them, but the practice is *dangerous* for a novice.

### Grinding Profile of the Bowl Gouge

Traditionally these were ground 'square across' and some manufacturers still supply them so. Specialist bowl turners usually possess several bowl gouges all ground to different profiles including square across, fingernail, and some ground back as much as 1" from the tip. This is done in the interests of speed and efficiency, but the beginner, with only one such gouge, will have to settle for a good, general profile.

My opinion is that a slight rounding of the cutting edge will prove to be the most useful and versatile grinding profile, easy to control and efficient in use.

To sharpen the tool, determine the correct angle on the grinding jig platform, see pages 37 and 38, (about 55°). Now offer the tool up well over on its side and roll it right over to its other side. The rolling should be accompanied by a slight swinging action to produce the slightly rounded profile. Continue (remembering to apply only gentle forward pressure on the stone) until the 'acceptable degree of sharpness' has been achieved, Fig 7.11 shows the suggested profile.

## Scrapers

These come in all shapes and sections and I possess probably twice as many scrapers as cutting tools, a strange admission from someone who has stressed the use of cutting tools wherever possible. However, I undertake a good deal of faceplate work in the form of plinths which are required with many different edge profiles, and my scrapers are ground to match the desired profiles. They are used to form the desired shape *after* I have removed as much waste as possible with gouges. The saving on marking out and execution is considerable.

It is obvious that scrapers can be used for two entirely different functions:

**As Forming Tools** The tool is ground to an exactly opposite profile to that required on the finished plinth, disc, or whatever, and is pushed straight into the work. Pattern makers use this method of shaping to a great extent, not only on faceplate work, but also on between centres turning where accuracy rather than quality of finish is of more importance, Figs 7.12, 7.13 and 7.14 show examples of such tool profiles.

**As Improvers** The attainment of a satisfactory finish straight from the gouge is in many cases extremely unlikely. The areas of end grain, particularly on the 'unsupported' fibres, tend to lift up under the action of the gouge. This will happen to some extent even when the sharpest of gouges is being used in extremely skilled hands.

This 'lifting' of the end grain is more pronounced in the coarse, open-grained timbers like elm and oak. Unskilled hands, employing a 'dull' gouge, will probably lift these fibres up to a depth of ¼", and thus nowhere is the keenness of the tool edge more urgently needed.

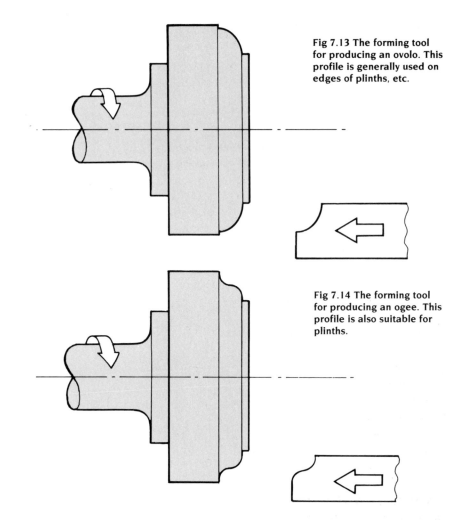

Fig 7.13 The forming tool for producing an ovolo. This profile is generally used on edges of plinths, etc.

Fig 7.14 The forming tool for producing an ogee. This profile is also suitable for plinths.

*Very sharp* scrapers will very often 'improve' the finish on the end grain. It has been said that there is no skill in using scrapers. I disagree! While I do accept considerably more skill is required to use the cutting tools correctly, to say *no* skill is required in scraping is bunkum. In the case of 'forming' scrapers, the demand on skill starts with the shaping of the tool on the grindstone. A 'feel' must be developed to get the best results, as with any

Fig 7.12 Selection of forming tools (scrapers) that can be used on both spindle and faceplate work.

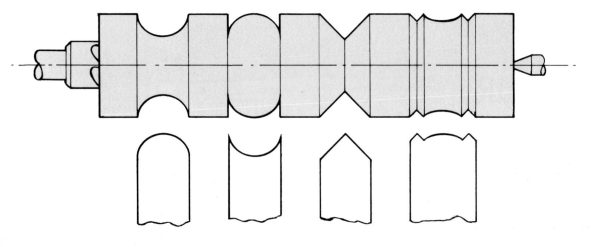

other tool, and this indefinable asset is even more difficult to attain when making use of scrapers as 'improvers'.

The amount of timber removed is directly proportional to how much forward pressure you exert. For 'improving' this must be very light and the scraper must be kept on the move. Shavings and not dust should leave the edge on all but the odd species of timber. If this is not happening, the scraper edge is dull.

Scrapers which are not extremely sharp will have a worse effect on the end grain than a 'dull' gouge, and no amount of sanding will remedy this.

Your recommended first set of tools contains three scrapers and these should prove adequate for some considerable time. If, however, you want a special profile of some kind, you can make use of a defunct carpenter's 'firmer' chisel and grind it to the required shape.

## Sharpening

For the reason discussed in great detail in Chapter 4, a grinding angle of about 80° is required on all scrapers. Adjust the platform on the grinding jig accordingly and offer the tool up very lightly on to the stone. Grinding the square ended scraper entails nothing more than traversing the tool parallel across the face of the stone. As with the smoothing plane blade, it is as well to slightly radius the ends of the square across scraper to prevent the tips scouring the work. Obviously the round nose scrapers must also be swung in an arc to maintain or form the desired profile. Again, the value of the large platform on the jig will be obvious.

The object is to throw up a butt on the edge of the scraper and the grindstone will produce this satisfactorily. It is not uncommon for some turners to improve the quality of this butt by 'ticketing' the edge over, in much the same way as cabinetmakers prepare their scrapers. This is time consuming and I personally do not find it necessary.

# TURNING YOUR FIRST BOWL

Not to be too ambitious, begin with a medium size blank of hardwood such as beech, sycamore or elm, about 8° diameter by about 3° thick, and the wetter

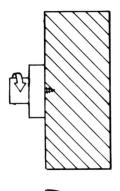

**Fig 7.15(a) Mount the bowl blank on the woodscrew chuck or faceplate and true up both the face and the edge with the ³⁄₈" bowl gouge.**

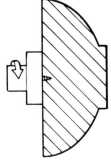

**Fig 7.15(b) Set out and form the plinth with the parting tool. Shape the outside of the bowl, sand and oil. (It is vital that the edge of the plinth is cut 'dead' square.) Now remove the blank from chuck or faceplate.**

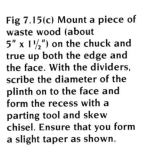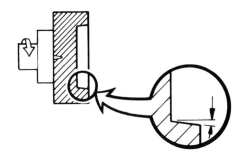

**Fig 7.15(c) Mount a piece of waste wood (about 5" x 1½") on the chuck and true up both the edge and the face. With the dividers, scribe the diameter of the plinth on to the face and form the recess with a parting tool and skew chisel. Ensure that you form a slight taper as shown.**

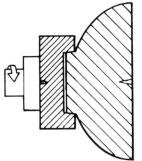

**Fig 7.15(d) A good tight fit is required. When this is achieved, true up the face and hollow it out with the bowl gouge. Start the cuts near the centre and gradually open out towards the rim.**

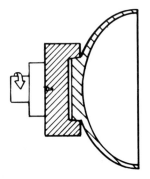

**Fig 7.15(e) Improve the internal finish with the domed scraper and sand and oil. The bowl is removed from the chuck by tapping with the heel of your hand.**

the better. The method of fixing is described on page 82, and Figs 7.15 (a) – (e) explain how it is done.

Ensure the screw chuck is accurately centred on the blank, or unnecessary vibration will be set up, and mount the wood on the lathe. It is as well to ensure that the surface receiving the screw chuck is planed flat to prevent any rocking.

Adjust the speed of the lathe to approximately 750-1000 rpm and position the toolrest across the edge of the stock, the first task being to reduce it to a true cylinder.

As it is absolutely *vital* in the interests of personal safety not to allow the tool to lift off the rest while being in contact with large diameter turnings, I recommend (and use to a great extent) the 'overhand' hold. This method of holding, as explained and illustrated in the preceding chapter, provides for the weight of the palm and fingers of the front hand to keep the tool pressed down on the rest. Again, nothing more than a normal, relaxed hold is called for.

## Gouge Presentation

Remember that the gouge is a cutting tool and all the relevant Laws must be complied with. Remember also to revolve the work freehand before starting the lathe. Vibration of some kind will be experienced when the lathe is started, however careful you were in centring. Offer the gouge up to the whirling wood, handle well down (safe angle of presentation), and pass it across the edge of the blank *without cutting*, just to get the feel. You will experience a certain amount of bumping until the blank is reduced to a true cylinder, but do not be alarmed. Gradually bring the cut on by lifting the handle until a fine shaving appears. Best results are obtained when the gouge is rolled well over on its side, flute facing the intended direction of traverse, and also angled in the same direction.

Having 'found the bevel' in your mind's eye, it is quite safe to start off the end of the wood and pick the cut up and traverse the gouge across the whole edge. Practise going from left to right and vice versa,

**Fig 7.16 Truing up the edge of the blank with the bowl gouge.**

taking only light shavings to avoid splitting the unsupported grain at the extremes. (In the case of plinths or discs requiring perfectly square edges, traversing the tool would need to be done from outside to centre from both ends, to avoid splitting, or alternatively the 'chamfering method' could be used.)

Correct presentation and angling of the gouge should result in the shavings leaving the edge *below* centre, that is where it is receiving optimum support. The angling of the tool and the slightly radiused edge assists in inducing a slicing action to minimize the lifting of the end grain fibres (Fig 7.16).

Stop the lathe and position the toolrest across the face of the bowl blank. The height needs to be adjusted so that the gouge can cut on the centre of the disc when pointing slightly upwards. Two methods can be used to true this face:

**(a)** With the handle held slightly down and the gouge rolled well over on its side (flute facing you), pull the tool from centre to the outside edge in a smooth traversing cut. Very flat and true surfaces can be cut in this manner, particularly when the 'underhand' hold is employed and the index finger bears on the toolrest that has been set parallel to the face of the wood. Unless the bevel is very short, stock removal will be part scraping, part cutting, but don't let this bother you – the finish should be fine! (Fig 7.17).

**(b)** Again with the handle down, commence the cut on the outside of the blank and traverse towards centre. The bevel must be 'lined up' with the intended square face and the cut takes the form of a shallow arc, with bevel in contact throughout. The shallow arc is effected by pushing the tool edge towards centre, while at the same time the handle is levered upwards (Fig 7.18).

This method is perhaps a little more difficult than **(a)**, but in both cases it is usual to remove any slight nipples or undulators with a square ended scraper.

This facing off is not absolutely vital on a bowl, as most of the wood is cut away, but it is good practice for when a flat surface is required, such as when turning wine table tops.

The bottom and plinth can now be set out. For this size of bowl a base about 2¾" will ensure the development of a nice flowing curve on the bowl wall. With the lathe running, pencil in this

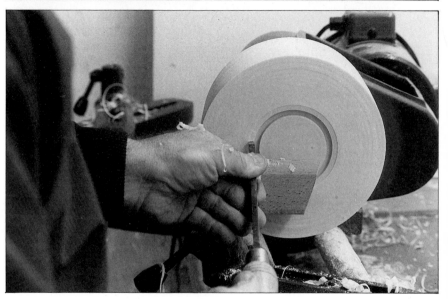

**Fig 7.17 Truing up the face from centre to rim, method 1.**

**Fig 7.18 Truing up the face from rim to centre, method 2.**

**Fig 7.19 Forming the plinth with the parting tool.**

measurement and with the parting tool, handle slightly down, go in to a depth of about ¼". Make a couple more identical cuts in the 'waste' side and then remove the remainder with the bowl gouge (Fig 7.19).

To fashion a flowing curve on the outside of the bowl, commence the cutting on the square edge you have just formed and remember to cut (where possible) from small to large diameter, with the gouge well over on its side, flute facing the direction of cut. The tool will need to be swung round the developing curve and if you stand in close you should be able to see the bevel rubbing behind the cut, supporting the tool edge. If you swing the handle too quickly, bevel support will be lost and the tool will dig-in and kick back at you. The remedy is obvious (Fig 7.20).

**Fig 7.20 Developing the outside curve with the bowl gouge.**

**Fig 7.21 Gouging in the opposite direction up to the plinth.**

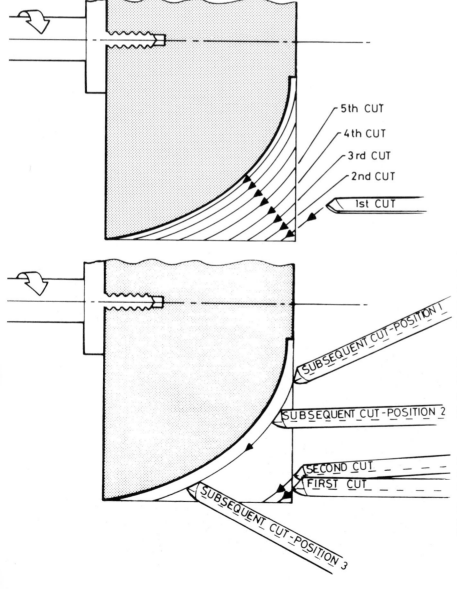

5th CUT
4th CUT
3rd CUT
2nd CUT
1st CUT

SUBSEQUENT CUT - POSITION 1
SUBSEQUENT CUT - POSITION 2
SECOND CUT
FIRST CUT
SUBSEQUENT CUT - POSITION 3

It is not possible to get the gouge on that area of the bowl wall adjacent to the plinth and observe the rule of cutting from small to large diameter. Consequently, light cuts in the other direction will have to be made, but with enough care no great damage will be done (Fig 7.21).

Fig 7.22 shows the order of cutting and the 'lining up' of the bevel on the outside of a bowl, while Fig 7.23 shows how the tool handle is swung as the cut progresses from near the plinth to the rim of the bowl.

**Fig 7.22 Order of cutting and lining up the bevel – outside of bowl.**

**Fig 7.23 Position of tool relevant to stage of cut – outside of bowl.**

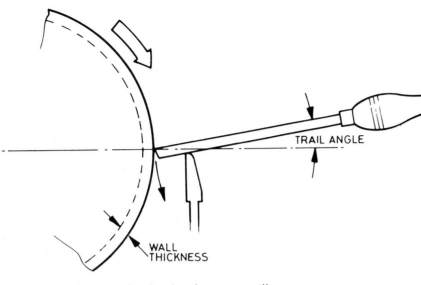

TRAIL ANGLE

WALL
THICKNESS

Fig 7.24 Scraping – outside of bowl. (i) The scraper must trail and be kept dead flat on the rest (Law 6). (ii) Adjust the rest height so that the scraper cuts on or just below centre. (iii) If the tool digs in the cutting edge will be forced downwards into fresh air.

Now stop the lathe and examine the work. You will be extremely fortunate if there are no rough areas of end grain. There are ways to improve this. One method is to power sand, which many bowl turners do. Another method is to soak the end grain with oil, sealer or wax (depending on your chosen finish), which has the effect of softening up the stubborn fibres.

Your first efforts with the bowl gouge will probably not leave a nice flowing curve and you will need to practise a good deal to develop the technique.

Do not despair. The square across scraper in your set will help put things right. Position the height of the toolrest so the scraper is 'cutting' dead on centre or slightly below. Should you have a dig-in, the tool will be knocked into fresh air and not deeper into the wood, which would increase the severity of the dig-in (Fig 7.24).

Keep the scraper perfectly flat on the rest and point it slightly downwards (trailing). For sweeping cuts like on the outside of a bowl, I place my fingers on top of the scraper, lock the handle to my side and let body movement pull the tool edge round in a flowing sweep. A few passes from centre to rim should give you a surface free from undulations (Fig 7.25).

The plinth now needs to be completed by slightly concaving the base. This again can be done with the square across scraper and in doing so you will understand why the extreme tips of the tool should be slightly radiused to prevent them scouring the wood. If you think this base is in need of a little decoration, a couple of shallow V-cuts with the toe of the ½" skew chisel, used on edge, will add to the effect as shown (Fig 7.26).

The sides of the plinth should be dead square or trouble will be experienced in obtaining a good 'friction' fit. My final cuts to achieve this are usually done with the toe of the small skew chisel, laid flat and used virtually scraper fashion. (Cutting tools are occasionally used as scrapers to good effect, Fig 7.27.)

Fig 7.25 Improving the finish with the 1" square scraper.

Fig 7.26 Forming decorative V-cuts in the base with the skew.

Fig 7.27 Accurate forming of the plinth edge with the skew.

Assuming you choose a Danish oil finish, which is suitable for most bowls, you can use the same product to soften the fibres. Apply a liberal coat of oil with a rag and allow a couple of minutes for penetration. Now take a freshly sharpened scraper and make a few light cuts around the bowl wall, traversing from the centre to the rim of the bowl. I would be very surprised if this treatment did not dramatically improve the finish. Bear in mind, however that the product used for the initial softening in this method must be chemically compatible with the product to be used as a finish.

The outside of the bowl can now be sanded and the chosen finish applied. Details of power sanding, hand sanding, polishing and finishing are given in Chapter 9, Sanding and Finishing. The completed outside of the bowl is shown in Fig 7.28.

Before reversing the bowl to gouge out the inside, it is best to plan ahead and determine the required internal depth, thus avoiding the mishap of gouging through the bottom. This is easily done if you get carried away with the sheer pleasure of 'sending the shavings flying'.

A simple but effective method is to prepare a piece of wood slightly longer than the diameter of

**Fig 7.28 The outside of the bowl completed.**

**Fig 7.29 The homemade depth gauge in use.**

the bowl and about 2" x 1" in section. Drill the appropriate sized hole in the centre to take a tight fitting length of dowel and determine the depth by tapping the dowel with a hammer until it is positioned as shown in Fig 7.29.

This measurement can then be transferred to the bowl gouge and indicated by means of a piece of tape stuck to the inside of the flute (Fig 7.30).

The next step is to remove the partly finished bowl from the screw chuck and replace it with a disc of wood intended for our friction drive chuck. A piece of softwood about 5" x 2" will do fine, so first of all true up both the edge and the face with bowl gouge and scraper. Measure the base of the bowl with dividers (Fig 7.31) and transfer this measurement to the wood now in the lathe. Be careful when doing this and allow *only one leg* (the one at 9 o'clock) to touch the whirling wood.

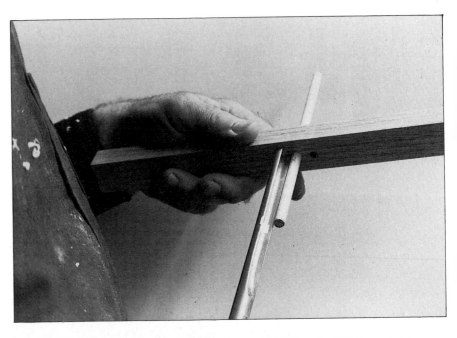

**Fig 7.30 Tape stuck to gouge on same depth.**

**Fig 7.31 Determining plinth diameter with dividers.**

This operation is difficult for beginners and an aid to 'marrying up' the points of the dividers is to pencil-in concentric rings on the intended friction chuck while the lathe is running. This obviously almost pinpoints where the dividers need to scribe the wood (Fig 7.32).

Another method used by many turners is to measure the radius of the base and set the dividers to this measurement. A pointed awl is used to make a small hole in the centre of the wood, allowing each leg of the dividers to be in contact with both wood and toolrest.

Whatever method you use, make sure the dividers point slightly down and both legs are firmly on the rest, otherwise you are inviting a dig-in.

Making use of the parting tool, go forward with a series of cuts just over ¼" deep (Fig 7.33).

For the final cuts adjacent to the scribed line, I prefer the toe of a skew chisel, scraper fashion again, to form a *gentle* decreasing bevel so the plinth tightens as it is inserted (Fig 7.34 and 7.15(c)).

Stop the lathe and try the fit (Fig 7.35). Further light cuts may be needed to arrive at a good friction fit. I do not mean the bowl has to be hammered into the recess; a good push fit will prove more than secure. For those in doubt of the effectiveness of this method, and most people are until it has been demonstrated, wetting the recess in the chuck will allow the wood to expand and grip even better.

Where the fit is a little sloppier than desired, it can be remedied by packing the recess with damp newspaper. With a little experience, however, the need to resort to such tactics will decrease. It does look a trifle 'greenhorn', but it does work!

**Fig 7.32 Scribing plinth diameter on intended chuck.**

**Fig 7.33 Forming the chuck recess with the parting tool.**

**Fig 7.34 Forming a slight inward taper on the chuck with the skew.**

**Fig 7.35 Testing the fit.**

Fig 7.36 Boring with the bowl gouge up to the tape mark.

Fig 7.37 Beginning the hollowing.

Fig 7.38 Forming V-cuts with the skew to prevent skids.

Fig 7.39 Arcing cut with the gouge from the rim to centre.

Now start the lathe and the bowl should be running dead true. If it is not, stop the lathe and a moderate blow with a light hammer, directed at the centre of the bowl face, will quickly remedy the situation. Turning can now commence and the first thing to do is dress the face of the bowl as with the bottom of the bowl.

Bore a hole in the centre of the workpiece in the same way as in the 'hollowing out' process on pages 74-5. Lay the gouge horizontally on the toolrest and positioned so the tip is in line with the centre of the wood. The tool is almost on its side (flute facing 1 o'clock), and a positive pushing action combined with a 'wiggle' from side to side will bore the hole up to the tape mark on the gouge (Fig 7.36).

Before beginning the hollowing process, just refresh your memory on grain direction. Remember that on the inside of a bowl, cutting with the grain is achieved by working from large to small diameter. With this in mind, start gouging just left of centre as you look at it and gradually widen the bowl out with a series of arcing cuts. Use the 'overhand' hold and present the gouge well over on its side, flute facing away from you and for the initial cuts the gouge is

almost at right angles to the wood (Fig 7.37).

To achieve the bevel rubbing mode, the handle needs to be well down, but remember how in spindle turning the gouge had a tendency to skid sideways until entry had been made? The same problem will be encountered here and the nearer we get to the rim, the greater the tendency to skid and inflict serious damage to the bowl rim. This can be avoided by making a series of V-cuts with the tip of the square across scraper or skew chisel near to the rim. These will afford immediate support to the bevel of the gouge, thus preventing the skid (Fig 7.38).

The professional way to do it, or rather my way, is to present the gouge just below the horizontal and boldly lever upwards and forwards, in much the same way as described for the spindle gouge. As soon as entry to the wood is effected, the handle should be dropped and the path of the cut should be in the form of a shallow arc, finishing at the centre of the bowl. The shaving, as always, should be coming from below the centre of the tool (i.e. the part receiving direct support) and used in this manner a dig-in is averted (Fig 7.39).

As the bowl widens and deepens, substantial

Fig 7.40 Lining up the bevel near the rim.

swinging movements will be necessary to make the shape 'flow'. Fig 7.40 shows the start of a cut near to the rim and the tool handle is well over towards the right-hand side of the bowl, as it must be in order to 'line the bevel up'. As the cut proceeds the handle will need to be swung towards the operator's body (Fig 7.41).

To maintain these substantial swinging movements, body movement, balance and weight transference are very important if a flowing internal shape is to be arrived at. For the final cuts with the gouge, ensure that the bevel is lined up with the outside profile and aim for an even wall thickness. Fingers can be used as a means to 'calip' the wall thickness, but the more accurate way is to make use of the commercial double-ended calipers (Fig 7.42). (Do not forget occasionally to offer your depth gauge up to the bowl. When the 2" x 1" touches the rim, you will have gone deep enough.)

Fig 7.43 should assist in explaining the 'order of cutting' and Fig 7.44 shows the angle of presentation: **(a)** for the commencing cuts and **(b)** for the swinging movements of the gouge from the rim to the centre.

Fig 7.41 The gouge in mid cut, the handle being swung towards the body.

Fig 7.42 Testing for even wall thickness with calipers.

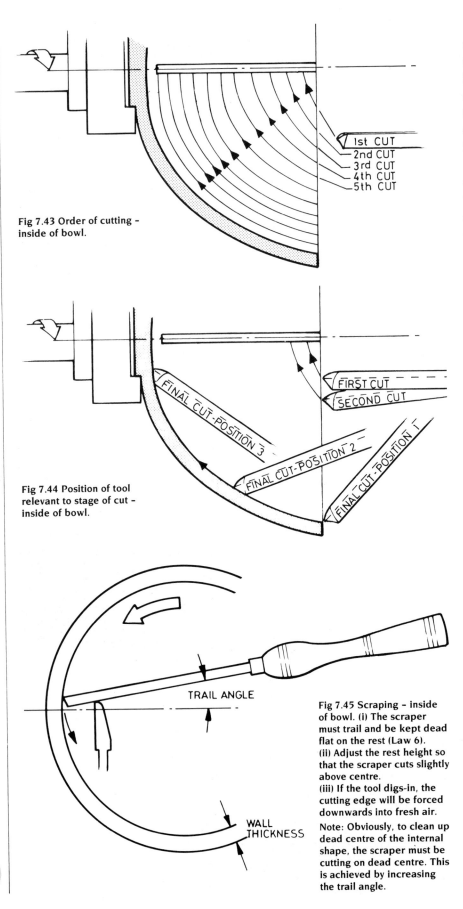

**Fig 7.43 Order of cutting – inside of bowl.**

1st CUT
2nd CUT
3rd CUT
4th CUT
5th CUT

FIRST CUT
SECOND CUT
FINAL CUT-POSITION 3
FINAL CUT-POSITION 2
FINAL CUT-POSITION 1

**Fig 7.44 Position of tool relevant to stage of cut – inside of bowl.**

TRAIL ANGLE

WALL THICKNESS

**Fig 7.45 Scraping – inside of bowl. (i) The scraper must trail and be kept dead flat on the rest (Law 6).**
**(ii) Adjust the rest height so that the scraper cuts slightly above centre.**
**(iii) If the tool digs-in, the cutting edge will be forced downwards into fresh air.**

**Note: Obviously, to clean up dead centre of the internal shape, the scraper must be cutting on dead centre. This is achieved by increasing the trail angle.**

Finishing touches to the inside of the bowl to remove any undulations are carried out with the I domed scraper. The toolrest must be positioned so it affords maximum support and at a height that enables the cutting edge of the scraper to engage the wood slightly above centre. Again, if a dig-in is experienced the scraper will be forced downwards into fresh air and not wood (Fig 7.45).

Remember to traverse from the rim towards the centre. Such traversing should be smooth and flowing if a smooth, flowing internal profile is to be arrived at. Keep the scrapers dead flat and limit the overhang to as little as possible. On internal shapes, always ensure that the radius of the tool is slightly 'quicker' than the internal shape, or the tips will almost certainly dig-in (Fig 7.46).

The process of soaking the end grain with oil can now be repeated on the inside of the bowl and the work is completed by skimming with a freshly ground scraper and then of course sanding and final oiling.

I do not recommend trying to make the bowl walls too thin during the learning process. Bowls of this size look and feel right if the finished thickness is about ¼". Even with this thickness, you will need to steady the bowl wall with your fingers to prevent the tools chattering, which would of course impair the finish (Fig 7.47).

I do recommend your early bowls be similar to the finished example, Fig 7.48, which has 'slow' flowing shapes and no tight curves. Bevel contact is much easier to maintain and confidence and proficiency should quickly increase. A final word on bevel rubbing. Many turners are over zealous in their application of the bevel when bowl turning, which

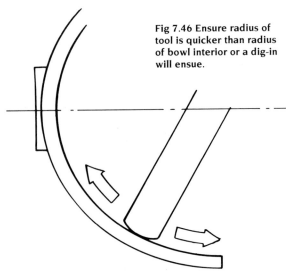

**Fig 7.46 Ensure radius of tool is quicker than radius of bowl interior or a dig-in will ensue.**

Fig 7.47 Using the left hand to support the bowl wall when scraping near the rim.

results in the tool edge becoming hot. While it is true to say that the bevel must rub behind the cut, a better description might be that it should 'glide' along behind the cut.

There is obviously a great deal more to faceplate work than bowl turning, but if the basic techniques are mastered, then the making of such things as bases for standard and table lamps, candlesticks and wall clocks, pot stands, bread boards, platters, etc. will present few problems.

# SUMMARY OF CHAPTER

**1** Ensure that the bowl blank or disc is sound and free from shakes and 'dead' knots.

**2** Study the end-grain formation, remembering it is normal to have the heart side up to avoid the bowl base becoming rounded.

**3** Cutting 'with the grain' on the *outside* of a bowl is achieved by working from *small* to *large* diameter.

**4** Cutting 'with the grain' on the *inside* of a bowl is achieved by working from *large* to *small* diameter.

**5** The best finish is achieved by the gouge being used well over on its side and presented at an angle with strict bevel rubbing.

**6** Scrapers can be used as 'forming' shapes or as 'improvers'. They lose their edge rapidly and need constant sharpening.

Fig 7.48 The completed bowl.

# Chapter 8

## COPY
## WOODTURNING

Travelling up and down the country and demonstrating woodturning at various shows is physically exhausting, but extremely satisfying and enjoyable.

Certainly, there are few who would question the physical demands on the demonstrator engaged in woodturning some eight or nine hours a day at venues which are always crowded, sometimes claustrophobic and invariably excessively warm.

While I am well used to beavering away for such periods of time, it is a different matter to work in these conditions and also give a running commentary, answering a multitude of questions on both the lathes and techniques.

Not that I don't enjoy the dialogue with the 'punters'. I most certainly do. However, taking into account the prevailing conditions, I have been known to suddenly take off for the nearest bar to partake of 'Bacchus' treasures'. This is neither because I am of immoderate habits nor because someone has posed a question I know not the answer to. It is simply that I must 'oil my larynx' to be able to continue talking!

The advantages of demonstrating are many. First of all it gets me amongst my favourite people, that is workers in wood, who by and and large are a happy breed only too willing to discuss techniques, methods, successes and failures.

Second, it is beneficial to me in my capacity as a woodturning instructor; not only because I am able personally to promote my courses, but mainly to identify, through continued dialogue with the enthusiasts, the most common problems they are encountering. I can therefore incorporate the causes and remedies of these problems into my teaching methods and general approach.

Another great advantage, of course, is that it gets you known. I do not think I would have written this book had I not been demonstrating one year for the Coronet Lathe and Tool Company at the Woodworker Show at Alexandra Palace.

In Chapter 4, On Sharpening, I mentioned that my research (based on dialogue with the hundreds of aspiring turners with whom I have come into contact) indicated that the greatest single problem in the learning stages is the accurate grinding and sharpening of the tools.

This research and collating of facts also reveals that most beginners have great difficulty in making two or more identical items. Time after time I am approached and asked how to go about making a set of matching chair or table legs, spindles for hour glasses, for staircases, etc.

There is no doubt that the ability to copy turn is a great asset, and once the basic techniques of cutting with the chisels and gouges are mastered, it is not as difficult as it is sometimes made out to be. I am firmly of the opinion that continued practice on simple copy work will inevitably lead to a student making rapid progress. I encourage beginners to practice simple copying exercises virtually from scratch, and certainly everyone who attends my courses is given an exercise that not only involves copying, but also provides practice in most of the techniques required in spindle turning.

I have heard established turners say that making say fifty table legs or staircase balusters is 'boring', I cannot for the life of me understand why! As I said in an earlier chapter, there is something uniquely satisfying about making a well-designed bowl. There is as much satisfaction for me in producing the turnings for a complete staircase, particularly when you have the opportunity of seeing the work in its completed state – that is, fixed and professionally polished.

Copy work certainly demands discipline and a great deal of concentration. I believe these two factors combine to make it the quickest means to improve your skills. The greater part of my output is this type of turning, such as bar, shop and staircase fittings, furniture components, etc. If you are skilful enough and can combine accuracy with speed, then such undertakings can be extremely profitable. Furthermore, the demand for your services will be constant and you may reach the happy state of being able to pick and choose what you want to do.

Such an assertion may sound rather extravagant, particularly in this age of the sophisticated automatic copy lathes which churn out this type of work in thousands. I can assure you it is not. There is still a demand for quality hand-turned work, for don't forget that the majority of the mass-produced items restrict the choice of timber to only two or three species. If the customer wants something different in the way of timber or design, he will seek the services of the hand turner. Bear in mind also that the 'automatic people' don't want to get involved in comparatively short production runs.

I have said that copy turning is not as difficult as some would have you believe, and I stick by that statement, assuming you possess the necessary determination, discipline and patience. I will not pretend combining speed with accuracy is other than difficult, and it only comes with experience and constant everyday practice.

Provided the beginner is prepared to work carefully and methodically, there is no reason why simple copy work should not be attempted very early in his woodturning career. Be reminded though that no one has yet found a way of replacing wood which has been cut away in error. I recall a lady onlooker at one of my demonstrations making the remark that woodturning was very similar to the potter working his lump of clay on the wheel. She couldn't have been further from the truth! When things go wrong for the potter, all that is required is for another piece of clay to be stuck to the original and off he goes again. With the turner, removing wood from the wrong place or too much of it in any part of the design means that particular piece of wood is destined for the scrap pile, accompanied by a few choice adjectives.

In simplistic terms, copy turning is merely repeating a pre-determined design, ensuring the design features are positioned in identical places and to the same width and diameter. While it is impossible to work to engineering tolerances, a good copy turner making use of a few simple aids, combined with a good eye, can produce copies that will stand up to close scrutiny. The development of a good eye comes with constant practice of course, and very often the experienced turner does not have to resort to calipers and the like to determine diameters.

Some may say that copy turning should not be included in a book aimed primarily at the newcomer to the craft, but I disagree. Beginners should be encouraged to 'have a bash', almost from day one, and personally I consider skills and technique will develop rapidly if the novice concentrates the majority of his time on this type of work.

Accordingly, I have set out three separate copying projects. The first is a fairly simple and straight-forward piece of spindle turning combined with faceplate work which can be developed into a very useful and saleable commodity, i.e. a child's three-legged stool. The second project, a staircase baluster, will be more of a challenge and also provide the opportunity to explain how to make and use a 'steady'. Finally, I describe the making of identical faceplate turnings, and the project is an attractive plinth or base that can be put to a variety of uses, e.g. for a lamp or candlestick.

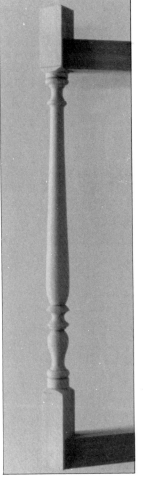

# PROJECT 1: CHILD'S STOOL

For this, choose some hardwood such as ash, beech or oak. I have made use of oak in the example. All that is required are three pieces 10" long by 1½" square for the legs and one piece 8½" square by 1¼" thick for the seat. The overall measurements can be drawn out full size on a piece of card or plywood from which we can determine the angle of splay for the legs (Fig 8.1).

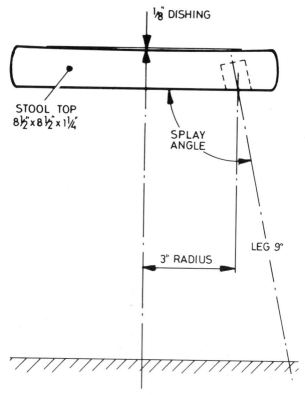

1/8" DISHING

STOOL TOP
8½ x 8½ x 1¼

SPLAY ANGLE

3" RADIUS

LEG 9"

## Legs

The profile of the legs is drawn separately on thick card and this is stuck to a piece of 1/8" plywood to serve as a 'rod' or marking stick. The salient points are then projected to the front edge of the plywood and a slight V-groove is made on these marks with a chisel or three-cornered file. The grooves will facilitate the accurate location of a pencil when marking the whirling timber. (Note that the

**Fig 8.2 Full-scale drawing of stool leg stuck to a piece of plywood to serve as a rod. Note the V-cuts on the front edge for pencil location.**

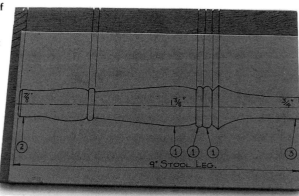

**Fig 8.1 Full-size layout to determine leg splay angle.**

**Fig 8.3 Plywood sizers to be used on the legs, numbered 1, 2 and 3 to accord with the diameters on the rod.**

**Fig 8.4 The rod being used to set out the stool leg.**

numbers on the rod indicate the three differing diameters, Fig 8.2). This device will of course only indicate where the main design features will be located. It will not assist with the various diameters that form part of the design. For this we need to make use of verniers, calipers, etc. to assist in sizing-in to the required depth. Alternatively, the appropriate diameters can be cut out of some 1/8" thick plywood, aluminium or brass sheet, or anything *less* than the width of the sizing tool, and they will have to be numbered to accord with the numbers on the rod (Fig 8.3).

Mount the first leg in the lathe (about 2000 rpm) and reduce the stock to a parallel cylinder with the roughing out gouge, making use of sizer No. 1 to arrive at diameter 1 (1⅜"), the thickest part of the leg. Move the toolrest close to the work and ledge

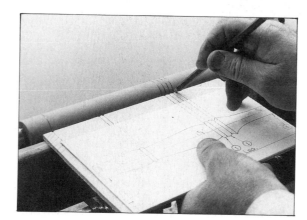

the rod on it and close to the whirling stock. The point of a pencil is then pushed into the V-grooves to scribe or mark the overall length and the position of the twin beads and V-cut near the top of the leg (Fig 8.4).

The other sizing cuts can now be made. (I have deliberately used only three different diameters so as to keep the first copying exercise simple. It is *method* I am concerned with at this juncture.) The parting tool should be used in the one-handed mode as described on page 59 with the sizers held in the other hand. First, part in on the waste side of the bottom of the leg (headstock end) to a diameter of about ½". (This diameter can be 'eyeballed' as it is not important.) Now use sizer No. 2 (a full ⅞") to determine the diameter of the base of the leg. Finally use sizer No. 3 (¾") to determine the diameter of the top of the leg. This measurement is critical as it forms the joint with the ¾" hole to be drilled in the underneath of the seat and it should be a good push fit.

When all the sizing cuts have been completed, the workpiece will be as shown in Fig 8.5.

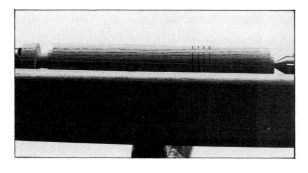

Fig 8.5 How the leg should look after the sizing cuts have been made.

The design of the legs, between the 'twin' beads and the bottom, is formed on a tapered line, so the first step in the shaping is to cut this taper with the roughing out gouge, followed by a planing cut with the 1" skew chisel. The rod can now be offered up and the position of the single bead can be marked in on the whirling wood (Fig 8.6).

The toe of the ½" skew can now be used to make V-cuts on the marks indicating the beads and to develop them into the finished profiles, after which the leg will be as shown in Fig 8.7.

The same tool or a spindle gouge can be used for the remainder of the shaping, although the

Fig 8.6 The rod being used (after the tapered section has been shaped) to mark the location of the single bead.

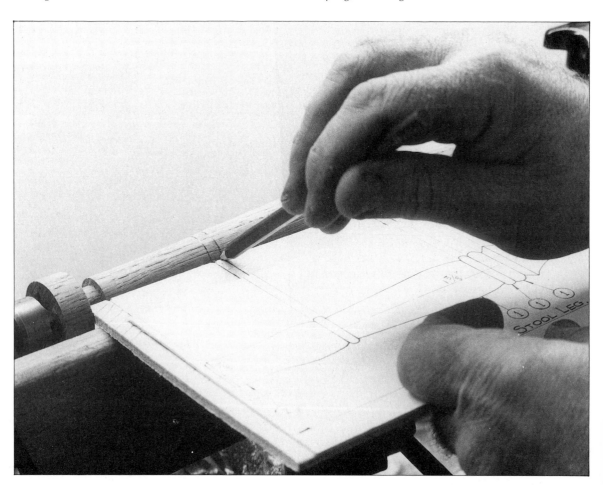

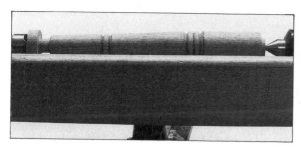

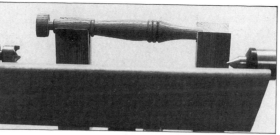

Fig 8.7 How the leg should look after all the beads and the taper have been formed.

Fig 8.8 The completed leg, sited behind the lathe on V-blocks, will serve as the master copy.

skew chisel will be needed to cut the tight intersections. The diameters adjacent to the beads are not determined by sizers. It is quite all right to 'eyeball' these, and you will be surprised how quickly you develop the ability to do this accurately. The slow hollow section between the twin beads and the top of the leg can be fashioned with the roughing out gouge.

If the tool work is good, sanding can be done with nothing coarser than 150 grit paper, followed by 220 grit. A handful of shavings will burnish oak to a pleasing shine. At this stage I would apply a coat of sanding sealer and 'cut it back' with 320 grit when dried, which is almost instantly. Now remove it from the lathe and position it on a couple of V-blocks in front of you so that you can keep glancing at the master copy when turning the other legs. Fig 8.8 shows the finished leg mounted on the blocks behind the lathe.

## Seat

A block of wood slightly over 8½" square is prepared and the underside planed flat. Determine the centre and set out the circumference with a pair of dividers. Now scribe a concentric circle 1¼" in from this line, which will be the line on which the holes for the legs will be bored.

The dividers (set at the same radius) can now be used to 'step out' six equal points on the inner circle, alternate marks indicating the position of the holes. All these marks should be joined up to each other by pencil lines and then a pilot hole drilled in the centre for the woodscrew chuck (Fig 8.9).

The blank can now be cut to a circle on the bandsaw (or by hand), following which the angled holes can be bored. There are several ways of doing this and probably the easiest is to use the drill press with the table suitably canted. Very few beginners will possess such equipment, so I shall explain how to do it by hand using a brace and bit. (It can also be done by making a boring jig that fits on the lathe, and this method is described in Chapter 10, Boring and Routing on the Lathe.)

The angled holes need to be accurately bored and this can be achieved by making a simple jig with a ¾" hole bored at the required angle, determined from

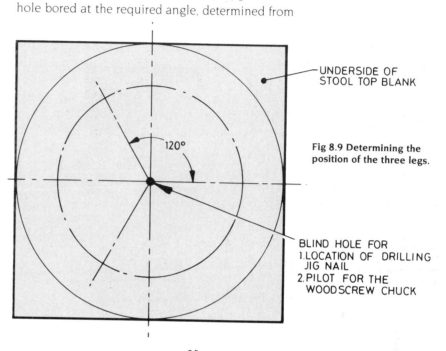

Fig 8.9 Determining the position of the three legs.

UNDERSIDE OF STOOL TOP BLANK

BLIND HOLE FOR
1. LOCATION OF DRILLING JIG NAIL
2. PILOT FOR THE WOODSCREW CHUCK

120°

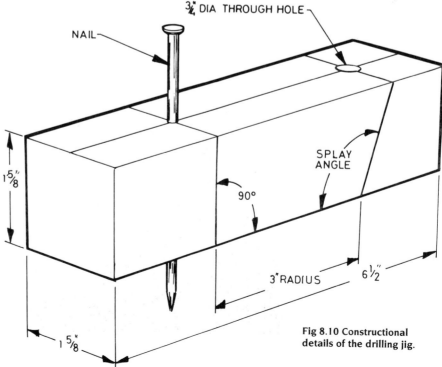

Fig 8.10 Constructional details of the drilling jig.

Fig 8.11 Method for
producing the splayed
holes.

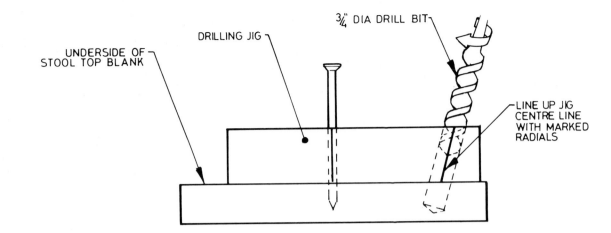

UNDERSIDE OF
STOOL TOP BLANK

DRILLING JIG

¾" DIA DRILL BIT

LINE UP JIG
CENTRE LINE
WITH MARKED
RADIALS

Fig 8.12 Boring jig in use.
Note the G-cramp and
depth stop.

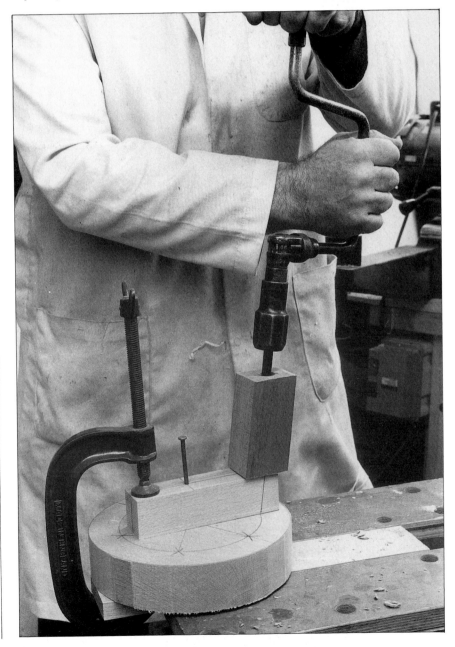

the original drawing and transferred with an
adjustable bevel. Figs 8.10 and 8.11 give the relevant
measurements and it is important to gauge in a
centre line on the top and ends so as to line up the
jig with the marks on the seat. The holes are blind;
so to prevent boring right through, a piece of wood
of the calculated length is cut and bored all the way
through. This is then slipped on to the bit and used
as a depth gauge. Fig 8.12 shows the boring jig
clamped to the workpiece with the brace and bit in
use.

After the holes have been bored out, mount the
seat on the woodscrew chuck and set the speed of
the lathe to 1000 rpm. True up the edge and top of
the stool with the bowl gouge, using the methods
described on pages 83 and 84.

Fig 8.13 The completed
seat section.

**Fig 8.14 The completed stool.**

The radius on the edge is formed by gouging from small to large diameter, the gouge held well over on its side and pulled towards you. The shape can be refined with a 1" square scraper if necessary. The slight dishing of the seat to make it more comfortable is again fashioned with the bowl gouge and cleaned up with the 1" domed scraper. The seat can now be sanded, burnished with shavings and given a coat of sanding sealer. Fig 8.13 shows the completed seat section.

## Assembly

Apply a coat of glue to the joints and hammer the legs to the bottom of the holes. Allow the glue to set and a final light sanding with a piece of worn 320 grit paper will prepare the stool for a couple of coats of Danish oil. These pieces are extremely saleable, and as well as being used by a child, they can become footstools or plant stands. Fig 8.14 shows the completed stool.

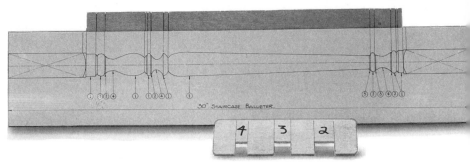

Fig 8.15 The full-size
drawing of the rod and
sizers used in making a
baluster.

# PROJECT 2: STAIRCASE BALUSTER

The design of these is usually determined by the architect or customer. A typical example is the one illustrated, which was made following a drawing supplied by a firm of shopfitters. The drawing was small scale so the first task was to reproduce it full size on some thick card and number the various key diameters.

As with the stool project, the card was stuck to a piece of plywood, the length of which should correspond with the measurement *between* the square sections, and the salient points projected to the front edge and V-grooved to take a pencil. The next step was to prepare the sizers, again making use of some ⅛″ plywood, taking care to number them to accord with the numbers and diameters on the rod. Fig 8.15 shows the drawing, the rod and the various sizers.

marking of the pummels is to lay about ten pieces of wood on a sheet of plywood or chipboard on to which I have screwed three pieces of wood to form 90° angles. The intended balusters are laid out on the device and secured with a pair of folding wedges. It is necessary to initially mark out two of the balusters with pencil and try square, and these must be positioned one at either side. The intermediate pieces are marked by laying a straightedge across these marks and pencilling all the way across (Fig 8.16).

Marking the centres on every spindle using the method of drawing diagonal lines would be time consuming and extremely tedious. There are several quicker, still accurate, methods. Perhaps the easiest

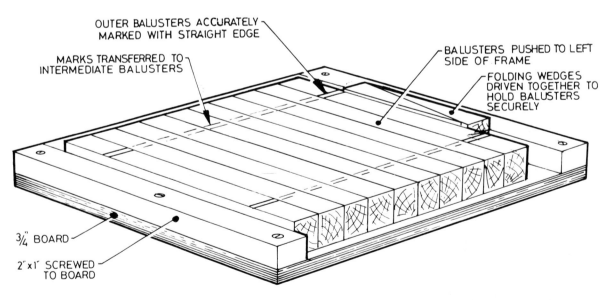

OUTER BALUSTERS ACCURATELY MARKED WITH STRAIGHT EDGE

MARKS TRANSFERRED TO INTERMEDIATE BALUSTERS

BALUSTERS PUSHED TO LEFT SIDE OF FRAME

FOLDING WEDGES DRIVEN TOGETHER TO HOLD BALUSTERS SECURELY

¾″ BOARD

2″ x 1″ SCREWED TO BOARD

For this particular order, 48 balusters were required. It is essential in this type of work for each piece of wood to be accurately centred, and also the extent of the 'pummels' or square sections needs to be carefully marked. My method of speeding up the

is to mount a piece of wood on the screw chuck, turn it to a cylinder and then form a tapered hole in the 'open end' large enough to take the square section of the baluster. The hole must be deep enough for the tip of the woodscrew to be exposed so that it can

**Fig 8.16 Method of setting out pummels.**

prick the end of the inserted baluster. Fig 8.17 gives details of how it is made and Fig 8.18 shows the 'centre finder' in use.

**Fig 8.17 A home-made centre finder.**

construction and subsequent photographs show it in use.

The problems associated with long slender turnings are that the tools tend to deflect the wood from its true axial path. Also, in many cases the

TAP BALUSTER TO MARK
TRUE CENTRE ON END

TURNED CUP-

SLIGHT TAPER-
ON BORE

BALUSTER END LOCATES-
ACROSS CORNERS AT
THIS POSITION

WOODSCREW CHUCK BODY-

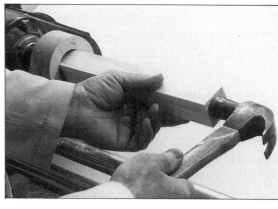

**Fig 8.18 The home-made centre finder in use.**

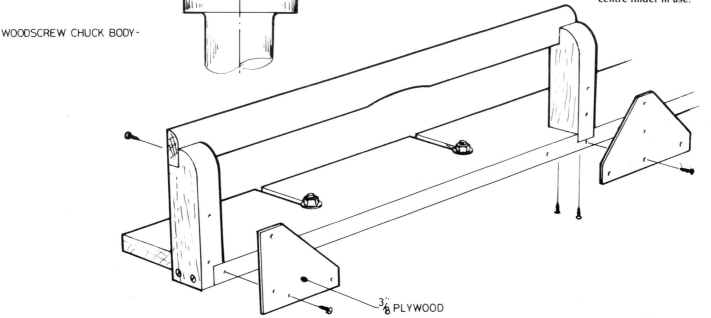

**Fig 8.19 A home-made wooden toolrest.**

$\frac{3}{8}$" PLYWOOD

Turnings of this length and section (the example is 30" long, $1\frac{5}{8}$" square) can even present problems for the experienced turner. The greatest of these problems is 'whip'. Additionally, unless you have a toolrest which spans the length of the work, you will be forever moving the toolrest about, which is both time consuming and frustrating. The problem can be overcome by making a wooden toolrest that bolts to the bench. This device is adjustable because of the slots in the base. The piece forming the actual rest is interchangeable for different rest lengths if necessary. Fig 8.19 provides details of

wood starts to whip even without the application of the tools. If this is not prevented in some way, the wood will bounce off the tools and most likely grab and dig-in. The surface of the timber will also take on a shallow, spiral effect and will not be turned truly round.

There are several things that can be done to minimize these problems:

**1** Reduce the speed of the lathe.

**2** Slacken off the tailstock pressure as much as possible.

**3** Leave the smallest diameters in the design till the end.

**4** Break the design down into sections and join afterwards. (Turnings with square sections, like balusters and newel posts, lend themselves to this, and the joining method is described in Chapter 10, Boring and Routing on the Lathe.)

**5** Make use of a back stay or 'steady'.

**6** Use one of your hands in the 'supporting technique', see page 56.

**7** Take fine cuts with sharp tools used in strict bevel rubbing mode. (Scraping methods mean that there is more resistance to the tool and the workpiece will be deflected a great deal more. This inevitably leads to a dig-in. Be aware that blunt tools, particularly the skew chisel, can also produce this spiralling effect, even when the work is not slender.)

various forms and you will need to design one to suit your particular lathe. The example shown in Fig 8.20 is suitable for lathes with twin bed bars and it is not difficult to construct. It is important that any steady is easy to move from side to side and with this in mind the two pieces with the V-notches are clamped to the bed with a bolt and wing nut. Wing nuts are also used on the two bolts securing the slotted cross piece to the upright. The slot in the cross piece is cut out by boring a series of holes and squaring out with a carpenter's chisel. This slot allows for movement back and forth for varying diameters. The castors need to be tightly embedded, and accordingly the holes for the shanks must be slightly undersize. It is *vital* that the castors are positioned so that a centre line drawn between them is exactly in line with the centre of the wood.

Fig 8.20 provides details of construction and Fig 8.21 shows the steady and also a home-made, full-length toolrest in use.

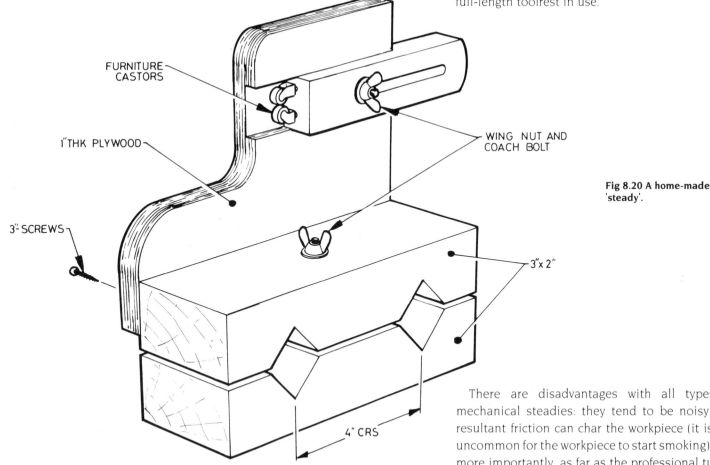

FURNITURE CASTORS

1" THK PLYWOOD

3" SCREWS

WING NUT AND COACH BOLT

**Fig 8.20 A home-made 'steady'.**

3" x 2"

4" CRS

There are disadvantages with all types of mechanical steadies: they tend to be noisy; the resultant friction can char the workpiece (it is not uncommon for the workpiece to start smoking); and more importantly, as far as the professional turner is concerned, they most certainly slow down the rate of output.

To make use of the home-made steady described above, it is necessary to first of all turn the stock (or

There are several types of 'steadies' on the market but they tend to be extremely expensive, and the alternative is to make your own. These can take

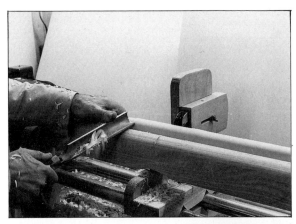

Fig 8.21 The home-made steady in use.

Fig 8.22 The rod being used to mark salient points on the baluster.

Fig 8.23 The baluster after the sizing in has been completed.

Fig 8.24 A skew chisel being used to make a planing cut on the tapered section.

part of it) to a cylinder. The steady is then positioned in the most advantageous place, usually somewhere near to the middle of the length of wood.

Because of the disadvantages mentioned, the professional turner will do his utmost to manage without a mechanical steady and rely purely on the supporting technique. To be able to do so requires a great deal of practice, but perseverance and determination will be rewarded.

Having prepared your stock ready to be turned, mount a piece in the lathe and set the speed between 1000 and 1500 rpm. I normally arrange for the thickest part of the baluster to be nearest to the headstock because I prefer to steady with my left hand and work from left to right. The pencilled lines indicating the pummels should be clearly seen on the whirling wood and the first step is to cut these with the toe of the ½" skew chisel. Start with light cuts taking out small chips, repeating the process from either side of the inside line until the cut is continuous round the wood and to the desired depth. The action of the skew to produce a radiused shoulder is, if you recall, one of rolling and lifting. The area between the pummels is then reduced to a cylinder with a roughing out gouge, rolling it well over on its side when cutting adjacent to the square sections to avoid fouling the whirling corners.

The rod and pencil can now be used, lathe running, to mark the salient design features. (It will be obvious now why the plywood should be cut to the length of the turned section, for otherwise it would foul the square pummels, Fig 8.22.)

If you intend making use of a steady, now is the time to position it to your best advantage, lathe not running of course. Making use of the previously prepared sizers and ¼" parting tool, cut in the key diameters at the appropriate places. When these have been completed the workpiece will be as shown in Fig 8.23. (**NB** There is no need to prepare a 'sizer' for diameter No. 1, as this is the *full* diameter of the wood after the square section has been reduced to a true cylinder.)

The beads and coves are then cut with chisels and gouges and the long taper can be fashioned with the roughing out gouge. Remember that this tool, if very sharp, will produce an acceptable finish on many kinds of wood if it is angled to induce a paring action and the bevel pushed boldly on to the surface of the wood. Fig 8.24 shows a skew chisel being used to make a planing cut from left to right (downhill) along the tapered section.

**Fig 8.25 Burnishing the finished turning with a handful of shavings.**

The necessary sanding can now be done and a handful of shavings can be used to burnish up the surface as shown in Fig 8.25. The completed baluster can now be sited at the back of the lathe on a pair of V-blocks to act as your master copy, Fig 8.26.

With continued practice at this type of turning, not only will your skills improve rapidly, you will develop a good eye that will eventually eliminate the need to do other than a very little sizing in.

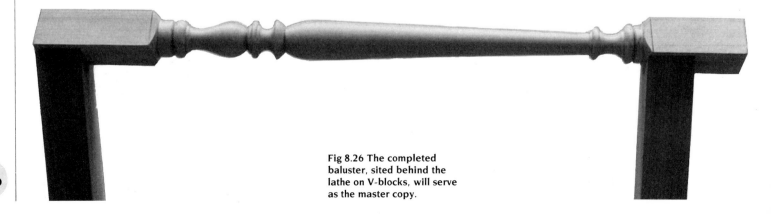

**Fig 8.26 The completed baluster, sited behind the lathe on V-blocks, will serve as the master copy.**

# PROJECT 3: A PLINTH

Most people associate copy turning with turning between centres only. It is true that the bulk of my copy work falls under this heading, but nevertheless, a good deal of faceplate work also needs to be copied. As an introduction to the methods I use, I shall describe the making of an attractive plinth/base which can be put to a variety of uses.

As always, the first step is to make a full-size drawing on a piece of card which can later be stuck to a piece of plywood. Project the salient points to both the edge and the side of the plywood and again make the V-notches for pencil location (Fig 8.27).

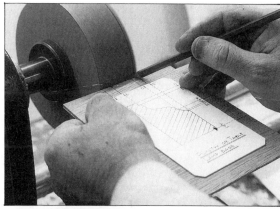

Fig 8.28 Rod and pencil being used to mark the thickness of the plinth.

Fig 8.29 The rod being used to mark out the face of the plinth.

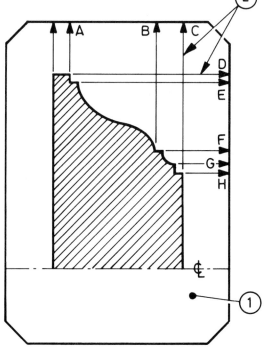

Fig 8.27 Preparing the rod.
**1** Produce a full-size 'half' template.
**2** Produce projection lines A, B, C, D, E, F, G, H.

The face of the disc can now be marked out using the rod and pencil (Fig 8.29). The sequence of cutting as shown in Figs 8.30 to 8.35 can now be

The disc, which should be slightly oversize both in thickness and diameter, is first of all turned to a true cylinder with the ³⁄₈″ bowl gouge (lathe speed about 1000 rpm). The rod and pencil are now used to mark the desired thickness (Fig 8.28). After positioning the toolrest across the face of the disc, the waste can be removed with the bowl gouge and square ended scraper.

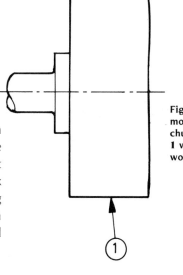

Fig 8.30 With the blank mounted on the screw chuck, true up the edge **1** with the ³⁄₈″ bowl gouge, working from left to right.

**107**

**Fig 8.31 1** The rod is offered up to the whirling disc and the finished thickness C is pencilled in.

**2** Remove the waste wood with the bowl gouge and square ended scraper.

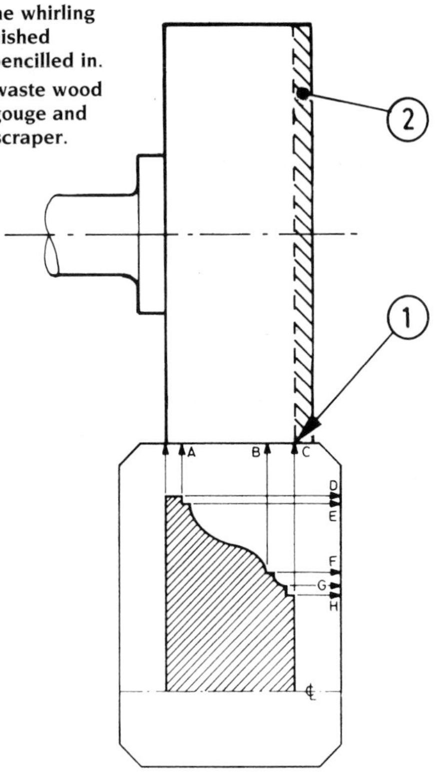

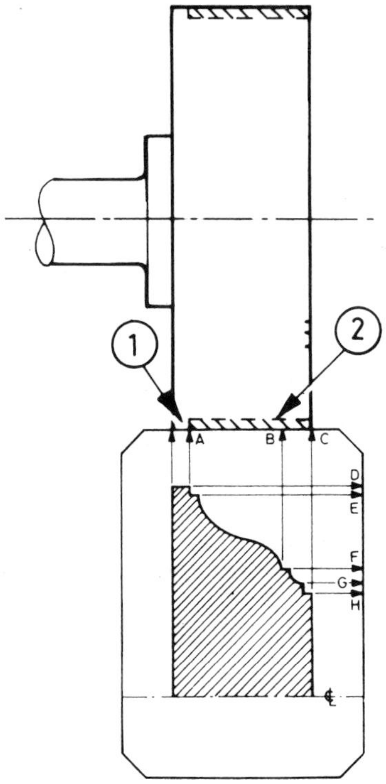

**Fig 8.33 1** Pencil in point A.

**2** Remove the waste wood with a parting tool, cutting from E to A.

**Fig 8.34 1** Pencil in point B.

**2** Remove the waste wood with a parting tool, cutting from F to B.

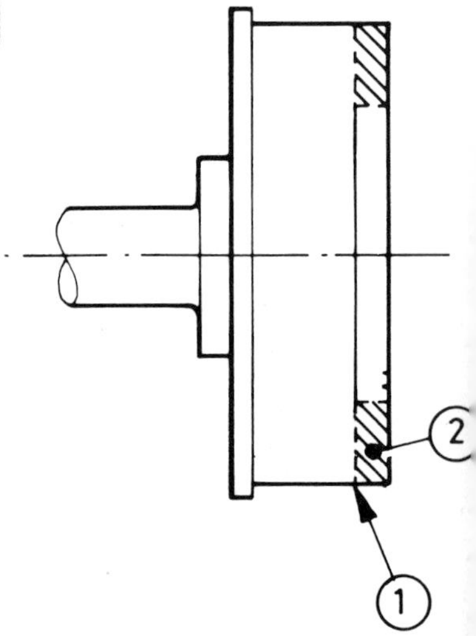

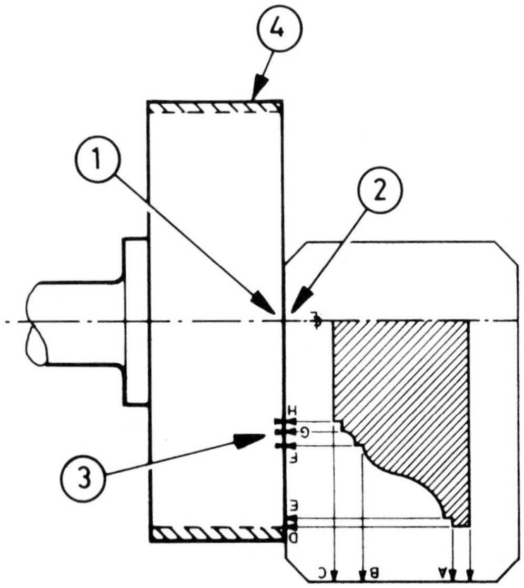

**Fig 8.32 1** Mark the exact centre on the face of the plinth.

**2** Line up the centre of the rod with the centre mark on the wood.

**3** Pencil in intermediate points E, F, G, H.

**4** Pencil in the finished diameter D and remove the waste wood with the bowl gouge, working from left to right.

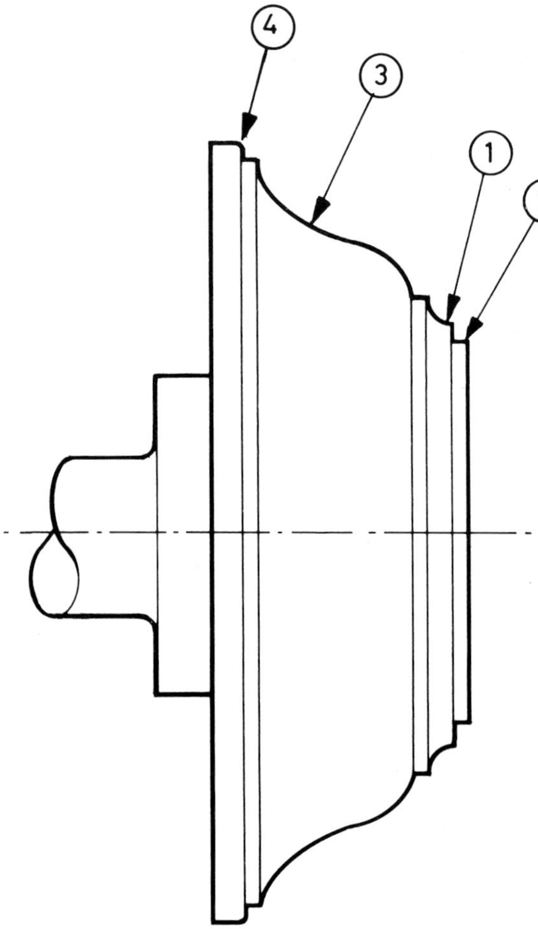

**Fig 8.35 1** The half round is shaped with either a small gouge or a small round nose scraper.

**2** The outer fillet is cut with the toe of the skew chisel.

**3** The ogee section is formed with a small gouge and scrapers.

**4** The small radius is formed with either gouge or scraper.

**Fig 8.36 The completed plinth.**

undertaken making use of the bowl gouge, parting tool and scrapers. Fig 8.36 shows the completed plinth.

All the above projects are fairly straightforward, but the reader will have learned something about the methods used and the simple appliances which can be made to assist. (There are other methods of copying of course and all kinds of other gadgets that may assist.)

# SUMMARY OF CHAPTER

**1** Students should attempt simple copy turning virtually from day one.

**2** Planning and setting out are vital stages in the process.

**3** Always make a full-size drawing of the project from which the rod is prepared.

**4** Speed is not important in the learning process, but accuracy and concentration are essential.

**5** Home-made wooden toolrests to span the full length of a project are simple to make and avoid the irritation of constantly moving the short rests from side to side.

**6** The 'steadying' of long slender turnings can be achieved either by using the supporting technique or by means of a home-made mechanical steady.

# Chapter 9

## SANDING AND FINISHING

It is said that the finish can make or mar any woodworking project, and wood-turning is no exception. It is also true to say that no matter how well any finish is applied, it will not disguise poor workmanship and the lack of care that has gone before. A good finish/polish applied to any piece of poor quality turnery will not improve the appearance. In fact, it will have the opposite effect — that is, it will only serve to highlight the shortcomings of the turner.

It follows, therefore, that both the turning and the finishing techniques must be of a high standard if the maker's reputation is to remain 'untarnished'.

Equally important is the *durability* of the finish or polish. You will certainly not have customers coming back for more if you make use of a finish that will not stand up to its intended use and becomes tatty after a short while.

# THE NEED FOR A FINISH

Very few woodworking projects of any kind are left in their natural state and there are several reasons why a suitable finish must be applied.

**1** To enhance the beauty of the wood by bringing out the grain and colour.

**2** To protect the surface from dust, grime, finger marks, etc.

**3** To seal the surface. This helps to limit the amount of moisture absorbed.

**4** To enable domestic artifacts to be wiped with damp cloths or even washed.

**5** To change the colour by staining.

In short, the object of applying a finish to woodwork is to seal, protect and enhance its beauty.

However, as emphasized above, a 'good finish' applied to poor work is no better than a 'poor finish' applied to a piece of exquisite turning. The success or otherwise of a piece of completed turnery depends on *every step* from preparation to finish!

# WHAT ARE THESE STEPS?

Most of these steps have already been dealt with. I have stressed the need to make use of quality tools that have been carefully and accurately ground to the 'acceptable degree of sharpness'. I have urged you to discipline yourself to *practise, practise, practise* in the forming of the basic profiles using cutting techniques, wherever possible, to leave the best possible surface finish straight off the tools.

Without such preparation you will need to spend a disproportionate amount of time sanding your work to get a reasonable surface to apply the finish/polish.

Too much sanding destroys the 'crispness' of a piece, so it must be your aim to minimize this step towards your goal.

In most cases, however, it is inevitable that a certain amount of sanding will have to be done (this amount being directly proportional to the ability of the turner) to remove surface blemishes. It should not be used to *shape* the wood, but merely to improve the surface.

Sanding is a boring, tedious chore and I loathe it. Nevertheless, you must discipline yourself to patiently go through the correct sequence of procedures if the best results are to be achieved.

You will discover faceplate work will require considerably more sanding than spindle turning, and side grain sands much more easily than end grain.

Experience will teach you that sanding can sometimes make the surface more uneven than it was before. For example, knots, being harder than the surrounding wood, will tend to become 'raised'. Timbers in which there is a pronounced difference in density between the quick growing spring growth and slower forming summer growth will sand unevenly. The darker rings (the hardest and densest) will also become raised. As an experiment, turn a small bowl in Columbian pine and sand it with some 100 grit paper. You will only have to run your fingers over the surface to realize how uneven and 'rippled' the surfaces of such timbers can become.

Unnecessary sanding should obviously be avoided. For example, I turn a good many newel posts and balusters in Scots pine which I know will be painted. If the timber is of good quality, I am able to avoid any sanding at all, the finish from the tool being more than satisfactory for a painted finish. Similar work in hemlock, which usually has little 'life' in it, gets a quick application of 100 grit paper, again good enough for paint application.

Such work carried out in oak or mahogany, or any timber where a 'clear finish' is to be applied, demands a much more sympathetic approach, and several grades of paper may be needed to achieve the desired finish.

*Before* we come to the sanding stage, the first step is to closely examine your piece of turnery for any defects such as worm, insect or nail holes, slight cracks or shakes. These will need to be 'stopped' and there are many proprietary brands of 'stopping' on the market. This needs to be pressed well into the defect (use a waste piece of wood, not a tool blade) and it is as well to leave it slightly proud of the surface to take account of any shrinkage in the drying process. Most of these products are fairly slow drying and it may be necessary to leave the piece overnight before commencing the sanding.

Many different shades of stopping are available, but even so, on special projects it is advisable to test for colour matching on a waste piece of identical wood. Mixing two colours together sometimes gives a better match.

# TYPES OF ABRASIVE MATERIAL

Although we invariably use the term 'sanding', modern woodturners rarely use either sand or glass paper. These have been superseded by garnet paper, aluminium oxide and silicone carbide papers. All are quite suitable and the latter is made up of waterproof backing and glue, being more commonly known as 'wet and dry' paper.

Abrasives are graded by numbers, the higher the number, the finer the paper. I normally make use of four grades of paper in my complete finishing process. For between centres turning, I rarely use anything coarser than 150 grit, other than on turnings to be painted. The sanding is completed by

then making use of 220 grit, which on some timbers is the only grade I use. After the application of sealer or polish, I generally use 320 grit to 'cut it back'. (**NB** Any liquid applied to timber has the effect of raising the grain, this effect varying from timber to timber. The term 'cutting back' merely means sanding very lightly with a fine abrasive to restore the original smoothness.)

On faceplate turnings, I generally start the sanding process with 100 grit (if I am hand sanding), and then go on to the finer 150 and 220 grits to obtain the desired finish. The 320 grit is used as described above.

The selection of grit size for the initial sanding is important and only experience and knowledge of timber will provide an adequate guide. Too fine a paper may not remove the blemishes but too coarse a paper will inflict more damage than was originally on the surface. For example, I turn a good deal of mahogany for cabinetmaking projects and I know making use of anything coarser than 220 grit will mean circular scratches will be visible when the project is polished.

It must be appreciated that nearly all sanding is *across* the grain and the depth of the circular scratches is increased as grit size is increased. To avoid these unsightly scratches, my advice is to use nothing coarser than the grit sizes I have mentioned. Wherever possible, it is advisable, before going to the next finer grade of paper, to stop the lathe and sand *along* the grain. It does help!

For best results, before proceeding to the finer papers, all the scratch marks from the initial sanding should have been obliterated by the intermediate sanding.

# METHODS OF SANDING

In the interests of safety, the toolrest must be removed. Prepare the paper by tearing it neatly into four equal parts and then fold each piece into three. This provides three sanding faces and helps to prevent the frictional heat becoming too uncomfortable for the supporting fingers.

Where the lathe has a good range of speeds (and it is not a major operation to change them), I

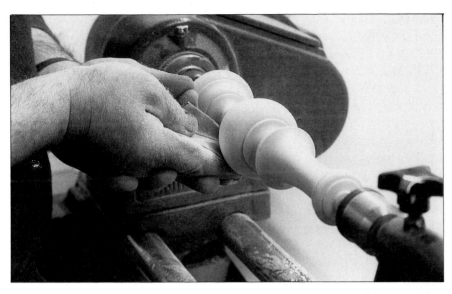

normally 'drop down a cog' from the turning speed. I find it more efficient and the frictional heat transmitted to the supporting fingers is certainly reduced.

For the majority of the sanding, the paper can be held between the fingers and the thumb and additional support can be given by the other hand clasping the wrist.

Wherever possible, sand *underneath* the whirling wood, because in the event of the paper or fingers 'grabbing', the centrifugal force throws both clear of trouble. (You can see now why the toolrest must be removed, Fig 9.1.)

I find the sanding of beads is best done by holding the paper in two hands and, again, underneath the whirling wood (Fig 9.2).

**Fig 9.1 Sanding in the 'safe position'. Note that the toolrest has been removed.**

**Fig 9.2 Using two hands to sand beads, again in the safe position.**

**Fig 9.3 Making use of a spindle gouge to sand a cove.**

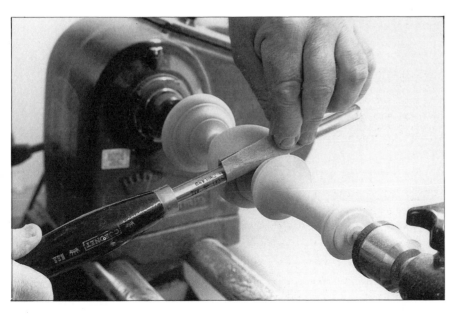

For sanding covers, I wrap the paper round an appropriately sized spindle gouge to ensure the desired profile is maintained (Fig 9.3).

V-cuts and fillets are sanded with the edges of the paper, but great care is needed so as not to destroy the crisp intersections.

On long cylinders or flowing shapes, do not dwell in one position. Keep the paper on the move and traversing in both directions to prevent scratching and the build-up of frictional heat. A trick used by some turners to prevent the fingers becoming uncomfortably hot is to use a piece of thin leather between the fingers and the paper.

A technique I employ for top quality cabinet turnings is to wipe the whole of the turning with a damp cloth. This raises the grain and will need 'cutting back' when dry with 320 grade paper. This process is sometimes repeated several times and always done when the work is to be stained (mahogany and oak are often stained). Otherwise the application of the stain would raise the grain and the subsequent cutting back might well expose bare wood. Make sure clean water is used, particularly on mahogany.

On the safety aspect, be extremely careful where squares or pummels form part of the workpiece. Contact with these while sanding can lead to a severe rap on the fingers. In fact, such features are often referred to as 'knuckle knockers' in the trade.

Directing our attention now to the sanding of faceplate turnings, it will soon be evident that this is even more loathsome than sanding spindle turning. Why? Because, as mentioned earlier, end grain is much more difficult to sand satisfactorily than side grain and therefore more sanding needs to be done, particularly if tool work is less than perfect.

**Fig 9.4 Sanding in the safe area – faceplate work. (Note the fingers pointing downwards.)**

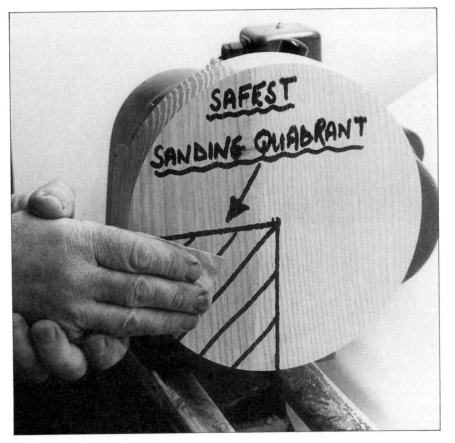

Because of my loathing of sanding, I always do my best to achieve the best possible finish on bowls and any type of faceplate work before I start the sanding. Here are a couple of tips to help towards that better finish.

Stop the lathe and examine the bowl for rough patches of end grain. Some timbers are notorious for this, but it can be improved as follows:

**1** Soak the rough patches with sanding sealer. I prefer the cellulose-based variety and I always thin it down with cellulose thinners (about 50-50) for this purpose. (Danish oil can also be used, providing it is compatible with the intended finishing product.) The reason why I prefer the sanding sealer is that I use it as a basecoat for *every* finish I use, be it wax, friction polish, pre-catalysed lacquer or Danish oil.

The soaking of the end grain has the effect of softening the fibres and a newly sharpened scraper — I personally use a small spindle gouge, but this is not recommended for the beginner — should remove the trouble and leave a nice, smooth surface. Some timbers even resist this method, and you may have to resort to:

**2** Repeating the soaking process, but this time use some kind of tool to scrape the affected area 'locally'; that means, without the lathe running. You can use either your normal turning scraper or a cabinetmaker's scraper. Sometimes I make use of a piece of broken glass, but be very careful if you do!

The bowl can now be sanded, starting with 100 grit paper. (I must confess that on really stubborn end grain I sometimes resort to 80 grit.) The safe area to sand faceplate work is in the quadrant between 6 and 9 o'clock. It is also advisable to have the fingers pointing downwards so they cannot be bent backwards against the joints, which can be very painful (Fig 9.4).

Initially, the paper will fetch off a considerable amount of dust, but gradually this diminishes to a point where virtually no dust at all is evident. This is the time to stop and go to the next grade of paper, repeating this process until the desired surface finish is arrived at.

Finally, and on all categories of turning, I always burnish the surface with a handful of shavings which makes the piece more pleasing to the eye.

# POWER SANDING

Many bowl turners now use this system, which consists of foam-backed abrasive disc pads

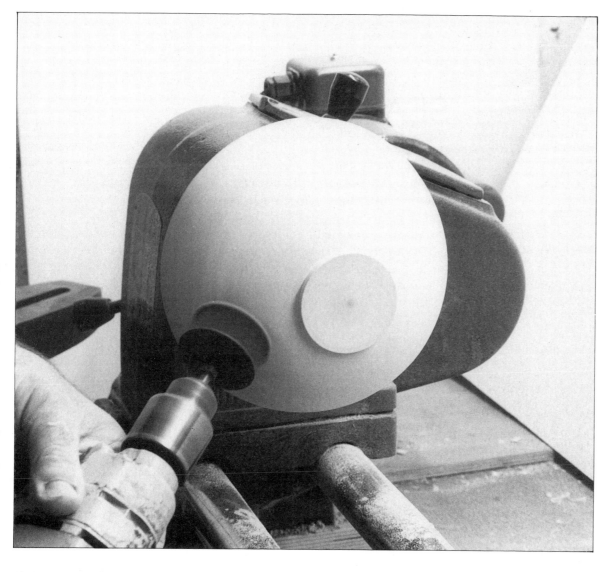

Fig 9.6 Method of using a dust extractor on a piece of spindle turning so as to ensure optimum dust collection.

Fig 9.5 Power sanding the outside of the bowl.

mounted in an electric drill. The abrasive discs are interchangeable by means of the Velcro system, and are available in grit sizes ranging from 60 grit to 400 grit. As the lathe and drill are rotating in opposite directions, frictional heat is minimized, as are the chances of inflicting those irritating scratch marks which are always likely when hand sanding. This method is obviously much quicker than hand sanding and flowing-shaped bowls can be completely sanded without resorting to hand methods. Obviously, very small, ornamental or detailed bowls cannot be power sanded, but the saving on time on many bowls is tremendous.

You will need considerable practice before you become proficient in its use, but it is worth persevering. In the interests of safety, do not try to use other than the bottom half of the disc, and sand in the quadrant described above for hand sanding

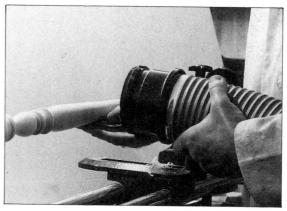

methods. Fig 9.5 shows the outside of a bowl being sanded with this method.

*Be warned*, however, because you may think you are in the Sahara Desert with a sand storm raging. The dust cloud can be considerable.

115

## The Perils of Dust

Power sanding conveniently leads me to the problems and perils associated with dust, which is the scourge of all woodturners. Mention was made in Chapter 1, Trees and Wood, that the dust from some species, particularly the tropical hardwoods, can be harmful. I think it true to say that while some timbers are more likely to give trouble than others, dust from any source will do nothing to improve your health. Everything possible should therefore be done to minimize exposure to and inhalation of fine dust. The least that can be done is to wear a face mask when sanding. These are available from most hardware shops and are inexpensive.

If the turner intends to specialize in bowl work, I believe a portable dust extractor is an absolute must, but even these have their limitations. While they will efficiently collect dust from a localized area, such as when sanding a bowl, they are not so effective in collecting dust on spindle work over about 15" long.

To overcome this problem I hold the hose in one hand and sand with the other, keeping the hands close together to ensure optimum dust collection. This method is very tiring, but it is the most efficient way I know (Fig 9.6).

# STAINING

Many turners do not stain their turned objects at all, relying on the natural colour and beauty of the wood to speak for itself. I too avoid staining wherever possible, but some timbers – and mahogany is a perfect example – look better for it. On this and similar timbers, the colour of the wood can vary tremendously even from different parts of the same bole. The colour can be brought to a better degree of uniformity by making use of stain.

Bear in mind that staining can only make the wood a *darker* shade than the original colour, it cannot lighten it. Faceplate turnings do not take kindly to staining as the end grain absorbs more stain than the side grain and therefore tends to go much darker in colour. Any areas of torn grain are also likely to stain darker than the surrounding wood, which means that the preparation must be perfect.

There are many types of stains available, and I use an industrial cellulose-based stain which is easy to apply and dries evenly. It can either be ragged or sprayed on, with good results from both methods.

# SEALING

As stated earlier, I use a cellulose sanding sealer as a base coat for *every* finish I use. It seals the grain and prevents dust, finger marks, smudges, etc. from soiling the wood. It also provides for uniform absorbency of the final finishing/polishing application. Like any liquid it will raise the grain of most timbers, but this is easily cut back to the original smooth finish with some 320 grit paper or wire wool.

Sealer can also be applied either with rag or brush. I prefer to use a good quality varnish brush which makes it easy to get into the nooks and crannies. The powder additive mixed in the sealer during manufacture provides for easy cutting back and the application of two coats of sealer is not a bad finish in itself.

When applying sealer, polish, oil, etc. to a piece of wood that is mounted in the lathe, it is as well to cover the lathe bed with a dust sheet or newspaper to prevent the substance soiling the bed. It can set very hard, and movement of the toolrest and tailstock can become very difficult.

# POLISHING/ FINISHING

Beginners to the craft can be forgiven if they are perplexed by the problem of choosing the most suitable finish from the bewildering variety available. Finishing woodwork of any kind is a subject and trade on its own and whole books are devoted to it. All I can hope to do is provide a summary of the finishes I consider to be the most suitable for woodturning projects.

The first piece of advice I can offer is to keep the finish as simple as possible. If you use a cellulose sanding sealer as a base coat, as I recommend, on top of this you can choose a type of finish suitable for each particular project.

# CHOICE OF FINISH

In deciding what kind of finish to apply, the following points must be considered:

**1** Is the piece of turning intended to contain food? If so, you are restricted to a finish that does not smell or taste and is non-toxic.

**2** Will the finished product be likely to be washed or wiped with a damp cloth?

**3** How much handling is the object likely to get?

**4** Do you require a glossy, satin or matt finish?

**5** For drinking vessels, special treatment is required.

## Products I Use

**Danish Oil** I use this for turnings that come under **1** and **2** above, such as salad bowls, platters, cheese and breadboards, decorative bowls, etc. It can be applied (lathe stationary) with either rag or brush. Immediately after application I sand it in with some 320 grit 'wet and dry' and then burnish it with a handful of shavings (lathe running). Successive coats can be applied at 24-hour intervals which will produce a pleasing satin finish that will not peel, crack or chip. It is also heat and water resistant.

**Wax** I prefer to use pure carnauba wax on extremely dense timbers and a mixture of this and beeswax for less dense timbers. Choose a fast lathe speed and melt the wax on to the whirling wood, but take care not to overload. It can be immediately burnished up to a high gloss by using a clean rag. There are also some excellent proprietory brands of wax avaialble, such as Bri-Wax, Liberon, Mr Jamiesons and Rustins, and these come either coloured or clear. Wax finishes are suitable for articles that are not likely to be handled too much and which are intended for ornamental purposes.

**Friction Polish** The advantage of this type of polish is that it is simple to apply and an extremely glossy shine can be achieved in a couple of minutes. Products such as Speedaneeze and Crafteeze are tried and trusted polishes, but because they are not particularly durable, again they are more suited to ornamental turnings which are unlikely to be continually handled.

Apply it while the wood is stationary. (I think a more even coat can be applied this way.) Then start the lathe and, using the same rag, apply an even pressure along the span of your turning until the desired shine is achieved. (If you wear spectacles, make sure you are standing to one side when you start the lathe up. The centrifugal force sends a fine shower of polish flying in your direction and this can set very hard on the lenses and take some moving.)

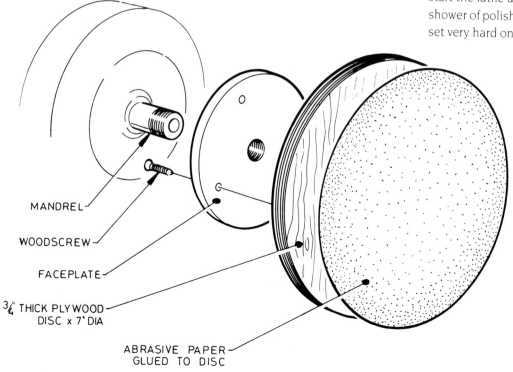

MANDREL

WOODSCREW

FACEPLATE

³⁄₄" THICK PLYWOOD DISC x 7" DIA

ABRASIVE PAPER GLUED TO DISC

**Fig 9.7 Constructional details of the sanding plate.**

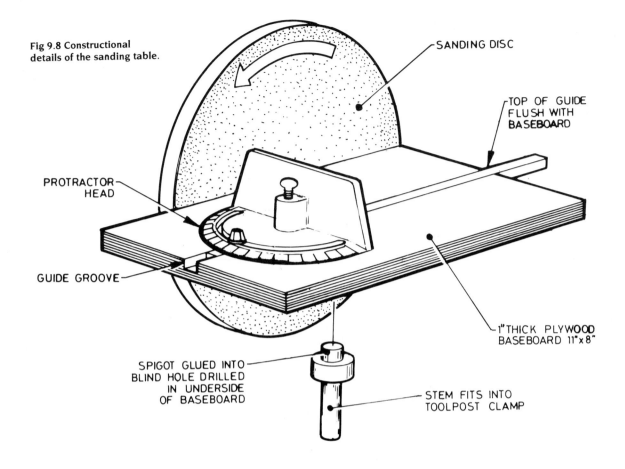

Fig 9.8 Constructional
details of the sanding table.

SANDING DISC

TOP OF GUIDE
FLUSH WITH
BASEBOARD

PROTRACTOR
HEAD

GUIDE GROOVE

1" THICK PLYWOOD
BASEBOARD 11" x 8"

SPIGOT GLUED INTO
BLIND HOLE DRILLED
IN UNDERSIDE
OF BASEBOARD

STEM FITS INTO
TOOLPOST CLAMP

**Rustins Plastic Coating** This is absolutely ideal for drinking vessels and although it is quite expensive and the finishing process can take some considerable time, it is worth both the expense and the effort involved. It produces a tough, mirror-like finish that is heat- and solvent-resistant. The bare wood can be stained (use the same brand) before applying the coating with either brush or spray gun. Several coats may be necessary and full instructions are included with the product.

**Pre-catalysed Lacquers** These are really industrial finishes and intended to be sprayed on to the work. They provide a tough and durable surface. Although best results are achieved by spraying, they can be brushed on if they are thinned down. I use them quite frequently for polishing standard lamps, reproduction tables, etc., but then I have a spray booth providing ideal facilities.

There are numerous other types of polish, many of which are no doubt equally suitable, but I can only comment on those I have personally used. My advice is to keep the polishing process as limited and simple as possible.

**DIY Sanding Table** Such an attachment for the lathe is extremely useful for sanding the bottom of boxes and the underneath sections of lids, plinths, bowls, etc. It is very simple to construct and the components required are a faceplate, a few discs of ¾" plywood (on which to stick the various grades of abrasive paper), a plywood platform, and a turned stem. One end of the stem is joined to the platform and the other end is turned to a diameter that will provide a good fit in the toolrest holder on your lathe.

Fig 9.7 shows how the sanding plate is constructed and Fig. 9.8 shows constructional details of the sanding table, together with a Picador protractor mitre fence. This accessory is invaluable for such jobs as truing up the edges of laminated or built-up work and sanding mitre joints. The top of the platform will require routing out to a depth and width suitable to accommodate the mitre fence as shown in the drawing. Fig 9.9 shows the attachment being used to true up a mitre joint.

# SUMMARY

1 The success or otherwise of any finish is totally dependent on every step which leads up to it being done to the best of your ability.

2 Sanding is boring, dusty and tedious, and must be kept to a minimum by aiming for the best possible finish straight off the tool.

3 In normal circumstances, grit sizes 100, 150, 220 and 320 should be adequate to achieve the most satisfactory surface for the finish.

4 Always remove the toolrest when sanding, and wherever possible sand in the 'safe' areas.

5 Always wear a dust mask and if possible use a dust extractor.

6 The choice of finish is influenced to a great extent by the intended use of the turned piece.

7 Ensure that the final polish/finish is compatible with any base coat that has been applied.

**Fig 9.9 DIY sanding table being used to accurately sand a mitre joint.**

## Chapter 10

# BORING AND ROUTING ON THE LATHE

B oring holes in turned projects plays an important part in my everyday commercial turning, and this chapter describes the various types of boring bits and drills which I consider suitable for such work. Sharpening techniques and optimum speeds for boring are described, together with the use of simple jigs.

Additionally, I show how that most useful of power tools, the hand-held router, can be put to good effect for fluting and reeding straight or tapered sections of turned work in conjunction with a simple jig that fits on the lathe.

Finally, several projects embracing the use of boring tools and the router are included.

# TYPES OF DRILLS/BITS

### Engineer's Twist Drills

These are available in very small sizes and are suitable for drilling holes in both wood and metal (Figs 10.1(a)). I personally do not use sizes exceeding ¼″ diameter for wood boring because I consider that larger holes can be made more efficiently with some of the bits described later. Nevertheless, twist drills are particularly useful for boring small holes in such projects as condiment sets, and for small inlay work. They are normally sold in high speed steel and are perhaps best purchased in sets contained in revolving drum holders; these are easily stored and inexpensive.

**Fig 10.1 (a) Engineer's twist drill.**

**Sharpening** Traditionally, this type of drill was always sharpened on the grindstone by offering the drill up to the face of the grindstone so as to maintain the original angle. A rolling action is then required to maintain the existing profile, this process being repeated on both cutting edges.

It is easy to destroy the original profiles and this will render the bit ineffective. Due to the difficulties involved, it may be an advantage to make use of one of several types of sharpening jigs available on the market which are specially made for this type of bit. They are not expensive and make sharpening quick, simple and accurate.

**Suggested Speeds for Boring** Best results will be obtained with this type of bit if the lathe is set to run at its fastest speed. These bits may be used in the hand-held electric drill to bore holes in wood mounted on the lathe (not running of course), in conjunction with various types of drilling jigs, when undertaking inlay work, but the fast speed of the electric drill will not harm the bit.

**Useful Tip** As there is no pronounced point on this type of bit, they have a tendency to 'skid', particularly on other than flat surfaces. This of course means that the hole will not be accurately located, but the problem can be prevented by making a small hole with a pointed awl to give the bit a start.

### Flatbits

These (Fig 10.1(b)) were originally intended to be used in portable electric drills, but they are also suitable for boring in the lathe. The long point

**Fig 10.1 (b) Flatbit.**

facilitates accurate location even when angle drilling, although for many boring operations connected with woodturning the point is too long and needs to be shortened to prevent 'bursting through' the bottom of intended blind holes. As the wood is bored with a scraping action, the bits will require frequent sharpening, but they produce a reasonably clean hole and are not expensive.

Flatbits also lend themselves to modification such as being ground to a taper shape for boring out the insides of thimbles, etc. For special jobs where only a shallow hole is required, it is an advantage to cut down the length of the shaft to provide maximum stability and prevent flexing. They are available in sizes ranging from ¼″ to 1½″.

121

**Sharpening** The bit should be secured in a vice and a fine knife-edged file should be used to lightly touch up the forward cutting edges, taking care to maintain the original angle and to make an equal number of strokes on both, otherwise the cutters will become imbalanced and will not perform satisfactorily. If the point needs to be shortened, it is essential that centricity be maintained by sharpening both sides equally, counting the number of strokes with the file. The same principle applies if it is decided to put a taper on the bit.

**Suggested Speeds for Boring** As mentioned above, these bits were originally designed for use in electric drills and consequently all sizes can be used with the lathe adjusted to its fastest speed.

**Useful Tip** Whether this type of bit is used in the headstock or tailstock, I always ensure that the nose or tip is located in the centre mark of the wood before I start the lathe. In the interests of safety, I consider it best to stop the lathe before withdrawing the bit from the completed hole.

## Lip and Spur Bits

These (Fig 10.1(c)) are also known as 'brad point drills' and 'dowel bits', and are available in sizes ranging from ¼" to 1". The brad point allows for very accurate location and also prevents 'skid'. They perform well in both side and end grain and are particularly suited to deep hole boring. The angled chipping bevel produces clean, accurate holes *if* the bit is entered slowly and evenly to allow the spurs to score the circumference of the hole. They are not too expensive and, apart from the sawtooth machine bits, they are probably the most useful bits to purchase.

**Fig 10.1 (c) Lip and spur bit.**

**Sharpening** Use a fine flat file to sharpen the cutters and the spurs, again ensuring an equal number of strokes is used on each so that both are kept at the same height. The brad point will only occasionally need filing, but take care to maintain centricity.

**Suggested Speeds for Boring**

| Bit Size | Speed (rpm) |
|---|---|
| Up to ½" | Approx. 1500 |
| Over ½" | Approx. 1000 |

## Saw Tooth Machine Bits

These (Fig 10.1(d)) are without doubt the best and most useful to the woodturner. They also happen to be the most expensive, but as in most cases with tools and equipment, you get what you pay for. Wherever possible I prefer to make use of them, as

**Fig 10.1 (d) Saw tooth machine bit.**

they will bore holes quickly, cleanly and accurately in end and side grain. Their efficient action requires little power and if well maintained they are a joy to use. They are available in sizes ranging from ⅜" to 4" and they all come with a ½" shank.

**Sharpening** Secure the bit in a vice and sharpen as follows:

**(a)** The teeth should be sharpened with a small, three-cornered file, each tooth receiving the same number of strokes to maintain the equal height.

**(b)** The cutters or lifters should be sharpened with a narrow flat file, working it through the throat of the cutter, never from the top. Take the utmost care to maintain the original angle and straight edges.

**(c)** The brad point can be sharpened occasionally with a flat file, but it is essential that centricity is maintained.

**Suggested Speeds for Boring** The general rule is the larger the hole to be bored, the lower the speed of the lathe, although it is appreciated that most lathes will not have the range of speeds to run at the exact rpm recommended.

| Sawtooth Bit Size | Speed (rpm) |
|---|---|
| ⅜" to ⅞" | 1000 |
| 1" to 2" | 500 |
| Over 2" | Slowest speed available |

## William Ridgeway Power Expansive Bits

These (Fig 10.1(e)) are designed to produce flat, clean-bottomed holes in wood, laminates and plastic. They are available in medium and heavy duty, the latter being the type shown in the photograph. The smaller of the two allows holes to be bored ranging from 7/8" to 2", while the larger one has a range from 1 3/8" to 3 1/8". There is no doubt that they provide a cost-effective alternative to buying a large number of the bits listed above.

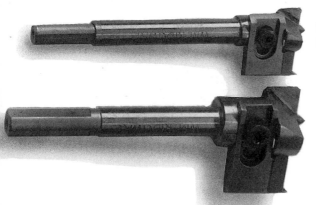

Fig 10.1 (e) Ridgeway power expansive bits.

**Sharpening** A flat file is used to lightly sharpen the inside of the spurs and the cutters or lifters from underneath, again taking care to maintain original angles.

**Suggested Speeds for Expansive Bits** The same for the sawtooth bits.

## Standard Lamp Shell Auger

This (Fig 10.1(f)) is the only tool designed purely for long hole boring in the lathe on such projects as table and standard lamps. Its special shape has been designed to cut into end grain easily, its central lip ensuring that long holes can be accurately bored to receive the electric cable. The

Fig 10.1 (f) Standard lamp shell auger.

auger is normally 30" long and is available in three sizes, but I use only the 5/16" size. It is employed in conjunction with a jig that fits in the toolrest holder, or alternatively lathes having a hollow tailstock can make use of a special hollow cup centre which allows the auger to pass through.

**Sharpening** I have had my long hole boring auger for many years and have never yet had occasion to sharpen it. When not in use, I hang it up and the business end is protected with a piece of wood, drilled out to receive the auger with a push fit. I understand resharpening is an exact science, for it is very easy to destroy the original profiles, and the consequences are that the auger will no longer bore accurately. If sharpening is attempted, great care must be taken not to alter the profile. A few light strokes with a fine file should be sufficient.

**Suggested Speed for Boring** The manufacturers recommend a speed of between 750 and 1000 rpm to be ideal.

# JACOBS CHUCK, ARBOR AND KEY

With the exception of the lamp standard shell auger (which is the only hand-held boring tool), all types of bits, when used in connection with woodturning projects, are normally held in a Jacobs chuck (Fig 10.2). As mentioned in Chapter 2, I consider this an essential accessory. They are available in two

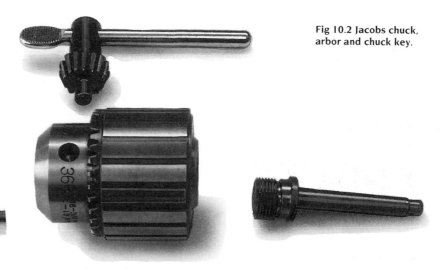

Fig 10.2 Jacobs chuck, arbor and chuck key.

sizes, 1/2" and 3/4" capacity. The arbor, which has a machined morse taper, is separate from the actual chuck. The appropriate size to fit your own lathe must be obtained, facilitating use in both the headstock and tailstock. In addition to being used for boring operations, it can of course be employed as an alternative to the woodscrew chuck, if a spigot is turned on one end of the workpiece to fit the chuck.

# HOME-MADE JIGS FOR BORING

A few simple jigs can assist boring operations by way of speed and accuracy. Most turners have dozens of jigs scattered about their workshops, not only for boring, but for all kinds of jobs. The most important demands on any jig are accuracy and speed of setting up. There is no need for them to look like works of art – some of mine look very crude, but they fulfil their purpose.

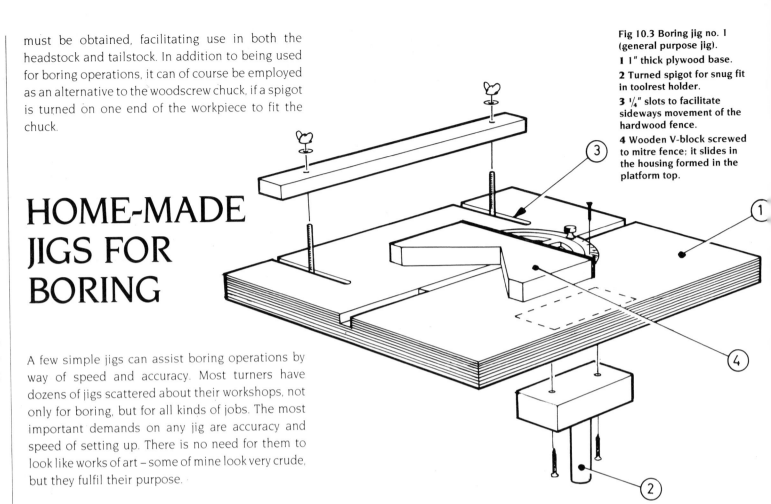

**Fig 10.3 Boring jig no. 1 (general purpose jig).**
**1** 1" thick plywood base.
**2** Turned spigot for snug fit in toolrest holder.
**3** ¼" slots to facilitate sideways movement of the hardwood fence.
**4** Wooden V-block screwed to mitre fence; it slides in the housing formed in the platform top.

## General Boring Jig

The type of jig shown in Fig 10.3 is extremely useful in many operations where the drill bit is held in the chuck secured to the headstock, enabling the wood to be fed on to it manually and without the assistance of the tailstock. This is an extremely slow method compared with manual feeding. (However, holes to be bored to a depth exceeding about 1½" are more accurately made by the support and advancement of the tailstock.)

Construction of the jig is fairly simple and similar in concept to the sanding table described in the previous chapter. One end of the turned stem is joined to the platform and the other end is turned to a diameter that will provide a good fit into the toolrest holder, which if turned upside down on the Coronet No. 3 lathe will increase the range of the up and down movement of the jig.

As mentioned in Chapter 8, Copy Woodturning, it is sometimes advisable to break down the design of long slender turnings into sections to prevent 'whip'. Turnings with square sections incorporated into the design, like balusters, lend themselves to

this. The square sections need to be cut to length, centred and then bored to take a tenon formed on both ends of the turned section.

To set up the jig, I mount a piece of wood of the same section to be bored between centres and adjust accordingly the height of the jig. The wooden fence is then pressed up to the workpiece and secured by nipping the two wing nuts. The depth of the hole can be gauged either by sticking some masking tape on the drill bit or by a pencil mark on the fence.

The boring can then begin, but remember to adjust the speed of the lathe according to the type and size of bit being used.

This same jig can also be used to bore the edges of discs such as table lamp bases. A piece of wood with a 45° V is prepared and screwed to the Picador mitre fence, enabling it to be slid back and forth in the matching housing cut in the platform top. When setting up, care must be taken to ensure that the centre of the V is dead in line with the tip of the drill and the jig is parallel to the lathe bed.

Fig 10.3 gives constructional details of the jig. Fig 10.4 shows the jig set up to bore a radial hole in the edge of a disc and Fig 10.5 shows it set up to bore a hole in the end grain of a piece of square section stock. Fig 10.6 also shows the jig in use.

## Jig for Angle and Round Section Boring

Another extremely useful jig is shown in Fig 10.7. This will facilitate the boring of holes at an angle (the underside of stool tops for example), and of course holes at right angles to the surface of the wood, efficiently and quickly. The design consists of a main platform of 1" plywood which is hinged to a piece of 2" x 2" hardwood. Into the centre of this, a hole is bored which must be exactly the same size as the tailstock barrel and about ¾" deep. This will ensure that the jig is accurately located every time it is used. The bottom of the platform should just clear the bed bars when it is suspended on the tailstock barrel.

The long angled slots allow for the two turned 'button' supports (secured with bolts and wing nuts) to be adjusted according to the diameter of the disc to be bored. (Various diameter button supports can be made to allow for a greater range of diameters to be bored.)

When boring angles, the bottom of the platform is obviously swung away from the lathe bed. To *keep* the jig at the required angle *and* prevent sideways

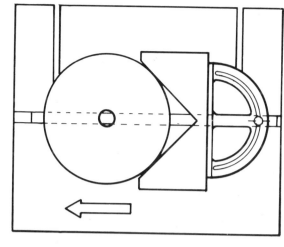

**Fig 10.4 Plan view of jig no. 1 showing the V-block being used to bore a flex hole in the edge of a table lamp base.**

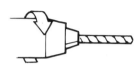

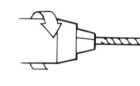

**Fig 10.5 Additional plan view of jig no. 1 showing the adjustable fence being used to bore a mortise in the end grain of a piece of square section stock. (The stock is advanced manually without assistance from the tailstock.)**

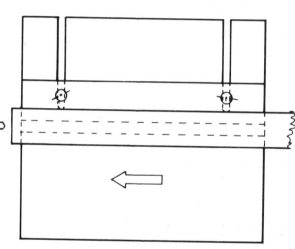

**Fig 10.6 Boring a hole in the edge of a table lamp base.**

movement, the adjustable support on the bottom edge of the jig will automatically gravitate and settle on the lathe bed bars. It is then secured in position by tightening the two wing nuts (Fig 10.10).

Fig 10.8 shows the jig being used to bore a 90° hole in the base of a napkin ring stand and Fig 10.9 shows it being used to bore the angled holes in the underside of a stool top.

**Fig 10.7 Boring jig no. 2, for angle and round section boring.**

**1** 1″ thick plywood backboard.

**2** 2″ x 2″ hardwood, full width of backboard and hinged to it, bored centrally with a hole that is a dead fit on the tailstock barrel.

**3** 45° slots to allow for the adjustment on the button supports.

**4** Button supports, adjusted and secured with bolts and wing nuts.

**5** Location holes for V-block attachment.

**6** 'Gravitating' support block secured with bolts and wing nuts.

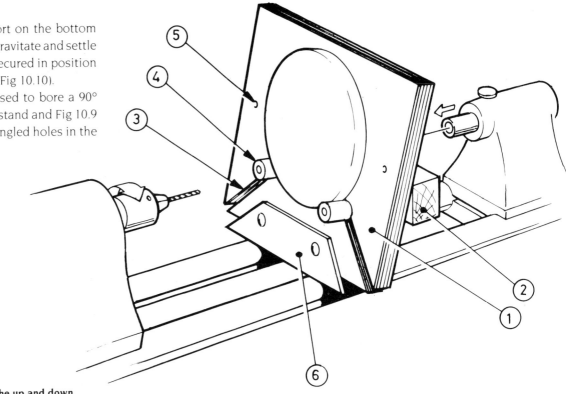

**(NB** The up and down movement is facilitated by two 90° slots cut in the base of the backboard.)

**Fig 10.8 Boring a hole in the base of a napkin ring stand.**

**Fig 10.9 Boring angled holes in a stool top.**

The same jig also allows for round section stock to be bored by making a V-block incorporating two ¼″ dowels that locate in corresponding holes bored in the main backboard. It is important that the centre of the V is exactly in line with the lathe centres, otherwise the resulting holes will not be radially true. Fig 10.12 shows how the V-block is constructed and located and Fig 10.11 shows it being used to bore a 90° hole in a round section

**Fig 10.10 Jig no. 2 being used to bore the underneath of a stool top.**

**1** G-cramp secures the stool top to the jig.

**2** Button supports ensure that the three holes are bored concentrically.

**3** The bottom support block has gravitated and settled on the bed bars. This provides stability and maintains the same angle of splay when the wing nuts are nipped.

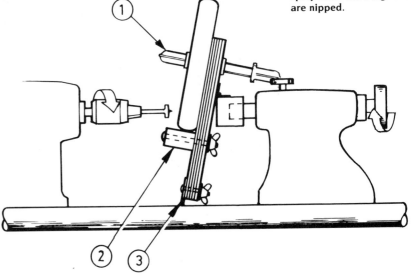

piece of wood. (Note that both buttons have been positioned to give added support to the V-block.)

Finally, the V-block principle can be used to bore holes at an angle in stool and chair legs to receive cross pieces or stretchers. It is necessary to prepare another V-block of identical proportions to the other, but minus the two locating dowels.

Fig 10.11 Boring a 90° hole in round section stock.

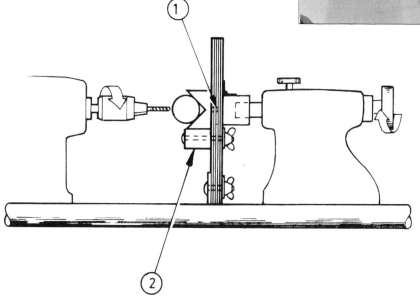

**Fig 10.12 Jig no. 2: elevation showing the V-block attachment being used to bore a 90° hole in a piece of round section stock.**

**1 The two dowels in the back of the V-block locate in the two holes in the** backboard. (It is vital that these two holes are precisely located so that the centre of the V-block is dead in line with the lathe centres.)

**2 The two button supports provide extra stability.**

is hinged to the backboard. (It only takes a couple of minutes to screw the hinge on and it does make things easier.)

A wedge, cut to an angle of about 11°, is located behind the V-block and secured to it by means of a 1¼" x 8" woodscrew. Fig 10.14 shows constructional details and Fig 10.13 shows a stool leg being angle bored in this manner.

To set the jig up, first of all fix the *dowelled* V-block to the jig. This will establish true centre height. Now bring up both button supports so that they just touch the V-block and secure them. Remove the block and replace it with the *undowelled* version which

Fig 10.13 Boring an angled hole in the stool leg. Note the wedge.

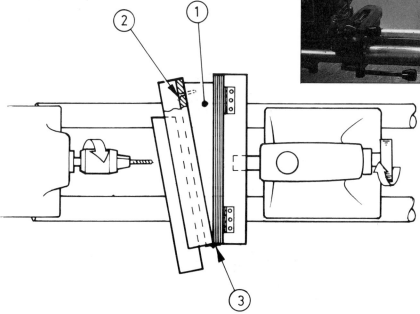

**Fig 10.14 Jig no. 2: plan view showing method of boring angled holes.**

**1 11° wedge fits between the backboard and the V-block.**

**2 The V-block is secured to the wedge with a 1¼" x 8" woodscrew.**

**3 The V-block is hinged to the backboard. (The button supports should also be used to stabilize the V-block.)**

# JIGS FOR INLAY WORK OR DECORATIVE TURNERY

As your turning skills improve, you will probably want to experiment with inlay work or, as it is sometimes called, decorative turnery. Extremely attractive pieces can be produced using plain timbers and inlaying them with contrasting varieties of wood.

So as to space the inlays equally around the circumference of any given circle, it is first of all necessary to fit what is called a 'dividing head' to the lathe. This can be made of wood or metal and its function is to divide the circumference of a piece of turning into equal spaces so as to allow equally spaced holes to be bored to take the inlay.

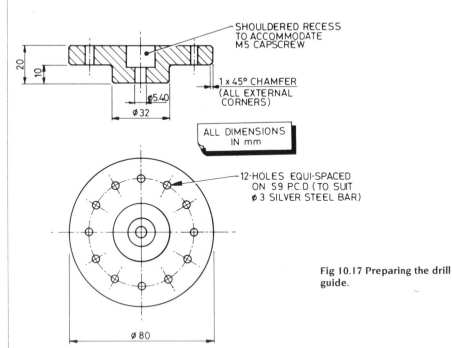

**Fig 10.15 Constructional details of the metal dividing head (all dimensions in millimetres).**

SHOULDERED RECESS TO ACCOMMODATE M5 CAPSCREW

1 x 45° CHAMFER (ALL EXTERNAL CORNERS)

ø5.40

ø 32

ALL DIMENSIONS IN mm

12-HOLES EQUI-SPACED ON 59 P.C.D ( TO SUIT ø 3 SILVER STEEL BAR)

ø 80

Fig 10.15 shows details of the metal dividing head I had made to fit my Coronet No. 3 lathe. The left-hand end of the headstock mandrel is conveniently tapped to take an M5 Allen screw and I made use of this to secure the dividing head to it. Using the appropriate size twist drill, I drilled a hole in the headstock casting to take the locating pin. (This is a piece of silver steel, obviously the same diameter as the holes in the head and in the casting, which serves to lock the head in any of the desired twelve positions.) Fig 10.16 shows the head fixed to the lathe.

In order to make sure the holes are bored radially, make a guide for the chosen size drill bit. This is simply a piece of square section wood with a tenon turned on one end to make a tight fit in the toolrest holder. (Ensure that the square shoulder is pushed right down on to the toolrest holder as this will give

**Fig 10.16 Dividing head affixed with the locating pin inserted. (The headstock has been swivelled for clarity.)**

accurate location every time the guide is used.) Now line up the centre of the wood with the drill bit fixed in the Jacobs chuck and mark the position of the hole (Fig 10.17). Complete the boring by using one of the jigs.

**Fig 10.17 Preparing the drill guide.**

The project for this example is a small nut bowl in oak. After turning the outside using the methods described in Chapter 7 you can position the boring jig and secure the dividing head with the locating pin. The bowl is to have six inlays, so after the first hole has been bored to a depth of about 1/8", the locating pin is removed and located in the *next but one* hole. (The dividing head can be used to bore 12, 6, 4, 3 or 2 equally spaced holes.) The process is repeated until all six holes have been bored.

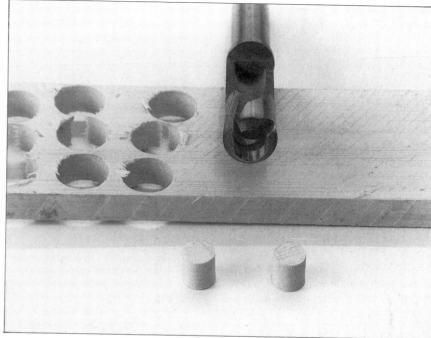

Fig 10.18 Boring the holes for the inlays.

To help make all the holes the same depth of $\frac{1}{8}''$, either use an appropriate length of scrap wood, centrally bored, to fit over the drill bit, or some masking tape. (Old corks also make very good 'spacers', and I use them frequently.) (Fig 10.18).

The next step is to prepare the inlays, sycamore in this case, and these can be turned between centres in batches of six. The grain must be arranged so that it runs along the *face* of the inlays, for end grain should not be showing on the finished project. A much better and quicker method is to use a plug cutter. These are expensive but very good (Fig 10.19). The inlays are glued in, and after being allowed to set the turning, sanding and polishing can be completed. Fig 10.20 shows the finished article. (This method can be used to build up intricate patterns of inlay, and the example is only intended as an introduction.)

Fig 10.19 Plug cutter in use.

Fig 10.20 The completed inlaid bowl.

# ROUTING ON THE LATHE

The hand router can be used to good effect on the lathe, particularly for fluting and reeding straight and tapered sections of turned work such as table legs, standard lamps, pedestals, bar supports and shop fittings. Figs 10.21(a) and 10.21(b) show sections of reeded and fluted profiles respectively.

Use the dividing head to accurately space the desired number of flutes or reeds round the circumference of the work. A jig in the form of a box-like construction for the router to sit in is required, enabling the router to traverse the full length of the workpiece between two guides.

Different size boxes can be made up to suit the work in hand and Figs 10.22(a) and 10.22(b) show details of construction of the one I use for routing

**Fig 10.22(b) Section through routing jig.**

**The bed bars 1 are 1½" in diameter and the spacer 2 is fractionally less in thickness. This means that the two cross pieces 3 tighten on to the bed bars by means of the bolt and wing nut 4.**

**Fig 10.22(a) Constructional details of the routing jig.**

**1 This full-length piece of wood needs to be a snug fit between the bed bars and deep enough to allow the cross pieces 2 to tighten on to the bed bars by means of the bolts and wing nuts 3.**

**4 The 'body' of the jig can be made up of several thicknesses of chipboard.**

**5 The rebates in the two full-length guides (one is cut away for clarity in the drawing) should be formed to ensure that the router slides freely between them.**

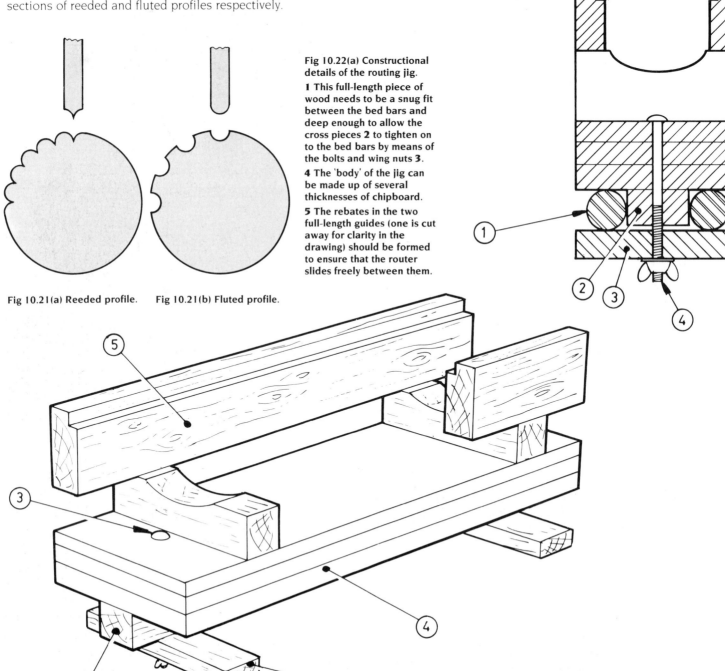

**Fig 10.21(a) Reeded profile.**   **Fig 10.21(b) Fluted profile.**

pedestals and standard lamp sections. The twin bars of my No. 3 lathe provide for accurate location and the jig is therefore self aligning, *provided* the guides for the router are precisely located.

If the turning is tapered in length, the box can be packed up at one end to compensate. Alternatively, the top of the box can be cut on the desired taper.

It is essential that the workpiece is securely fixed and stable. On the more slender turnings it may be necessary to pack the workpiece with wedges to prevent it flexing under the power of the router. The most important requirement is to ensure that the exact centre of any cutter used in the router is precisely in line with the lathe centres, or the profiles will not be radially cut and will look awful. Figs 10.23(a) and 10.23(b) show the router being used to flute a section of a standard lamp and Fig 10.24 shows the completed piece.

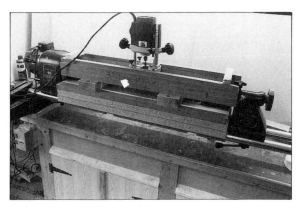

**Figs 10.23 (a) and (b) The router being used to flute a section of a standard lamp.**

**Fig 10.24 The completed fluted section.**

# PROJECTS INVOLVING BORING OR ROUTING

## Bud Vase

**Design** The project must be designed round the 4" x ½" glass tube which will hold water for the buds. I think it makes sense to draw out these dimensions full size and then design the profiles round it (Fig 10.25).

**Wood** Any close-grained hardwood. The example is a yew wood limb, 7" long by 3" diameter.

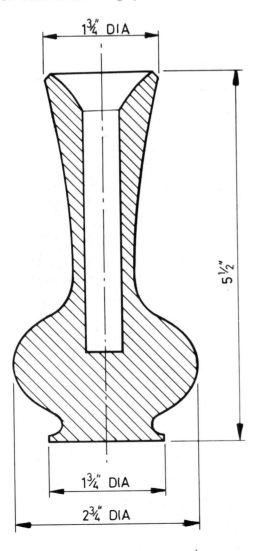

1¾" DIA

5½"

1¾" DIA

2¾" DIA

## Method

**1** The turning will be done on the woodscrew chuck, but first of all mount the stock between centres and undercut the end supported by the tailstock. Remove the wood from the lathe, pare away the small nib left on the undercut end and make a pilot hole for remounting on the screw chuck (Fig 10.26).

**Fig 10.26 The stock is mounted between centres, turned to a cylinder and undercut at B, then mounted on the woodscrew chuck.**

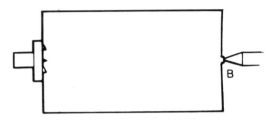

B

**Fig 10.25 A typical bud vase.**

**2** With the wood mounted on the chuck and the lathe set to about 1500 rpm, use the roughing out gouge to bring it to a true cylinder. The 'open end' can now be faced off with a ⅜" spindle gouge, working from outside to centre, the gouge being held well over on its side. A shallow impression can now be cut with the toe of the ½" skew chisel in the dead centre of the work. This will allow the drill bit to get a positive start. (All the above techniques are described and illustrated in Chapter 6, Turning Between Centres.)

**3** The appropriate size drill is secured in the Jacobs chuck, mounted in the tailstock. Adjust the speed of the lathe so that it is suitable for the drill bit size, and drill the hole to the required depth, indicated by a piece of masking tape stuck on the bit (Fig 10.27).

**Fig 10.27 The stock has been mounted on the chuck and is bored to the required depth.**

B

**4** Adjust the speed of the lathe back to about 1500 rpm, pencil in the design features, and size in the only crucial diameter (the base of the tapered neck) with parting tool and calipers (Fig 10.28).

**Fig 10.28 A parting cut is made at P to limit the length and diameter of the neck.**

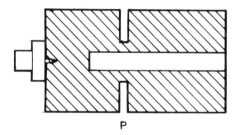

**5** The shaping is now undertaken, using gouges and chisels. The flare on the inside of the neck can either be fashioned with a spindle gouge or a half round scraper if preferred (Fig 10.29).

**Fig 10.29 Complete the profiling using gouges and chisels.**

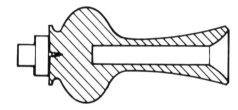

**6** The project is sanded and the finish applied, after which it should look something like the one shown in Fig 10.30.

**Fig 10.30 The completed bud vase.**

## Table Napkin Rings and Stand

**Design** The holes are bored with a 1⅜" drill bit and the thickest section of the walls should be ¼". This allows a pleasing profile on the outside without bursting through the wood. This project is also an exercise in copy turning, as all the rings will be stacked on a simple stand. As always, the first task is to draw the project full size (Fig 10.31).

**Fig 10.31 Typical table napkin ring and stand.**

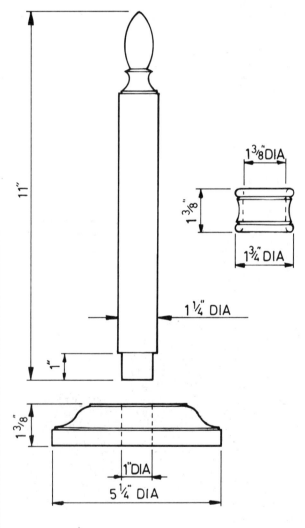

**Wood** A close-grained hardwood, the example again is yew. Three pieces, 5" x 2" x 2", are required for the rings (each piece will make two), one piece 5" diameter x 1¼" thick for the base and one piece 12" long x 1½" square for the stem.

## Method

**1** Prepare the stock for the woodscrew chuck as in project 1 and reduce it to a cylinder with the roughing out gouge. Set out the workpiece with dividers, marking the length of each ring, but leaving a full ¼" between them to allow for parting off. Bore the hole with the 1⅜" sawtooth machine bit (don't forget to adjust the lathe to a slow speed) to a depth just below the extent of the second ring. Here again a piece of masking tape stuck to the bit will determine this depth (Fig 10.32).

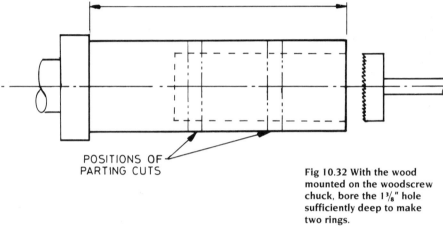

POSITIONS OF PARTING CUTS

**Fig 10.32 With the wood mounted on the woodscrew chuck, bore the 1⅜" hole sufficiently deep to make two rings.**

**2** The outside profile of the first ring is fashioned using spindle gouges and the ½" skew chisel. When you are happy with the shape, part it off and use it as your master copy, positioning it in front of you where you can see it clearly. Repeat this process with the other ring and also with the two other pieces of wood (Fig 10.33).

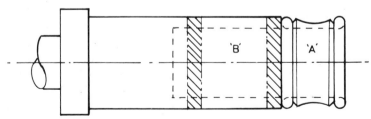

**Fig 10.33 (i) Shape the outside of A and then part it off.**

**(ii) Repeat the process at B.**

**3** When the sixth and last ring has been parted off, make use of the stub left on the screw chuck to turn a ½" long spigot (with a slight taper) for the napkin rings to be snugly pushed on to. This enables the rings to be cleaned up, sanded, and polished both inside and out. (Don't make the spigot an overtight fit or you will split the rings.) (Fig 10.34.)

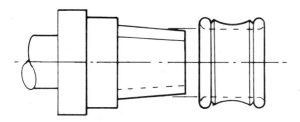

Fig 10.34 Turn a spigot with a slight taper on the waste piece, so that it will receive each ring with a snug fit. Sand and polish the inside and outside of each ring.

**4** Turn the base of the stand to the desired shape and bore a central hole, 1" diameter, with the aid of the boring jig.

**5** Turn the stem between centres, ensuring that the tenon is a snug fit in the base. The finished project is shown in Fig 10.35.

Fig 10.35 The completed rings and stand.

## Pepper Mill

**Design** In this case the design is based on a 7"
mechanism marketed by Craft Supplies Ltd and
Fig 10.36, showing the component parts and how
they are assembled, is reproduced by courtesy of
this company.

**Fig 10.36 Pepper mill
mechanism (minus the top
retaining plate, which is not
required if this method is
adopted).**

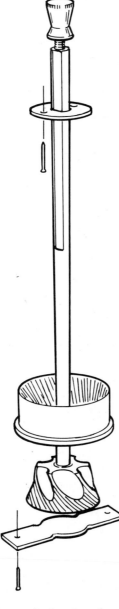

A variety of shapes can be made, but I prefer to
keep the profiles of the body fairly simple, avoiding
too much adornment. I always ensure that the
largest diameter on the finished turning is at the
base, or the project will look top-heavy and out of
proportion.

**Wood** Teak, oak, walnut and sycamore are all
suitable.

## Method

**1** Draw out the project full size (Fig 10.37).

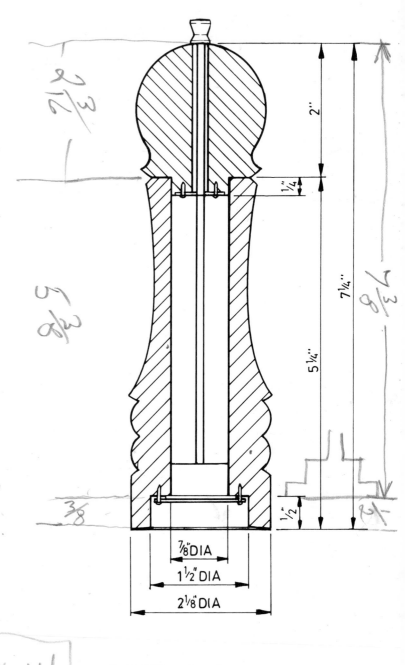

**Fig 10.37 Dimensions of a
typical pepper mill.**

**2** Mount the stock on the screw chuck and reduce it to a cylinder (Fig 10.38).

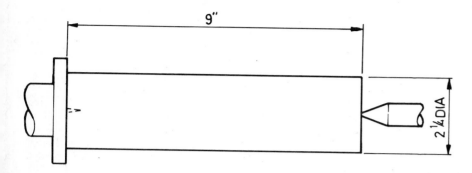

9"

2¼"DIA

Fig 10.38 Mount the stock on the woodscrew chuck; bring up the tailstock for support and reduce it to a cylinder.

**3** Fix the Jacobs chuck with a ⅞" bit to the tailstock. Reduce the lathe speed to between 500 and 1000 rpm. Wind in the tailstock to bore the hole to a depth just over half-way up the body. To prevent the drill bit binding, it is advisable to withdraw it from time to time to remove the waste. It should also be noted that the traverse on most tailstocks is insufficient to bore the full depth hole on one winding. It is therefore necessary to stop the lathe and reposition the tailstock further in towards the headstock when the hole has been part bored (Fig 10.39).

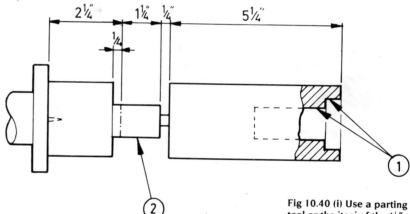

2¼"   1¼"   ¼"   5¼"

¼"

①

②

Fig 10.40 (i) Use a parting tool or the 'toe' of the ½" skew to form the rebate to take the bottom retaining plate. Also, very slightly open the ⅞" bore to house the female part of the mechanism.

(ii) Set out the parting cut and the spigot (which must be a good push fit in the ⅞" main bore) and then part it off.

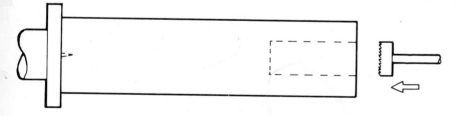

**4** The rebate to take the bottom retaining plate is formed with either a parting tool or the toe of the ½" skew chisel (scraper fashion). Remember that the stock is only supported on a single woodscrew, so do not try to remove too much wood at a time. Light cuts and patience are the order of the day. It will be found that a ⅞" hole will not quite accommodate the female part of the mechanism, so this needs to be enlarged slightly with the skew (Fig 10.40).

Fig 10.39 Fix the Jacobs chuck in the tailstock and bore the ⅞" hole just over half-way up the body.

The capstan, the parting cuts and the spigot are set out at the headstock end, following which the main body is parted off. (Ensure that the spigot is a good fit in the partly bored main body.)

**5** The body is reversed, jammed on to the spigot and the main bore completed (Fig 10.41).

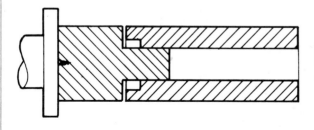

**Fig 10.41 Reverse the body on to the spigot and complete the main bore.**

**6** Remove the body and part the spigot off to about ¼" in length. A shallow recess is made in the face of the spigot (with the parting tool) to house the driving plate. This recess allows the driving plate to finish flush with the surface of the wood, and looks much more professional than simply tacking it in position (Fig 10.42).

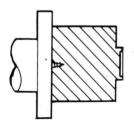

**Fig 10.42 Remove the body and part off the spigot to a length of about ¼". Form a shallow recess in the underside of the capstan to house the driving plate. Now remove the capstan from the chuck.**

**7** Remove the capstan from the woodscrew chuck and replace it with a piece of waste wood about 2½" square and of about the same length. On this a ⅞" spigot is required, which will receive the base of the mill on a good push fit. The ¼" hole can now be bored in the capstan (Jacobs chuck held in the tailstock) to take the spindle mechanism (Fig 10.43).

**Fig 10.43 Mount a waste piece of wood on the screw chuck and turn a spigot on it that will receive the whole body with a 'jam' fit. The ¼" hole for the capstan can now be bored.**

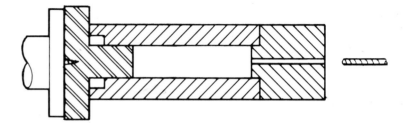

**8** The tailstock and live centre is brought up to give support and the profiling with gouges and chisels can be completed in preparation for sanding and polishing (Fig 10.44).

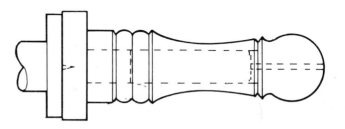

**Fig 10.44 Bring up the tailstock and live centre for support and complete the profiling using gouges and chisels.**

**9** The final step is to lightly sand the inside of the top of the main bore so that the spigot on the capstan can turn freely. Fig 10.45 shows the finished project.

**NB** With this spigot left on the underside of the capstan, there is no need for a top retaining plate to be fixed.

There are other and much quicker ways of making pepper mills, but this method requires minimal equipment. Some of the others involve several sizes of expensive drills and chucking equipment.

**Fig 10.45 The completed pepper mill.**

## Standard Lamp

With careful planning and patience, there is no reason why this should not be undertaken by a beginner. The reader may be encouraged to know that many inexperienced students at the college where I teach have successfully completed the project.

Additionally, this project provides the opportunity to use the long hole boring auger and also the router for making flutes around the central column.

**Design** The standard is of fairly traditional style, but modified to incorporate a central shelf. Fig 10.46 provides details of the design, the component parts and how the joints are arranged.

**Wood** A hardwood of your choice, but I use mahogany usually.

## Method

**1** Cut to length the three pieces that will form the stem and turn them all to a cylinder.

**2** Start the long hole boring operation. This can be achieved if either: **(a)** the tailstock barrel is hollow: a special ring centre can be inserted which allows the long auger to pass through, as is the case with the Coronet No. 3 lathe, or **(b)** the tailstock barrel is not hollow: make use of a jig that fits in the toolrest holder. (The former method is used in the example.)

**3** Bore each length to just over half-way, going forward no more than about 1½" a time, after which the auger must be withdrawn to remove the waste. Otherwise it will bind and may run off centre. It makes for smoother boring if the tip of the auger is occasionally dipped in a tin of wax.

**4** Replace the 4-pronged drive with the counterbore tool. The peg on this fits snugly into the part-bored hole and maintains centricity. The spurs, in addition to driving the stock, will also bore a 1" diameter hole to form a mortise. The holes are bored all the way through each piece.

**5** The mortises in the top and bottom sections are bored. Bring up the tailstock but let it just support the work without being tight up to it. Grasp the wood firmly and then switch on. The hole is bored by advancing the tailstock.

Fig 10.47 shows **x** a hollow ring centre; **y** a boring jig and centre finder intended for use in the toolrest holder; and **z** a counterbore tool.

Fig 10.48 shows a piece of wood that has been bored and counterbored. (For the purpose of

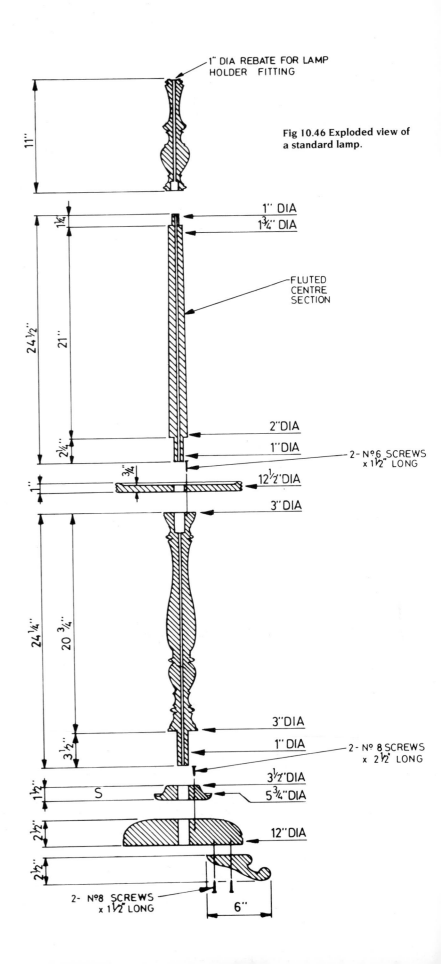

Fig 10.46 Exploded view of a standard lamp.

1" DIA REBATE FOR LAMP HOLDER FITTING

11"

1½"

24½"

21"

1" DIA
1¾" DIA

FLUTED CENTRE SECTION

2¼"

2" DIA
1" DIA

2 - N°6 SCREWS x 1½" LONG

3¼"

1"

12½" DIA

3" DIA

24¼"

20¾"

3½"

3" DIA
1" DIA

2 - N° 8 SCREWS x 2½" LONG

1½"

S

3½" DIA
5¾" DIA

2½"

12" DIA

2½"

2 - N°8 SCREWS x 1½" LONG

6"

Fig 10.47 **x** shows a hollow ring centre; **y** shows a tool post boring jig; **z** shows a counterbore tool.

**x**          **y**          **z**

clarifying the operation, it has been sawn down the centre.)

**6** Mount the middle section in the lathe, form the tenons on either end with the parting tool and vernier/calipers, and then fashion the long slow taper (2″ to 1¾″ diameter). It is advisable to slightly undercut the shoulders of all tenons to ensure a good joint with the mortised sections.

**7** Fix the router jig to the lathe. Making use of a radiused cutter in the router, complete the fluting on this centre piece as described earlier. If it is desired to 'stop' the flutes short of either end, as in this case, it is necessary to nail a couple of strips at either end of the router guides to limit the travel of the router.

**8** The top and bottom sections of the stem can now be shaped. The counterbore tool can be used to form the recess at the very top of the stem to house the brass fixing plate to which the lampholder is screwed. (The 1″ hole made by the counterbore is conveniently the right size to admit the brass lampholder fitting shown in Fig 10.49.)

Fig 10.48 'Split' turning, showing the method of boring the flex hole and the counterbore.

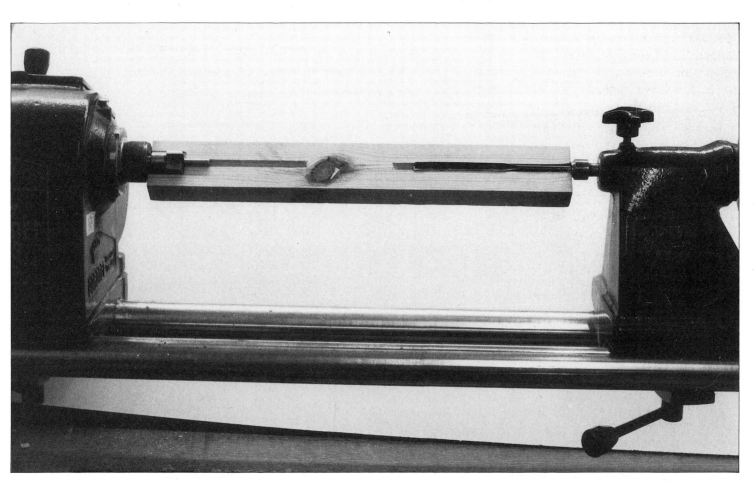

**Fig 10.49 The type of brass lampholder fitting I prefer.**

**9** Prepare the centre shelf for turning by first of all planing the underside flat and sawing it as close as possible to a true circle. Fix it to a faceplate, making sure that the securing woodscrews are short enough to avoid being exposed when turning the other side. Mount it on the lathe and complete the profiling, using a bowl gouge and scrapers. Before removing from the lathe, mark the dead centre with the toe of the skew chisel, so as to give a positive location for the drill bit. The shelf, being 12½″ diameter, cannot be swung over the bed of most lathes and the turning must obviously be done with the headstock swivelled or on the outboard end. This of course prevents the centre hole being bored by assistance from the tailstock, and consequently boring will have to be done off the lathe by hand methods. The two adjacent screw holes enabling the shelf to be securely fixed to the bottom section of the stem can also be drilled and countersunk to take something like a 1½″ x 6″ woodscrew. (These two holes must be located inside the diameter of the fluted column, or they will be exposed.)

**10** The design of the base has been influenced by two factors. First, the difficulty in obtaining stock large enough to make it in one piece. (I think that a one-piece base should be no less than 15″ diameter by 2½″ thick. The bases on many standards on sale in the shops are, in my opinion, too small, too light and consequently unstable.) Second, if such large sections of suitable stock are readily available, diameters over 12″ should not be tackled until a good deal of experience is attained.

Accordingly, the base has been designed to incorporate three sections. The spacer, shown in Fig 10.46, page 140, as **S**, adds to the appearance of solidity and stability. The 12″ x 2½″ main section of the base has been deliberately designed to be plain so as not to present the inexperienced turner with too many problems. Finally, the three feet, positioned at 120° intervals, provide for extra stability and interest. The feet can be sawn to shape on a band saw, jig saw or coping saw, and smoothed off with files and abrasive paper.

**Assembly** This must first of all be done 'dry' to check all the jointing is satisfactory. The next step is to screw the three feet to the underside of the base, then the 'spacer' is screwed to the base. The holes in the main base and the spacer should be exactly in line or there will be difficulty in fitting the tenon on the base of the stem. Alignment is achieved by making use of a piece of 1″ dowel that passes through both holes.

The whole project can now be glued up, starting from the bottom section of the stem. The centre shelf now needs to be positioned and screwed up, again making use of the piece of 1″ dowel to ensure proper alignment. The grain on the base and the shelf should be lined up to give the best effect. To prevent the glue seeping into the central bore, I insert a piece of ¼″ steel rod that passes all the way through the standard. If something like this is not done, you may have great difficulty in threading the lamp flex through the hole. Leave overnight, remove the steel rod, clean up and apply the finish of your choice. Fig 10.50 shows the finished project.

# SUMMARY

**1** As with all woodworking tools, drill bits must be maintained in good condition. To prevent damage to the cutters, some kind of drill stand is essential for storage.

**2** When sharpening, it is imperative that the original profile is maintained and the cutters are filed to the same height.

**3** Before the lathe is started, ensure the speed has been fixed to suit the type and size of drill bit being used.

**4** Boring jigs can be made up and with a little thought and ingenuity, most boring problems can be overcome.

**5** When boring deep holes, retract the bit from time to time to remove the waste, otherwise it will bind and overheat.

**6** A 'dividing head' or, as it is sometimes called, an 'indexing head' is an absolute must. It is essential that it is accurately made.

**7** Many hollow ware projects can be speeded up by boring away a great deal of the waste wood.

**Fig 10.50 The completed standard lamp.**

## Chapter 11

## SAFETY, DESIGN, COURSES . . .

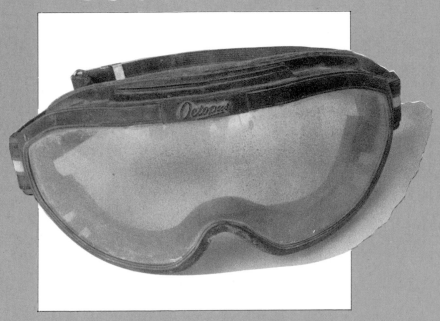

# SAFETY IN THE WORKSHOP

Safety is *the most important aspect of this book* and I considered long and hard whether it ought to be the subject of the first chapter. The reason for this not being so is that a good many of the safe working practices and measures described would not necessarily mean a great deal to the newcomer to the craft if they were merely included as a list without the relevant potentially dangerous operations, equipment and tools first being described.

While the woodturning lathe is arguably the safest of all woodworking machines, there have been instances of serious injury being caused to the operator. In my opinion, the reasons for this can be put down to one of three things:

**1** Ignorance of the correct techniques – incorrect methods are nearly always dangerous – and safety measures.

**2** Taking unnecessary risks, even when experienced. Most professional turners take 'acceptable' or 'calculated risks' to speed up production, but even so the chances of injury are increased particularly when combined with number 3 below.

**3** Tiredness or lack of concentration. The well-known saying 'familiarity breeds contempt' is particularly relevant to all wood machinists. It must be remembered that all machines can 'bite', and most accidents occur through lack of concentration and towards the end of the working day when tiredness has set in. My advice is to stop when you feel tired or if your mind is so engrossed on something else that it prevents you from applying maximum concentration.

The object of this section is to refresh the reader's memory on what has gone before relating to safety, and also to include one or two more points which have not been touched on. Remember, many of the following points are basically the application of common sense.

## Safety Rules

Ensure the electrics are safe – that is, the machine is properly earthed and installed in accordance with the maker's instructions. If a secondhand lathe is acquired, obtain the services of a qualified electrician to check it over. It will be money well spent.

• Rubber plugs should be fitted to all woodworking machines.

• Examine the electric cable from time to time to make sure it is in good order.

• Always isolate the lathe from the mains when changing speeds or applying the 'test of tightness'.

• Ensure that the lathe is securely bolted down to a good solid bench, in the case of a bench model, and occasionally check the tightness of the nuts.

• Sensible dress must be worn. Loose, dangling sleeves must be avoided at all costs. Good strong footwear is also very important. Tools are sometimes dropped or roll off the bench and can cause nasty wounds if you are shod in trainers or similar footwear.

• Use a purpose-built grindstone that is properly enclosed and designed to run at the correct speed. Occasionally check the soundness of the stone as described in Chapter 4 On Sharpening. Some form of eye protection must be worn when using the grindstone.

• Study the Laws of Woodturning, pages 41-49 as frequently as possible. Breaking any one of them can be dangerous.

• Always examine the wood for faults, such as dead knots, splits, shakes, etc. If any of these are evident, discard the timber and find some sound stock.

• Ensure that all the locking handles have been tightened and the work spins freely before switching on the power.

• Always stand to one side and out of the 'firing line' when starting the machine.

• Make sure that there is no less than ¾" of toolrest protruding by the end of the wood on which you are working.

• In the early learning stage, it is advisable to stop the lathe when making adjustments to the toolrest.

• Minimize the downward leverage on the tools by keeping the rest as close as possible to the workpiece.

• Always remove the toolrest when sanding. Wherever possible, sanding must be done in the 'safe' position.

- Some kind of protection against dust is essential. Make use of a dust mask and/or an extractor unit.
- Keep a fire extinguisher in the workshop and do not smoke or allow anyone else to smoke in the shop.

The above list is by no means exhaustive. Very often safety boils down to using your common sense, being patient and not taking risks.

# DESIGN

As your turning skills improve, you will automatically develop a good eye for shape and proportion (in other words, design), and now is the time to really use your eyes and observe the work of others.

There is no shortage of sources that will stimulate and generate design ideas. Visits to stately homes, museums, galleries, antique shops and craft centres can be a constant inspiration. Many books are devoted purely to the art of good design, architecture, classical Greek and Roman profiles, the 'Golden Ratio', etc. Most of the woodworking magazines regularly publish articles including the design for turning projects. The sources of design are endless and if the student is sufficiently enthusiastic and motivated to produce things of beauty, experience will enable him to tell when a project looks right.

# WOODTURNING COURSES

Since being pioneered by the late Peter Child, woodturning courses have sprung up in all parts of the country and certainly a good tutor can impart sufficient knowledge to a novice on a two-day course (the most popular duration) to allow him to develop his skills in a safe and confident manner.

These are not cheap and if I was paying out good money to go on such a course, I would want to know the answer to the following:

**1** How many other students will be on the course? My own view is that two is the optimum number. I previously did courses for a wood machine retailer where four people per course was the norm. I do not recall any complaints, but I felt I could have given better value for money if only two students had participated. In my capacity as a teacher at the local college of further education, I have had as many as sixteen students sharing four lathes. Progress can be made, but inevitably it is slow.

**2** How many lathes are available and what make are they? There is no substitute for 'hands on' experience (preceded of course by explanation and demonstration), so ensure that there is one lathe per student.

**3** How much time is actually allocated to 'hands on'? While it is inevitable that a certain amount of theory, explanation and demonstration is necessary, the amount of time spent on these must not be disproportionate to the hands on time allowed. In my opinion at least 80 per cent of the course time should be so allocated.

**4** Is the instructor articulate and able to explain things in a simple and easily understood manner? (Being a good woodturner does not necessarily mean you are a good teacher.) If possible, arrange a visit to the instructor's workshop. This will give you the opportunity to assess him and determine whether or not his personality is compatible with yours. Two days is a very long time to spend with someone you cannot take a liking to.

**5** Is his workshop well organized, tidy and comfortable? (The state of a workshop will provide many clues as to the instructor's attitudes, enthusiasm and teaching skills.) If the course is during the colder months, is there any heating in the place? There is nothing worse for the concentration than being cold.

**6** Is there a course syllabus and are there any course notes? Personally I would want to know exactly what topics are covered. I appreciate that the pace of every course needs to be adjusted to the receptivity and aptitude of the student, but this is no excuse for a 'let's see how we go' approach, with little or no planning. Inevitably some students will be a little slower than others, but would this mean that the whole of the syllabus would not be covered? Also, I would expect to be supplied with some fairly comprehensive course notes. No one can be expected to remember more than about 25 per cent of all he is told, therefore notes are an extremely useful means of revising everything that has been explained on the course.

Looking at it from the instructor's point of view, I do feel that many people expect too much from a two-day course of instruction. If the student has learned the basics, as outlined in this book, then I am more than satisfied that he or she will have created a solid *foundation* on which to build with confidence and optimism. Remember, no one can impart that indefinable *feel* into your hands – this can only come with constant educated practice.

# WAYS FORWARD

Learning the craft of woodturning is a gradual process. As with any form of learning there will inevitably be setbacks and occasions when you may well think you are not making the progress you should. Do not be downhearted, because *everyone* goes through such stages. There are ways forward, however, that can revitalize and perhaps inspire the student to 'keep right on to the end of the road'. Accordingly, I offer the following ideas to provide a much needed boost, which we all require from time to time.

**Evening classes** Some local authorities run woodturning classes. Despite the fact that it is more than likely you will be sharing a lathe with two or three others, much can be learned by listening and looking. A bonus is that many close friendships are forged and normally there exists an excellent camaraderie, each student swapping ideas and so on, to the benefit of all.

**Demonstrations** These are featured at all the major woodworking shows, and most of the demonstrators are only too willing to give advice and help out with any problem you might be encountering. Don't be afraid to ask. I for one certainly welcome any query and it is more than likely that a good many of the onlookers are experiencing similar problems. Some of the larger suppliers of woodturning equipment and accessories, such as Craft Supplies Ltd, also run regular demonstrations and they are well worth a visit. The same company publishes a quarterly magazine entitled *The Woodturner* which contains many useful and interesting projects.

**The Association of Woodturners of Great Britain** This association was formed at an international seminar at Loughborough in August 1987. It is organized and administered *by* woodturners *for* woodturners and membership is open to anyone interested in the craft, be they novice or professional.

The advantages of belonging to this association are many. Its aims and objectives can do nothing but improve the standing of the craft in the eyes of the public. The setting up of local 'chapters' provides the opportunity of meeting other members living in their area, so as to exchange ideas on techniques, developments and projects. Seminars and exhibitions are also organized, and internationally known turners are invited. Attending such gatherings can be a rewarding and stimulating experience, providing the chance to rub shoulders with the acclaimed. The association also publishes a newsletter from time to time, updating the membership on all that is happening in the world of woodturning.

# APPEAL

By now you will have gathered that I am a self-confessed 'wood nut'. Those of you just starting out on your woodturning venture will, I am almost certain, also develop a love for the material. The decimation of the world's rain forests and the destruction of trees by natural disasters such as the hurricane that swept across southern England in 1987 cause much alarm. I think it is incumbent on all of us to do our little bit to ensure that future generations of woodworkers can enjoy all the species of trees that we do.

Do you realize that for as little as £1 donated to the Woodland Trust, Autumn Park, Grantham, Lincs NG31 6LL, you can have a broadleaved tree planted where the need is greatest? What is more, your name will be included in the official *Book of Commemoration*. Please think about it, but not for too long – remember that some trees take 100 years to mature!

# INDEX